IN NO TIME

PC Basics

In No Time

PC Basics

Second Edition

Oliver Pott

Prentice Hall

AN IMPRINT OF PEARSON EDUCATION

PEARSON EDUCATION LIMITED

Head Office:
Edinburgh Gate
Harlow CM20 2JE
Tel: +44 (0)1279 623623
Fax: +44 (0)1279 431059

London Office:
128 Long Acre
London WC2E 9AN
Tel: +44 (0)20 7447 2000
Fax: +44 (0)20 7240 5771

First published in Germany in 1997

First published in 1997 as *PC-Grundlagen: leicht, klar, sofort*
by Markt & Technik Buch-und Software-Verlag GmbH
Martin-Kollar-Straße 10–12
D-81829 Munich
Germany

This edition published 2000 by Pearson Education
British Library Cataloguing in Publication Data
A CIP catalogue record for this book can be obtained from the British Library.

ISBN 0-13-031977-5

10 9 8 7 6 5 4 3 2 1

Translated and typeset by Cybertechnics, Sheffield.
Printed and bound in Great Britain by Henry Ling Ltd, at The Dorset Press, Dorchester, Dorset.

The publishers' policy is to use paper manufactured from sustainable forests.

Contents

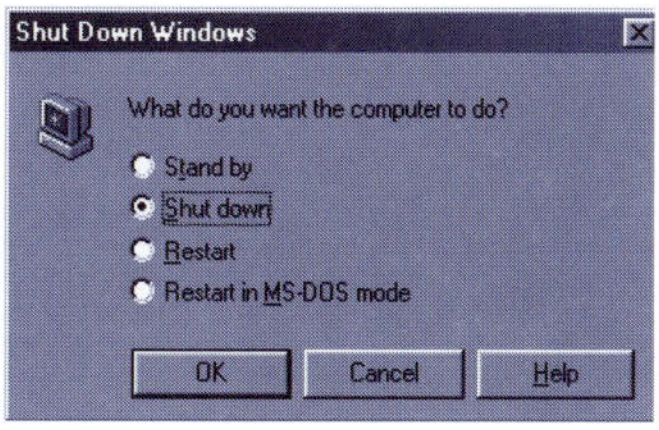

Shut Down Windows
What do you want the computer to do?
Stand by
Shut down
Restart
Restart in MS-DOS mode
OK
Cancel
Help

4 From man to computer 52

5 Digital documents 82

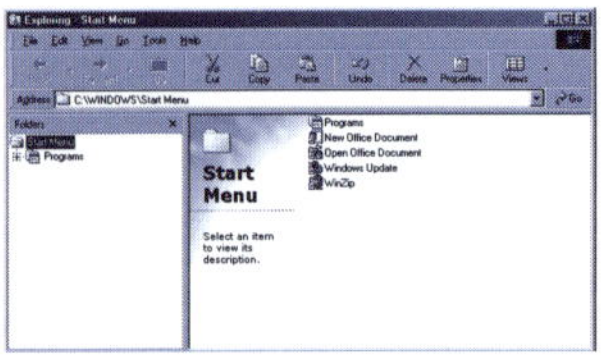

6 How does your computer work? 140

7 Printing 162

8 As fast as television 190

9 The Internet and going on-line 206

10 The “personal computer” 228

11 Software 242

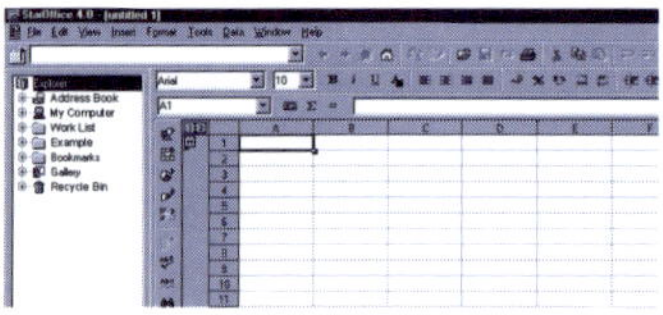

Glossary 252

Index 354

Dear Readers,

It is obvious that working with a PC has several advantages. Millions of professional users all over the world cannot be wrong.

Perhaps you are the type of PC owner who is in love with computer technology and always has the latest computer. Or you may just be forced to deal with technology for professional reasons, for example because you have had to switch your accounting over to a computerised system.

If you have not yet had any contact with the "super typewriter", which is after all what a computer appears to be, you have the right book in your hands. Or perhaps you already work with a PC and now you would like to get better acquainted with your electronic helper. This book will tell you all you need to know in order to function with a PC.

This book focuses on practical knowledge and hands-on experience. You will be able to gather the information you need for your daily work in easy and comprehensible learning steps. You can read and study this book while working on your computer, which is probably the most effective way to use the book.

The great advantage of working with this book is the concept of the "Market &Technology" production. In this book you will work mainly with Windows 98 and Internet Explorer 5, but of course you will be able to use the book even if you work with Windows 95, Windows NT or any other operating systems. In this edition, innovations in the PC world are also discussed.

When you have finished reading this book, email me with your comments, suggestions or even criticism. My email address is oliver@pott-it.de or you can write to the publishers and they will forward your comments on to me.

Have fun reading the book!

Oliver Pott

The keyboard

The following three pages show you how your computer keyboard is structured. Most of the computer keys are operated exactly as keys on a typewriter. However, there are a few additional keys, which are designed especially for computer work. See for yourself.

Typewriter keys

Use these keys exactly as you do on a typewriter.
The Enter key is also used to send commands to your computer.

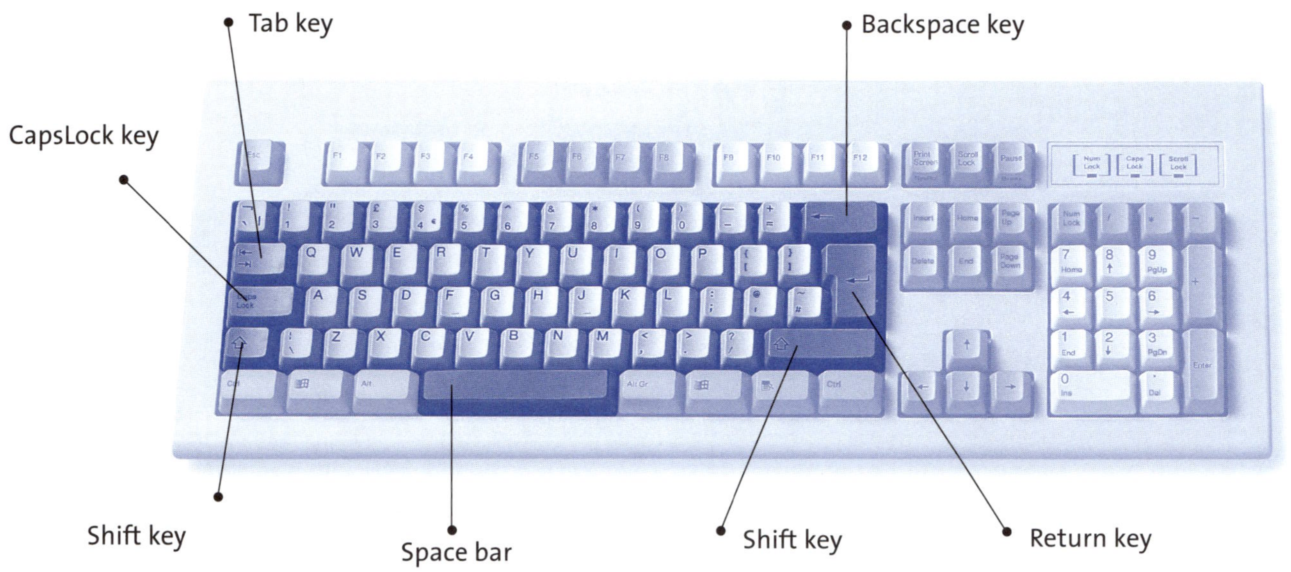

Special keys, function keys, status lights, numeric key pad

Special keys and function keys are used for special tasks in computer operation. The Ctrl, Alt and AltGr keys are usually used in combination with other keys. The Esc key can cancel commands. Insert and Delete can be used, amongst other things, to insert and delete text.

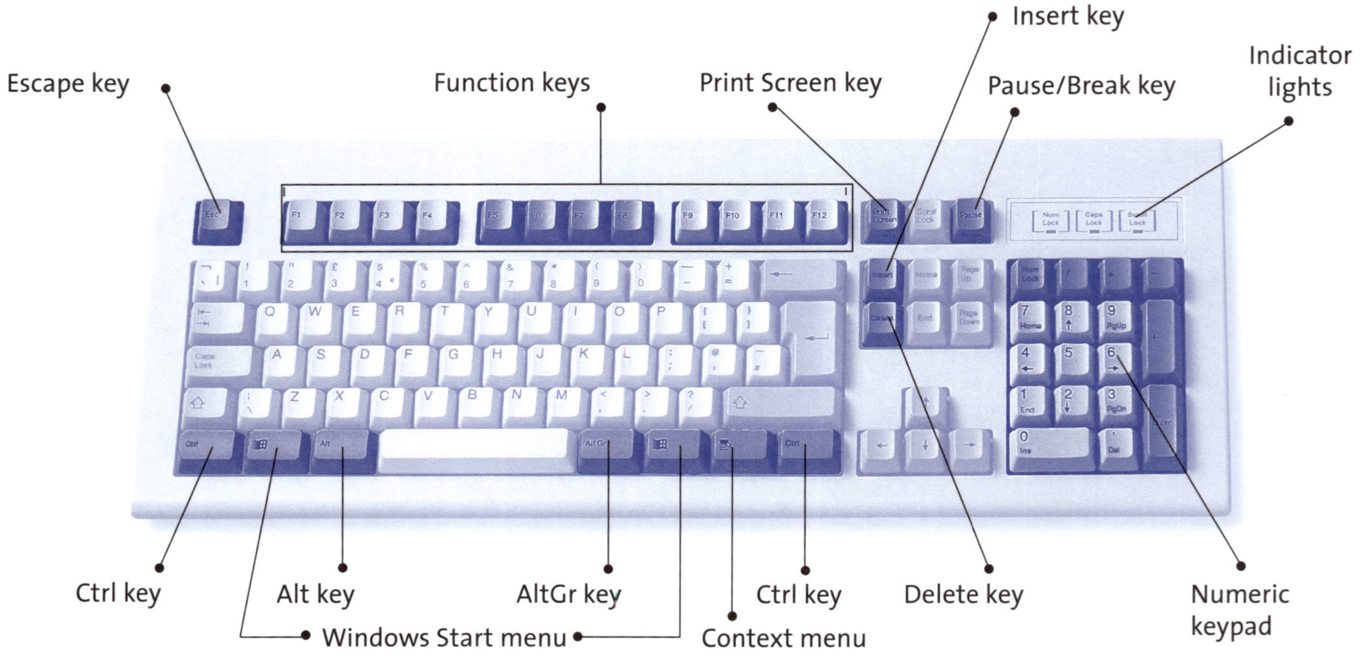

Navigation keys

These keys are used to move around the screen.

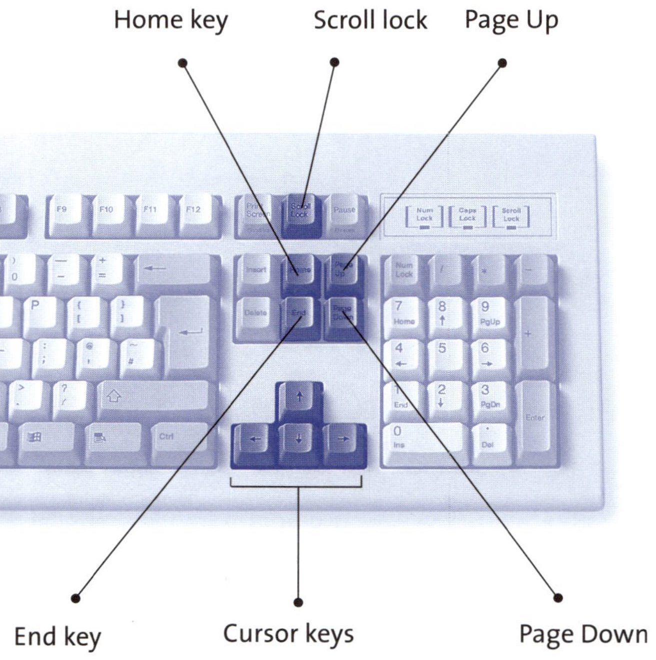

The mouse

'Click on...'

means press once briefly on a button.

Clicking with the left mouse button...

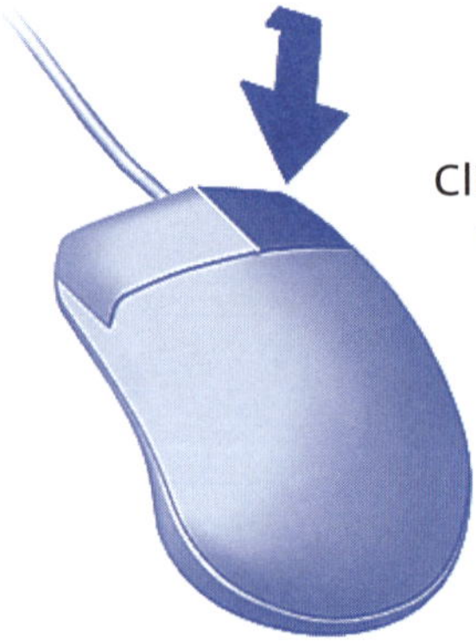

Clicking with the right mouse button...

'Double click on...'

means press the left button twice briefly in quick succession.

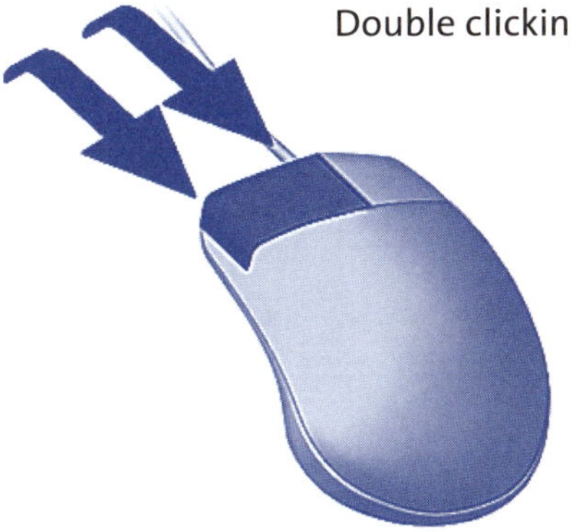

Double clicking

'Drag...'

means click on an object with the left mouse button, keep the button pressed, move the mouse and drag the item to another position.

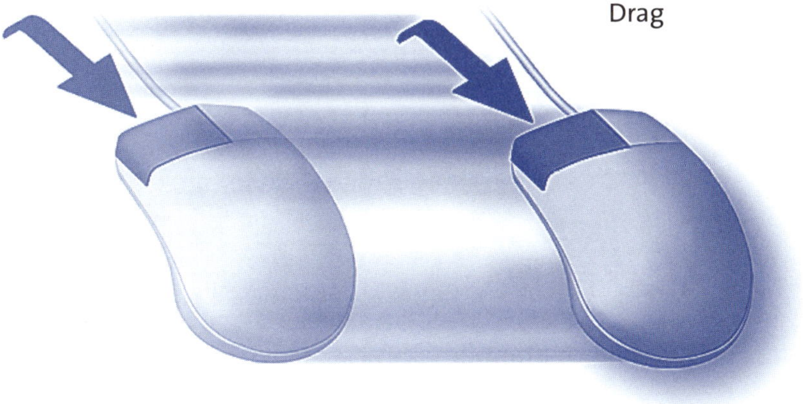

Drag

1 Unpacking and setting up your computer

What's in this chapter:

Before introducing you to the fascinating world of computers, we are going to show you how to unpack and assemble your PC. If you are already using your computer, and therefore just want to become better acquainted with how it works, you can skip this chapter.

You are going to learn about:

1st step: Peace & quiet, and Time

If you have collected your PC from the supplier or from the shop where you bought it and you would like to assemble it in your office or on your desk, you definitely need some:

Peace and quiet and a little bit of time!

WHAT'S THIS?

The technical term for connecting the individual devices is **installation.**

You cannot simply plug a PC into an electrical outlet and switch it on. If you have never worked with a PC before, try to keep a couple of hours free to install your new PC.

Take a couple of hours to get used to "the mysterious world of computers". All you need to do to make the system work properly is to make sure that all the pieces are assembled properly.

2nd step: Unpacking and assembling

WHAT'S THIS?

Hardware is the technical term for the individual components which together form the computer. The complete PC is described also as the **Computer system** or as the **System,** for short.

You should have a number of boxes from the computer shop. Each box contains a piece of hardware.

TIP

When you unpack the components, you will notice that the computer monitor and the PC are protected with styrofoam, inside their box; the styrofoam often sticks in the box.

Put the box on its side and slide out the styrofoam instead of lifting the heavy monitor from the box.

Now remove the hardware and put the styrofoam blocks back into the box.

Before unpacking the components, you must check that you have been provided with all the following boxes:

- **Computer box**: this box contains the PC itself. You will recognize the PC by the numerous sockets on the back. It is often surrounded by various bags which contain manuals, spare parts and a key. There will also be another box containing the keyboard.

- **Monitor box:** the monitor (or "screen") is packed in a different box. Be very careful not to damage the tube when unpacking the monitor.

- **Printer box:** your printer (if you have purchased one) is packaged in a separate box. The box with the printer should also contain some CD-ROMs, as well as a manual and an ink cartridge, ribbon or toner cartridge.

CAUTION

Always remember to buy a printer cable for the printer. This cable, which unfortunately is not supplied with your printer, is essential for connecting the printer to the computer.

Now place the computer where you want it to be. Position the monitor on your desk, allowing for a distance of at least 50 cm between your eyes and the screen. Put the keyboard on your desk, in the most comfortable position for you to be able to reach it and work without straining your back or your arms.

The mouse should be beside your keyboard, on the right (if you are right-handed), so that you can reach it easily while you're working. The mouse should always rest on a mouse pad.

You can position the printer wherever you like. But remember that a standard connection cable has a maximum length of 2 metres.

WHAT'S THIS?

A **mouse pad** is a pad of synthetic material on which you move the mouse. Mouse pads can be bought very cheaply in PC accessory shops.

WHAT'S THIS?

Data is the term used to define the "language" the PC uses to communicate. We will introduce you to this language in a later chapter.

3rd step: Connecting

As you unpacked, you will have noticed numerous cables which you will need to connect to your PC. Each piece of equipment, for example the printer, has a data cable and a power lead.

TIP

A "pin" is a metal point which you see when looking at a plug. Therefore, a "5-pin plug" is a plug in which you can see five metal points.

Follow these instructions to guide you through the connection process:

1 The power cables... supply your PC, your monitor and your printer with electrical current from the power supply socket. You need one cable for each piece of hardware. First, plug the matching ends into your PC (you cannot go wrong, only the correct cable will fit in to each socket), your monitor and your printer. Then connect the appliances to the power supply: a three-way adapter is helpful.

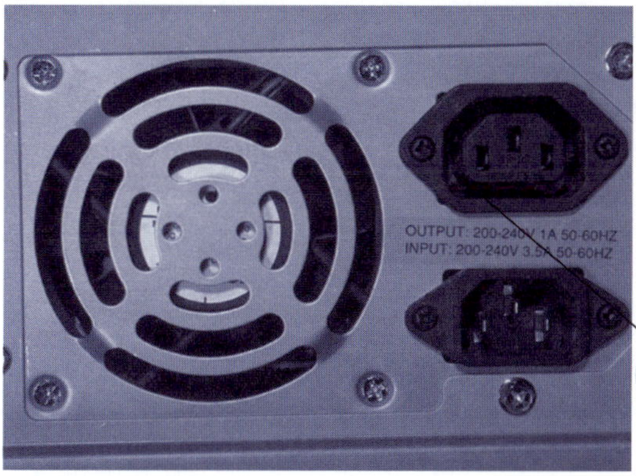

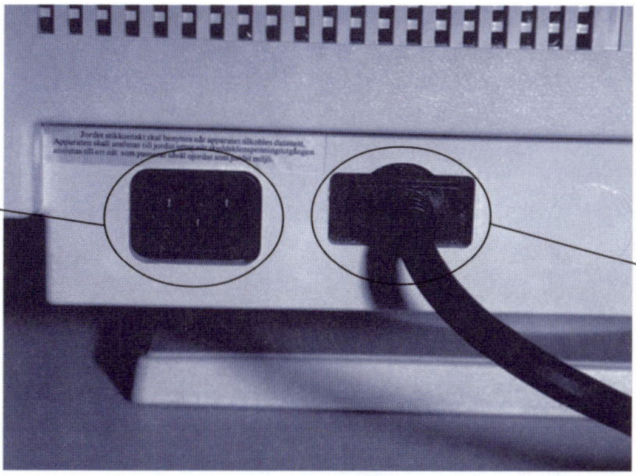

2 The monitor cable ...

.... connects your PC to the monitor. It is fixed at one end to the monitor and, at the other end, fits only in one socket on the back of the computer. Two fastening screws prevent the plug from slipping out; tighten these screws with your fingers.

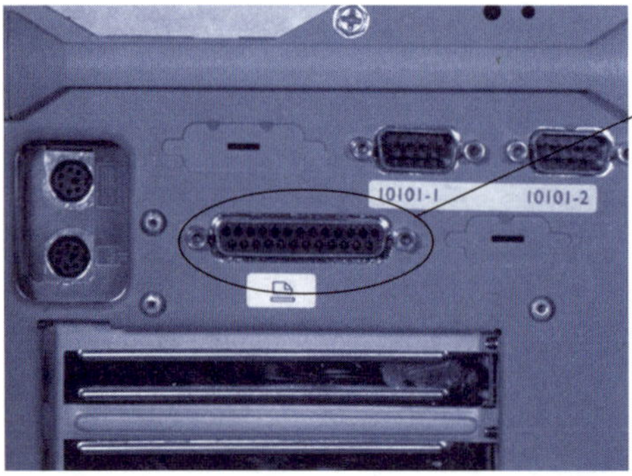

3 The printer cable ...

connects your printer to the PC. This large cable will only fit in one socket and has two wire clips (or screws) to prevent the plug from slipping out.

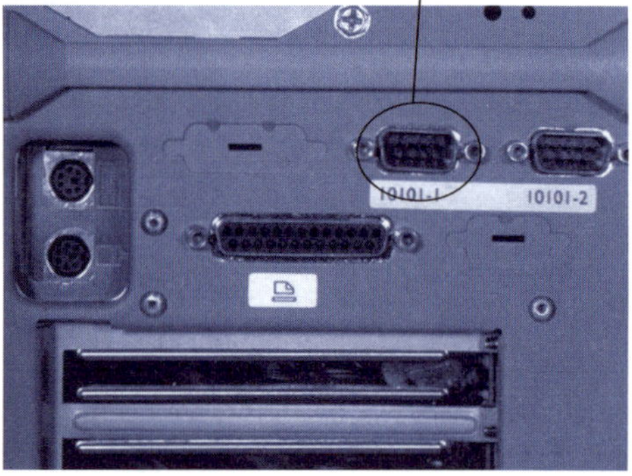

4 The mouse cable ...

also attaches to the back of your PC. It is narrower than the printer cable. You can see 9 pins. Sometimes this plug is small and round — just like the mouse.

5 The keyboard cable ...

connects the keyboard to the PC. It is a spiral cable and is fixed to the keyboard. The other end of the cable has a round plug which fits in the socket on the back of your PC.

4th step: The first time ...

you switch on your computer is an exciting moment. Push the "On" button on the front of your computer; sometimes this button is labelled "Power". A green light (the experts call it "a light-emitting diode") shows that your PC is now powered up.

WHAT'S THIS?

In technical jargon, starting your computer is called **Booting** or **Starting Up.**

Your monitor must be switched on separately. The Switch On button is usually on the front, but in some models the switch is on the right-hand side, or even on the back.

Do not press any key on the keyboard yet. Watch the PC coming to life. At first, the black screen fills up with a series of weird symbols and incomprehensible messages.

After one or two minutes the black screen changes to a coloured (and more friendly!) view.

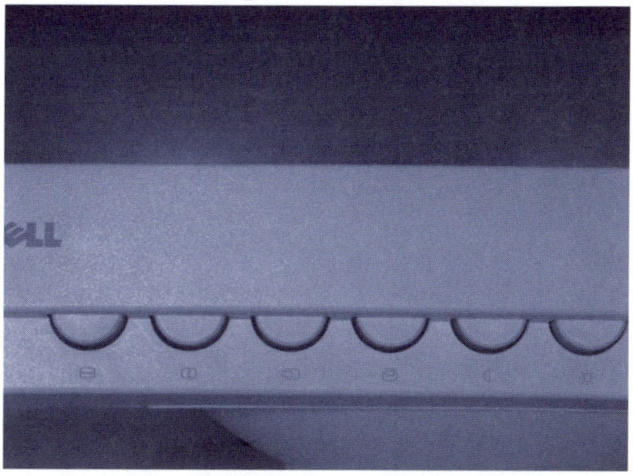

With the contrast and brightness controls on the monitor, you can adjust the picture, just as you do with your television set, as you wish.

Congratulations — Your PC is ready to work. In the next chapter we will give you some background information on computers and the history of computing.

2

Introduction

What's in this chapter:

You will see that man and computer have a special relationship.
You will learn how a computer processes information, which tasks a modern computer is able to undertake and which tasks are better left to man.
You will find out how a computer records and performs a piece of music.

You already know about:

You are going to learn about:

The history of the computer

Probably the question most frequently asked by computer beginners is "which tasks can computers undertake?"

This question cannot be answered in one sentence and PC experts are at a loss as to how to answer it. After all, modern computer technology has developed so much that it is very difficult to give a quick answer.

Let's look at the origins of modern computer technology; this will help us to find an answer to our question.

In 1936, Konrad Zuse, who is considered the father of computers, built the first computer with his own hands and called it "**Zuse 1**". Because there were no industrially manufactured products available, Zuse used telephone relays and connected 2,000 of these to an adding machine. Zuse's computer was so large that it filled a whole house.

And thus the theoretical foundations for the development of the computer were set. Early computers were simple objects, in terms of what they could do; any modern electronic calculator can do much more than the Zuse 1.

In 1946, the American Eckert Mauchley produced the **ENIAC computer**, which was already a big step ahead in this field. Unlike the Zuse 1, this new prototype did not function with telephone relays, but used electronic components.

Although the ENIAC had a fairly advanced functionality in some respects, it still had a number of disadvantages. The technology used was not easy to manage, was susceptible to interference and used up so much energy it almost required its own dedicated power station to work.

Computer development continued rapidly and in 1954 a new technology was introduced, one which is still used in today's computers: **the silicon chip**. These minute chips had qualities that made them perfect for computers. Development went on for about four years, until the company Texas Instruments finalised the development of the computer chip in 1958 and produced the predecessor of the modern computer.

The personal computer, in its current form, can therefore trace its first direct ancestors to about 20 years ago. In 1976, two American electronics students built the first personal computer. Steven Jobs and Steve Wozniak called the new system Apple and set up a company with the same name, which is still going strong.

Life for this new electronic 'miracle baby' was difficult at first, as it took some time for it to become accepted against other more established technologies.

It was only when the then market leader, IBM, introduced its own **personal computer** in 1981, that the world began to take notice of the new product.

The new computer was equipped with a computer chip (processor) manufactured by a company called Intel and came equipped with software produced by a company which, at the time, was virtually unknown, called Microsoft. IBM-Intel-Microsoft: the three new shining stars in the computer sky, so much so that, even today, we still refer to "IBM-compatible", "Intel processor" or "Microsoft Windows", and these phrases have become an integral part of computer jargon.

While Intel and Microsoft still occupy a substantial space in the crowded computer market of today, IBM lost its monopoly position a long time ago. Today IBM-compatible computers can be produced by any computer manufacturer.

What computers can do — and what they cannot do

We have not yet answered the question we asked at the beginning of this chapter: what could the first computers do, and, more important, what can computers do today?

The first instructions used for the Zuse 1, for example, were probably "add 0 and 1" or "subtract 5 from 6". There was nothing revolutionary about these operations, but what was revolutionary was the speed at which the computer would carry out these operations.

The first **operational** fields were simple arithmetical calculations which any first year student could just as easily do and which represented a minimum level in terms of meaningful work.

As computers became faster and more efficient, they were given new and more demanding tasks to perform. Computers could now record data and could therefore manage a client list, for example. They could also edit text and were far more flexible than any typewriter could ever possibly be. These are just two of the most typical computer application areas.

The following overview shows the tasks that a computer can tackle today.

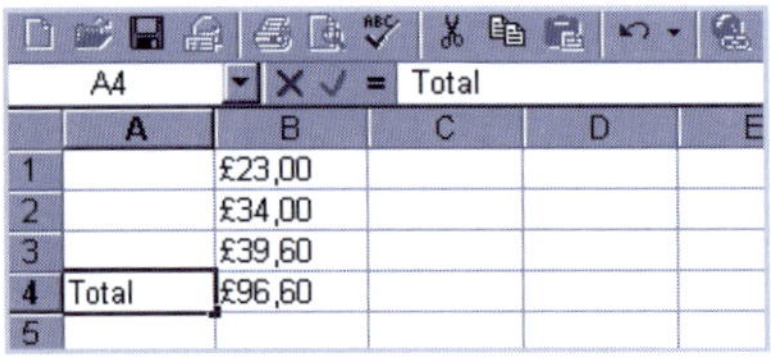

1 Computers can perform operations

As well as simple types of calculation (adding, multiplying), a modern computer can also handle complex types of calculation such as sine, root extraction, squares and percentages, including the calculation of interests.

Client List

Forname	Surname	Title	Client Data
Paul	Watkinson	Mr	23.10.73
Gareth	Scott	Mr	18.02.77
John	Mitton	Mr	19.09.78
Elena	Annunziato	Miss	24.08.75
Jas	Sehmi	Mr	19.09.76
Richard	Grayson	Mr	08.12.80

2 Computers can manage a database

You can manage a client database just like a store stock list. Databases can also be used to perform calculations, for example adding up stock levels.

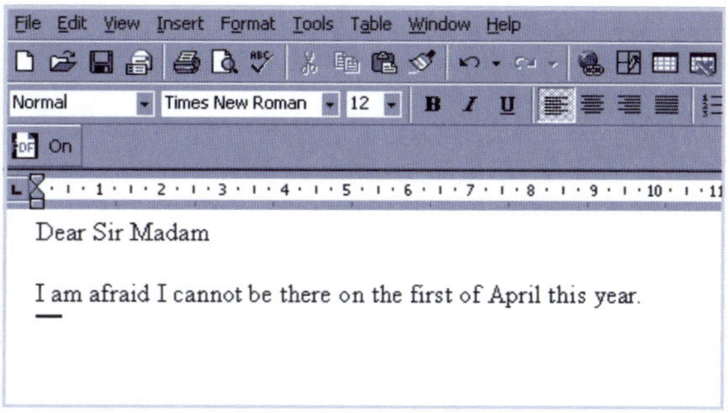

3 Computers can process text

Text entered with a keyboard can be stored in a data folder and, when required, it can be amended or changed and used as many times as it is needed.

4 Computers can work with graphics and photos

Photos can be put into a computer and manipulated. Graphics (such as company logos) can be made multi-coloured.

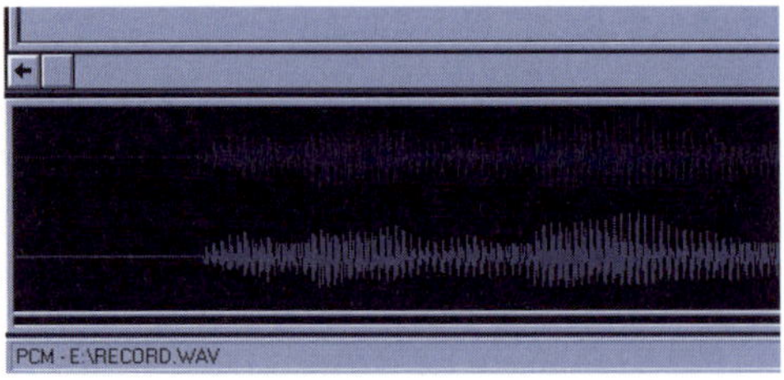

5 Computers can work on audio data

Computers can record music, voice and sound just like a cassette recorder, and allow users to modify the recorded data. So, for example, computers are able to add reverberation and echo, or delete specific sequences.

6 Computers can communicate

Computers can contact other computers in other parts of the world in the space of a few seconds and, for example, exchange data, through the World Wide Web.

7 Computers can measure, control and regulate

A computer can record and calculate weather data and provide data feedback in the form of a weather chart. It can manage a production line in a factory and control traffic with a computerised tracking system.

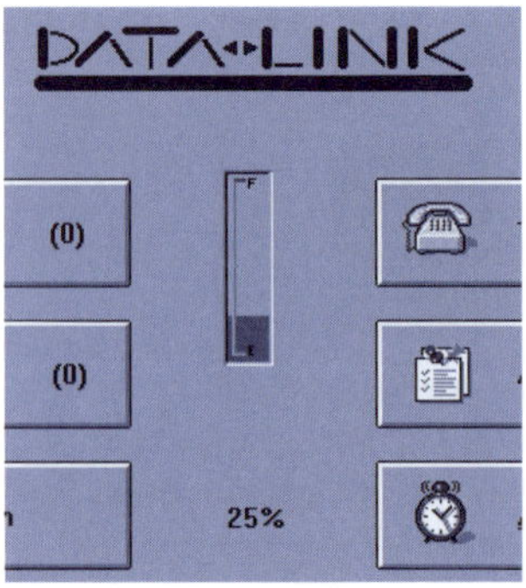

So, is the computer an electronic genius or is it just a useful slave? The fact is that computers may be able to do fast calculations, but they are not intelligent. All operations are filtered through a background program (**algorithm**) generated by a human user.

Some simple processes are an almost impossible obstacle even for a multi-million pound computer. **Recognition of human language**, for example, is only possible with great effort and it is still unreliable. **Handling handwriting** is still a great challenge for modern computers and software engineers.

In short, you are far superior to your computer, but your computer can relieve you from **routine and repetitive administration** work.

The way computers "think": the IPO principle

A computer works like a human being, at least in theory. This is understandable because, after all, computers have been designed by man and perform according to human criteria.

WHAT'S THIS?

Data processing consists of three single steps and is described briefly as the **IPO principle**. IPO is an acronym formed by the first letters of the individual steps: Input, Process and Output.

1 **Input**

Keyboard, mouse, scanner
Computers must receive data. Man too must receive information, for example aurally or visually. A computer receives information through input devices, such as the keyboard or a scanner (a specialised film reader).

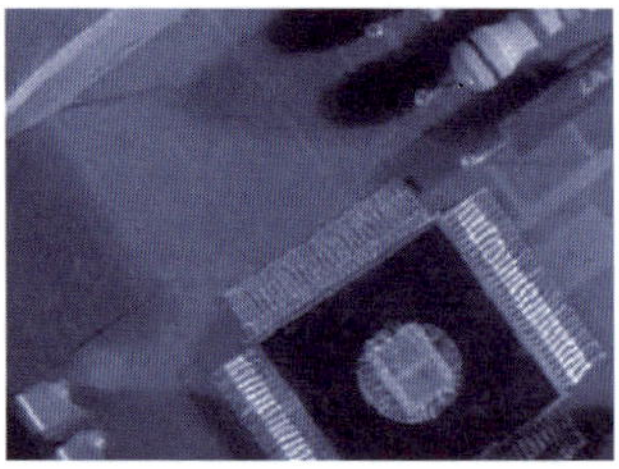

2 **Process**

Processor, memory
The second step is processing data. The human brain also processes data and can execute calculations or remember data. The processing unit of the computer — its brain – is called a processor.

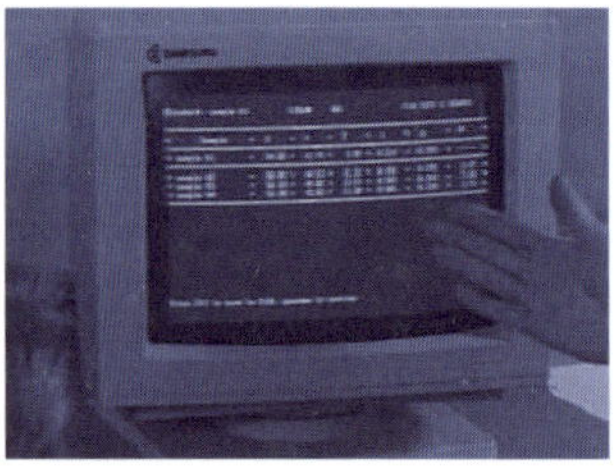

3 **Output**

Printer, monitor, hard disk
In the third and last step, the computer gives you the result of its calculations. The output device of a human being is first of all spoken language, but also mimicry, gestures and written language. The computer shows data on its monitor or by printing it out on its printer.

Analog and digital: the meeting of two worlds

Imagine you are listening to some music. The sound is carried to your ears by waves — sound waves transport information. Nature uses **waves** to transmit sound information.

As well as sound waves, even the light which is all around us is made of waves, where each colour is a different type of wave. Sight and hearing – two of the most basic forms of our communication – work by waves, too.

WHAT'S THIS?

When information is transferred in the form of waves, we call this an **analog signal**.

The first computers worked with analog signals too. The single elements were communicated through waves. Early experiments with this system showed that analog signals were inadequate for computer-supported information processing. Instead of a clear state, waves could also accept inter-states; so they could range between very high and very low interstates of an infinite number of inter-states of a sound wave, for example, a "medium high".

A computer can handle discrete information better and faster. All modern computers save data in two ways: as "binary", and as "ASCII", that is to say "zero" and "one".

And so two completely different worlds meet: the analog world of man and the digital world of computers.

If a continuous analog signal is to be converted into digital information, the analog wave is broken down into small segments. The computer distinguishes whether there is a "binary" or an "ASCII" state for every single segment with a limit. The result is a machine-readable digital format.

WHAT'S THIS?

When information is characterised by only two different states, we call it a **digital signal**.

WHAT'S THIS?

An analog signal can be translated into a digital signal. The translator is called an **analog digital converter** and is of vital importance for the entire computer world. A **digital analog transducer** performs the reverse operation.

With the help of an analog digital converter, man can connect to the computer and give instructions. Your computer communicates with you via a digital analog transducer in the opposite direction.

The following example shows a typical application when a digital signal is converted into an analog signal. A recorded piece of music will be recorded by the computer and then played through the computer speakers.

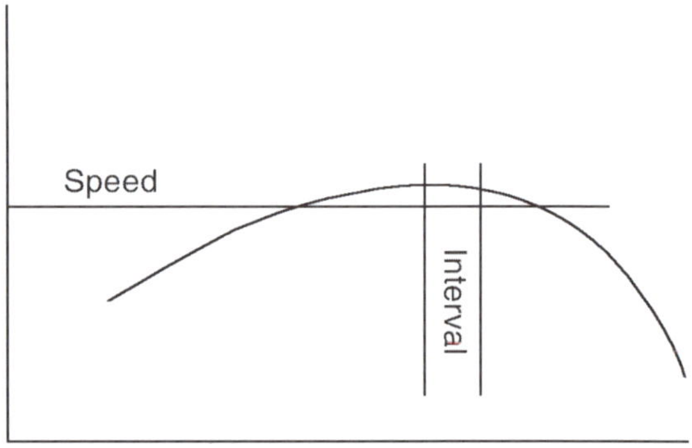

1 Recording a piece of music
The music is recorded with a microphone as an audio signal. This is an analog signal.

2 Transformation into a digital signal
Since the computer can only work with digital signals, an analog-digital converter translates the music into a digital signal. The translation takes only a fraction of a second.

3 Editing music

With the help of your computer, you can now edit music, for example, to alter the volume, delete sequences or insert an echo effect.

4 Back translation into an analog signal

Because a speaker can represent the music, the digital analog transducer translates the edited music back into an analog signal.

5 Reproduction of music tracks

The analog signal is played through the speakers of your computer.

The technical realisation of the conversion of analog into digital or vice versa is more complex and has some limitations. Because the analog wave is in definite **intervals**, there is a **loss of quality**. For example, a cheap analog digital converter may introduce some background noise as a result of the conversion.

It is interesting to note that the digital technique has also moved into other areas of our daily life. Your digital watch no longer shows the time with hands, but with figures. Audio CDs no longer record music as waves, but use digital signals.

Short- and long-term memory

How does a computer "remember" data? You know that, according to the IPO principle, data input is the necessary prerequisite for processing data. A computer can store information permanently or temporarily and work with it as requested.

WHAT'S THIS?

The standard way of storing information is called SAVE. Retrieving stored information is the opposite of saving and is called LOAD.

Here too, we can compare the memory of a computer to the human brain. If you look up the number of your business partner in the telephone directory, you will adopt a series of mnemonic combinations to remember the number. You will write the number down, make your telephone call – and then you will forget the number.

The **short-term memory** of the brain can save data and make it available for a short time. Data stored in this way fades fast and is deleted after the action. The computer also has a short-term memory.

WHAT'S THIS?

Temporary memory can only save short-term information.

You know the telephone number of your best friends without having to look it up. Even after many years you will not forget your partner's date of birth and you can usually remember your address without the help of your filofax. The brain also has a **long-term memory** that can save information without time limits.

If you happen to call the phone number you had looked up in the above example several times, the process we know as **"remembering"** is set in motion. Probably, after the fifth or sixth call, you will know the number off by heart.

In this case, some information was passed from the short-term memory to the long-term memory; your computer carries out the same operation as well.

But is it true that information can be retained without time limitations, as the definition seems to imply? Let us return to our example. If you have not called a specific telephone number for some time, you will forget it. Was it 45589 or 45859? The longer the time span, the less likely you are to remember the number.

WHAT'S THIS?

Permanent memory can only save long-term information.

However, research carried out in the USA confirms that the mind never forgets information and once information is in, it is available for life. What we know as "forgetting" is in fact the loss of access to specific data. If the access path is activated for any reason, the forgotten information is suddenly available again, a process know as a "memory flash".

Computers are not capable of having memory flashes, but they have specific data paths for storing information on a permanent basis. To retrieve information for processing purposes, the processor needs the exact address where the information was stored. If the address is missing, the data is still stored but is effectively lost, because the address reference is no longer known.

WHAT'S THIS?

Every item of memory data needs an **Address** so that the processor can access it.

If the processor requests some information, the data must reach the processor via the memory. The "data highway" in your computer connects all the parts of your computer's memory and transports information between them.

The language of the computer: the binary format

Why is the number system based on the number 10? The **decimal system** – as the system based on 10 numbers is called — has its origin in the number of fingers on our hands. Our ancestors added up and subtracted using their fingers to help them count.

WHAT'S THIS?

The computer transport information system is called a **Bus system** or simply **Bus.**

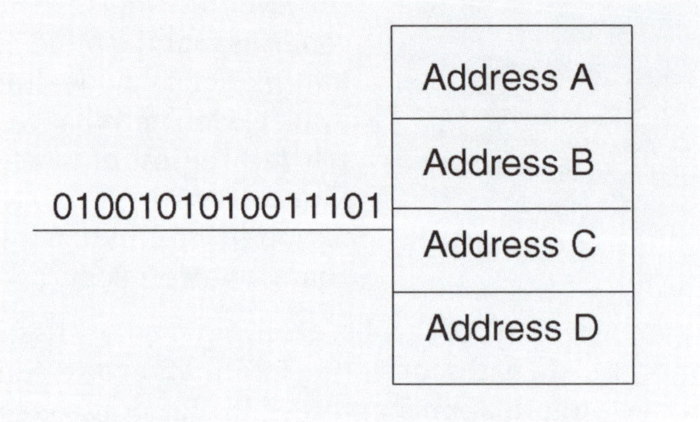

If the computer knows only the two states of binary and ASCII, which number format does it use? Computers work with a number system that takes this unusual feature into account.

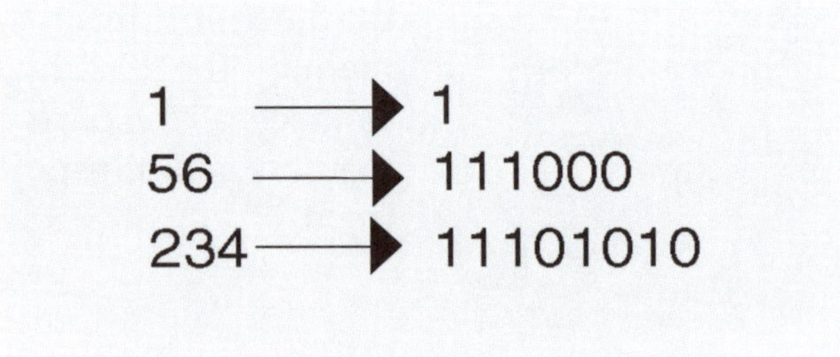

Each decimal number is perceived as a binary number. Binary numbers are made up of a string of zeros and ones; for human beings these numbers are incomprehensible. The computer **executes** the conversion and saves you the complex work. You can provide your computer with a plain text operation such as "add 50 plus 50" and get as a result "100". The computer has carried out its calculations using binary numbers, without you being aware of all this background work.

WHAT'S THIS?

The **binary system** is the number system of all computers and knows only two numbers: the one and the zero.

3 Start-up and shut-down

What's in this chapter:

You will now learn what happens between you switching on your PC and the graphic user interface starting. You will see that when you switch on your computer, it runs a self-diagnostic check and warns you of possible errors.
This chapter will also explain what an operating system is and describe what a driver is used for.

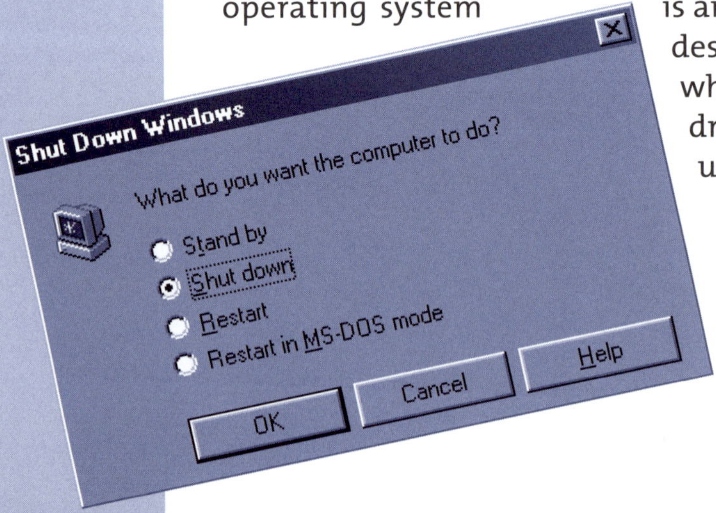

You already know about:

You are going to learn about:

The start routine

Switch on your computer. After a few seconds you will see the operating system start up and then the Desktop will appear.

The PC runs various important operations within a few seconds of the **start** (most of them in English). **Essential operations**, without which your computer would not start, are set up and run in this short period of time. These operations are often described as the "start-up" routine.

During the start, the computer runs and displays a report on the **hardware diagnostics** which will help your computer to start working safely and to avoid possible data loss.

The **shut-down** is also extremely important. If the computer is not shut down properly, data could be lost and your system could be damaged.

The summary at the beginning of this chapter tells you about the operation executed by your computer. The further learning steps in this chapter show you in detail what happens after switching your computer on.

At the end, the chapter explains why you cannot simply switch the computer off, but must first close all the applications that are currently open.

WHAT'S THIS?

Start-up means the effective start of the computer.

WHAT'S THIS?

Shut-down means an orderly termination of a working session with the computer, via an appropriate operating system within the computer.

1 Press the **“Power”** button of your computer.

A power supply built into the computer provides all components of the system with power. The hard disk spins with a whirring sound.

2 The computer starts a special diagnostic routine.

During the diagnostic routine the computer checks that all its systems are functioning correctly as well as identifying and notifying possible errors.

3 The computer reads information from a read-only memory.

In the third step, the computer reads the system settings from your hard disk or from other hardware equipment.

4 The computer loads basic routines.

Some routines, vital for running various basic operations, are loaded into memory.

5 The computer loads the operating system.

Windows 95, Windows 98, Linux, or other operating systems are loaded at a basic level.

6 Configuration files are loaded by the operating system.

Specific files adapt the operating system to the hardware.

7 The graphic user interface is loaded.

At the end, the popular Windows 98 interface (for example) appears. You may now start work.

Diagnostics: the POST routine

The computer starts a **special routine** when you switch on the power. While the computer is switched off a small program is stored in the read-only memory: this is called the POST routine. This abbreviation is made up of the first letters of the diagnostic **self-test run after switching on** ("Power On Self-Test").

WHAT'S THIS?

The **POST routine** tests the PC's systems and checks for errors.

This program generates a sequence of different codes which the PC evaluates internally and which trigger an immediate feedback. If, for example, there is a problem with the floppy disk drive, the POST routine reports "Floppy Disk Drive Failure". If no errors are selected, the PC reports "error code 00" and continues to boot up.

Your computer memory finds and displays the error code and can also determine the cause of the error using special **diagnostic hardware**. If the computer is equipped with the appropriate fault-fixing software, then it will repair the fault and the error message will disappear.

Although various errors can be recognised by the POST routine, the fact that the test is successful does not guarantee that your system is working fully and is completely error-free.

The ROM memory

The personal computer is an **open system,** which means that individual components can be shut down in different ways.

You may remember that, when you bought your PC, the salesperson asked you what size of hard disk you wanted, how much memory you needed and which graphic card you had selected.

How does your computer know the size of the hard disk you have installed or how many megabytes are available in the main memory? Another interesting question is how your PC can remember the date and time, if you stop its power supply.

WHAT'S THIS?

A **ROM memory** is a memory chip which retains information even if the computer is not switched on. No data can be written to this memory.

A Read-Only Memory, or **ROM** for short, contains information introduced by the manufacturer when the PC was built. Now, every time you switch on the PC, it accesses the ROM and selects information. Even the POST routine, which shuts down the different components of your computer, is stored in the ROM.

The name ROM underlines that you can **only read** from this memory, and that it is not possible to write to it. The ROM memory doesn't need any power once data has been written to it. Even after several years with no power supply, data can be retrieved in full from the ROM memory.

So far, everything sounds quite logical and easy to understand. However, what happens if your PC is fitted with **another hard disk** or additional main memory is installed? A small memory segment connected closely with the ROM can save specific parameters.

This memory is called **CMOS** and carries data to your hard disk or to the main memory. Every configuration is saved in CMOS.

> **WHAT'S THIS?**
> The **CMOS memory** contains important information about the components in your computer and cooperates closely with the ROM memory.

In this way, the data remains safe even after the power is turned off, because your PC has a small floating battery inside it. The battery provides the CMOS with power, and it also keeps the clock and the calendar running even while the PC is switched off.

When your computer is started, information is loaded from the PC's ROM and integrated with the data from CMOS.

> **WHAT'S THIS?**
> There is a small accumulator in the computer, called a **floating battery,** which powers some components of the PC.

If you haven't switched on your PC **for a few months**, the PC may well start with an error message and the operating system will not continue to load. The error message "CMOS Setup Checksum Error" is usually displayed when the floating battery is dead. This usually results in information being lost from the CMOS memory. If this happens, your computer is unable to recognise which hard disk and working memory are present.

> **TIP**
> If you only switch on your computer for short periods, such as half an hour every few months, it will cause problems. The floating battery is only recharged when the computer is on.

The RAM memory

WHAT'S THIS?

RAM is the abbreviation for "Random Access Memory". It only retains data and information when the power is switched on.

Your PC also has another type of memory, called RAM or main memory.

RAM is much faster than ROM but it is only able to save data for a long time when the PC is switched on.

The main memory has a central role. All data is saved in the main memory, and inputs are temporarily put in it. When the computer is switched on, ROM transfers speed-sensitive items into the faster RAM.

Because that data gets lost when you shut down the PC, a long-term memory is necessary. The main differences are explained later on in another chapter.

The BIOS: the core of the computer

WHAT'S THIS?

The BIOS checks that access to the hardware is loaded before the operating system.

Let's look more closely at what happens when you start your PC. So far, a self-diagnostic test has been executed, information has been loaded from the read-only memory and fed back as data to a configuration memory.

The default settings are now available; what is missing is a routine which makes **access** to the **main components** of the PC possible. For example, how is the PC going to know where to find the operating system?

The ROM memory also contains a number of programs which scan and control the hardware: **a save message** could appear at this point, such as: "instruction on the hard disk: save the document of the user in the memory area sector 3/track 4". We will explain later what a sector is. What is important here is that this routine communicates directly with the hardware.

This program deals with basic tasks and is called the **BIOS,** which stands for **Basic Input/Output System**. It is one of the programs stored in the ROM and is provided as part of the operating system by the manufacturer.

WHAT'S THIS?

An operating system is an interface between the user and the hardware. This is the sytem that talks to your printer, for example, and allows the printer to receive data files.

Boot sector and operating system

After loading the information from the ROM and the CMOS, your PC loads the operating system.

The operating system is like the soul inside the computer body. You will have been told about it when you bought your computer. You know that Windows 98 is one type of operating system.

An operating system gives information directly to the BIOS, and makes up an interface between you and the hardware. Because the BIOS of your computer communicates directly with the hardware, it sends an order to the operating system, for example: "message to BIOS: write the user's document on the hard disk". The translation into track and sectors is managed by the BIOS.

The main operating systems currently available are:

- Windows 3.x
- Windows 95
- Windows 98
- Windows 98 second edition
- Linux and UNIX
- Mac OS/2
- Windows NT 4
- Windows 2000

However, there are a number of other operating systems. They all provide the user with graphic and mouse interface, they organise and control data files, and can run several programs at the same time. Later chapters will give you more details.

WHAT'S THIS?

Resident programs are available permanently in the background to the memory. Operating systems are always resident.

At the back of the book you will find a detailed description of the essential performance features of individual operating systems.

To execute all the instructions that you give to the hardware (such as "Print document") the operating system must always be present. If the operating system is loaded, it guides you through to the shut-down and switching off of the computer. It will operate in the **background** while you, the user, write a letter with Word for Windows or create an illustration with CorelDraw in the **foreground**.

The technical term for this permanent presence is **resident**. The operating system is a resident program because it runs in the background.

WHAT'S THIS?

The **boot sector** is a small permanent area of a data file on which the operating system is stored.

How does the BIOS know which operating system you would like to load? In theory, you could use an alternative operating system, such as Linux instead of Windows 98.

Without the instruction "I use Windows", your computer doesn't know **the type of operating system**. At the start, it searches in the permanent area of the hard disk (and any floppy disk) for the operating system and the information it finds there provides the data about the operating system.

WHAT'S THIS?

Computer viruses are resident programs which may cause loss or corruption of data or other nasty effects. Boot sector viruses are a particularly dreaded species of computer virus.

This particular area of data files is called the **boot sector** and it always contains the operating system. "Booting" is a word borrowed from an American slang expression, and means the start-up of a computer. The BIOS loads

WHAT'S THIS?

The **kernel** is the smallest, but the most important, part of the operating system.

this permanent sector and interprets the stored data for the operating system.

Computer viruses nested in this area of the PC are particularly dangerous. They are loaded up directly at the start-up of the PC, and from here they can carry out their destructive work.

Of course, the entire operating system does not fit in the very small boot sector. Only a small part, known as the **kernel**, is loaded and the basic functions of the operating system are started.

Configuration and installation

So that the operating system can be adapted to your computer, many programs copy single files to your hard disk.

WHAT'S THIS?

When you install a new peripheral, the computer learns how to adjust to the changed environment created by, for example, a new hardware component.

For example, a new **computer mouse** comes with a floppy disk which must be "installed" after plugging in the mouse.

These files, which during the installation are stored on the hard disk, contain information about the new hardware and instructions for the operating system. This information defines the working of the new hardware. Such a file is also described as a **driver,** or hardware driver.

WHAT'S THIS?

A driver forms the basis for the integration of a new component into an existing computer system. Drivers are special files which are hidden on the hard disk during installation.

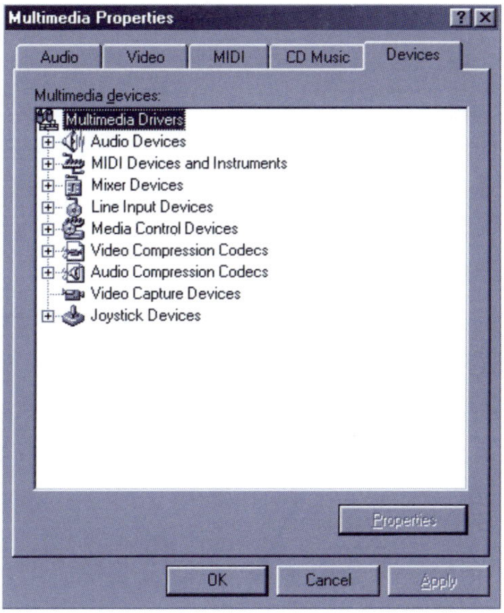

During installation, not only files are copied onto the hard disk, but the operating system is also adapted to the new conditions.

The **configuration files** will allow you to customise your computer to suit your needs and taste.

Every configuration alteration is recorded in a file which is therefore **dynamic**.

The CMOS is a kind of configuration file which does not form part of the operating system, but is loaded before the operating system.

The type and structure of the configuration files depend exclusively on the operating system. Several files can complement each other and interact with each other for configuration purposes.

WHAT'S THIS?

A **configuration file** contains information about the individual features and customising options of an operating system.

A configuration file may contain the following entry, for example: "This computer is equipped with a Logitech pilot computer mouse. When the computer is switched on, the suitable driver must first be loaded". To give you an idea of what this kind of information looks like in **computer language**, the next line shows the actual entry in the configuration file:

```
DEVICE=C:\CONFIG\LOGITECH.SYS
```

Other **programs** too are capable of identifying their own configuration file. So, for example, CorelDraw produces its own configuration file during installation.

In the Microsoft operating systems, which are MS-DOS, Windows 98, Windows NT, two typical configuration files are available. The file called **CONFIG.SYS** is complemented by a second configuration file, **AUTOEXEC.BAT**.

In addition, the Windows system works with a Windows-internal configuration file named **WIN.INI** which carries out tasks and specific functions.

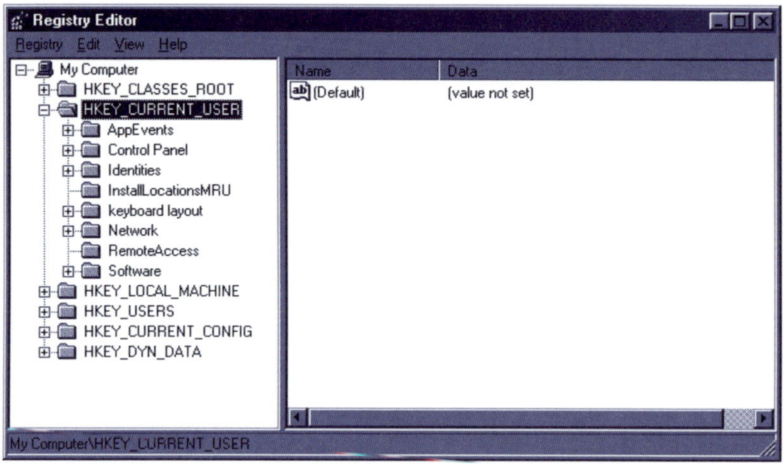

WHAT'S THIS?

The registration database is an extremely efficient form of configuration file.

Windows 95, Windows 98 and Windows NT 4.0 use a **registration database** which is in practice a more modern form of configuration file with additional features.

In the following pages you will see how an internal hardware driver is installed and how the Windows registration database is adjusted correspondingly. If you need to install a driver, you can use the following steps as a practical guide, to take you step-by-step through the installation process.

1 Close all programs which may be open because a system crash may occur during the installation of a driver.

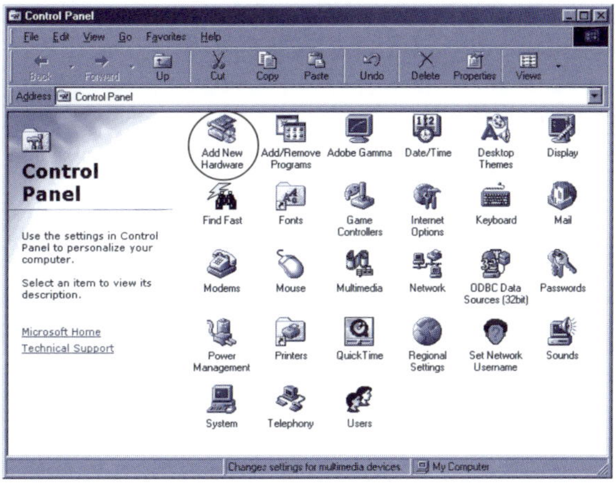

2 Click on the START button and choose the SETTINGS ENTRY. Click on CONTROL PANEL and choose the *Add New Hardware* icon.

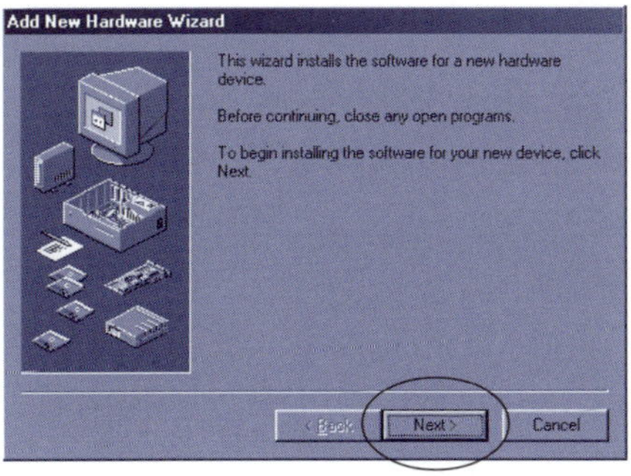

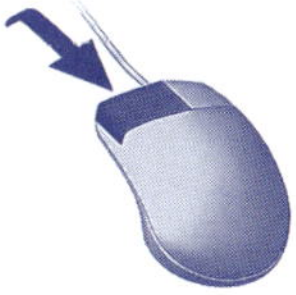

3 The *Add New Hardware Wizard* welcomes you. Confirm this window with a click on NEXT.

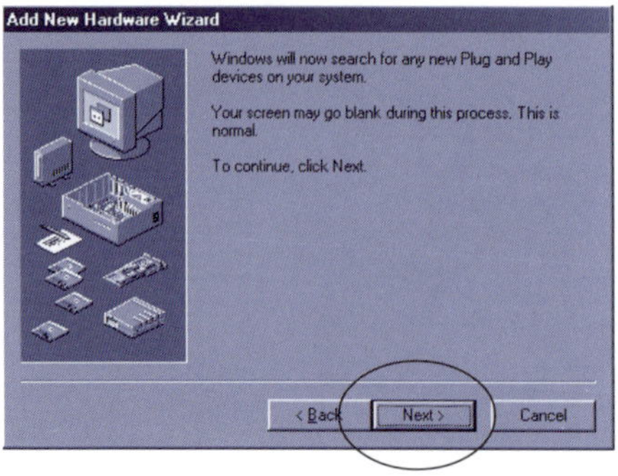

4 Windows asks you whether new hardware is going to be installed. Confirm this with a click on NEXT. You can confirm the following safety report also.

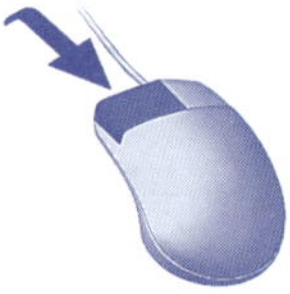

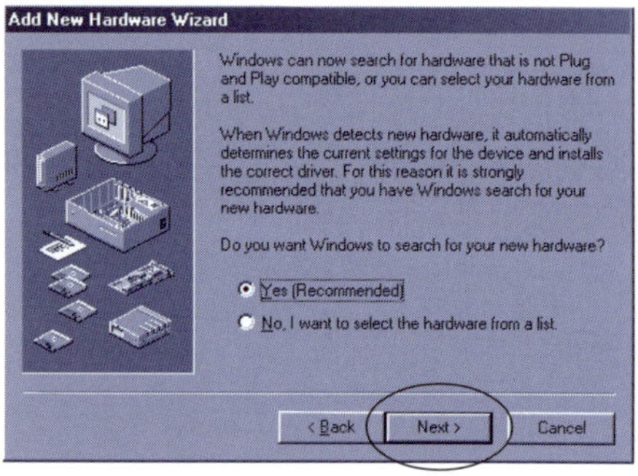

5 In this window, you can select hardware manually on older systems. Select "Yes" here and confirm with NEXT.

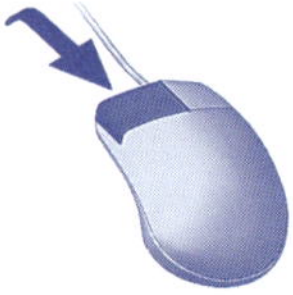

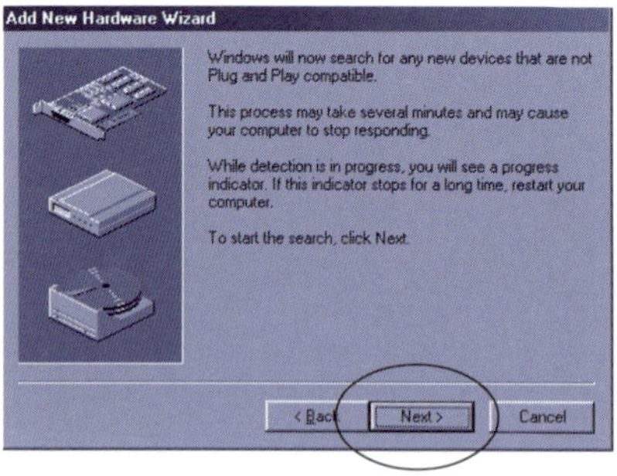

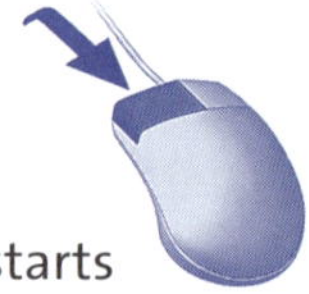

6 With the last dialog box, the hardware detection starts now on the monitor. Confirm with a click on NEXT.

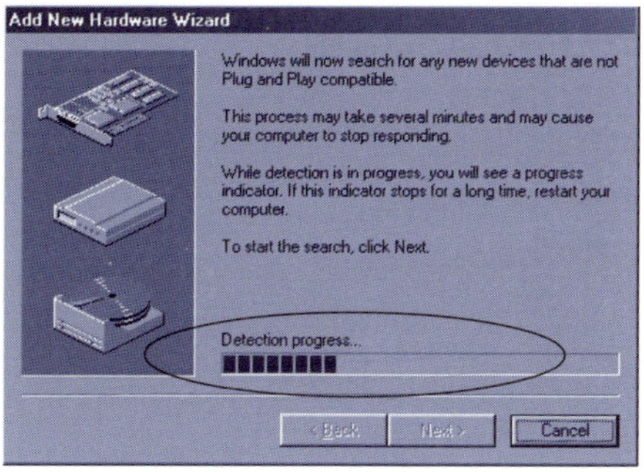

7 During the selection of new hardware, a progress bar which represents the installation process appears in the window, to show you the progress of the operation.

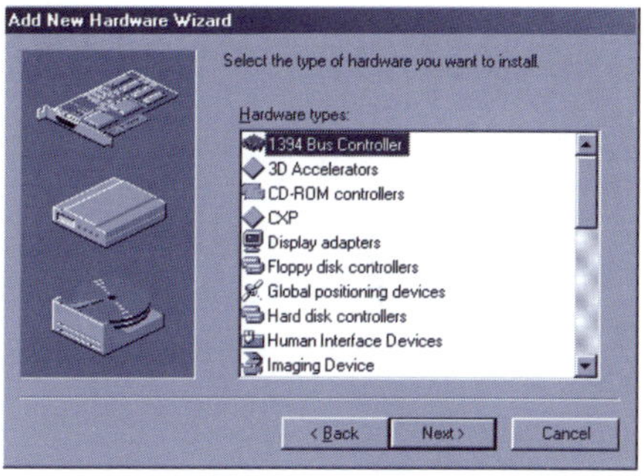

8 The hardware types are listed, so you can choose a specific type to assign to the driver.

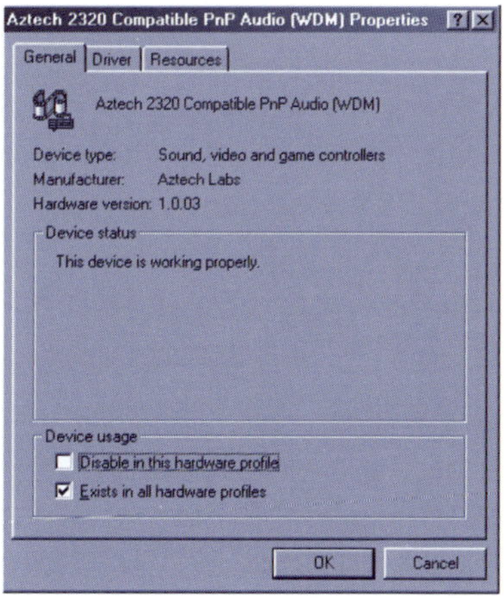

9 After installation, the hardware is operational and can be used by Windows.

Starting the Graphic Interface

After loading the kernels and all the necessary drivers, the **graphic interface** of the operating system is loaded.

While the configuration files AUTOEXEC.BAT and CONFIG.SYS were being loaded earlier, the **registration database** is only evaluated at this stage. This is how the driver, which is responsible for producing the soft copy, is loaded and can activate your printer driver.

Shutting down the operating system: finishing your work

A **basic mistake** which beginners are likely to make and which can lead to **serious system errors** is switching the computer off without shutting down the operating system.

Why is it so important that the computer should not just be switched off? Earlier **DOS versions** were less sensitive in this respect and did not have a specific function which could make them react negatively to being switched off abruptly. The entire DOS operating system covered only a small part of the area in the main memory which Windows 95 now requires. Windows 98 uses even more memory than Windows 95.

At the start, the main functions of the operating system are loaded into the main memory. As an "intelligent" operating system, its work is no longer transparent for you as the user. While you type text, for example, with MS Word in the foreground, Windows 98 may well be active in the background and start a maintenance process which you would not notice because it is working without you having any input into this activity.

It would be a **fatal** mistake to save your Word text and then switch off your PC. It would mean that the maintenance process running in the background would be interrupted with unforeseen consequences: the minimum that can occur is that some data would be lost, because you have interrupted an automatic background system operation which is vital to make sure that your computer carries on working as it should.

Users of older DOS versions always knew what their computer was up to. If Word was started in DOS, this maintenance process would not run in the background. Today, computers have a higher level of integration of functions, and are capable of executing several processes in parallel, therefore the danger of operations being executed without you realising it is also increased.

Sometimes you may have no control over whether your computer gets unintentionally switched off. For example, if a **power failure** occurs, or if you accidentally push the power switch of your PC.

Power failures which happen while a document is being saved or while other write processes are taking place are particularly dangerous and worrying for the user. A file which has not been saved is no longer readable by the computer. Although the file is useless, it still takes up space on the hard disk.

In this case, you should always run a routine test on the data files of your computer. **Corrupted** files are recognised and deleted by this check-up routine, so the hard disk is again returned to its original condition.

Windows 95, 98 and NT, for example, use a diagnostic program named SCANDISK, which is able to clear minor hard disk faults. Users of Windows 95 must start SCANDISK manually; Windows 98 detects minor system faults and automatically checks the local hard disks at the next start-up.

The following steps show you how a hard disk check-up is carried out. We have based our examples on Windows 95, but for more modern **operating systems** such as Windows 98, Windows NT, Apple Macintosh and OS/2 there are corresponding system tools available.

If you work with Windows 98 and you would like to check your **hard disk**, you can use the following steps as a practical guide, which will take you safely step-by-step through the hard disk checking process.

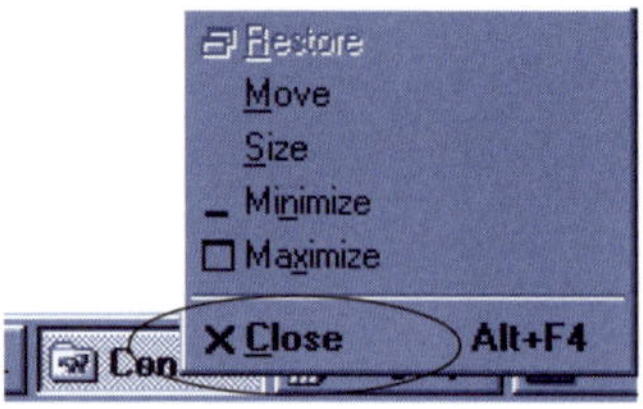

1 Shut down all open programs before starting the process, because the check run may well cause a system crash.

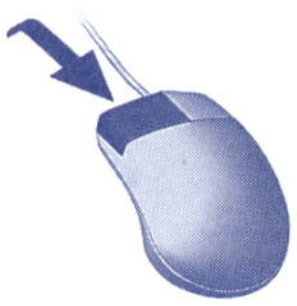

2 Click on the START menu button and choose PROGRAMS. First choose ACCESSORIES and then SYSTEM TOOLS in the menu that opens automatically. The hard disk checking program can be launched now with a click on SCANDISK.

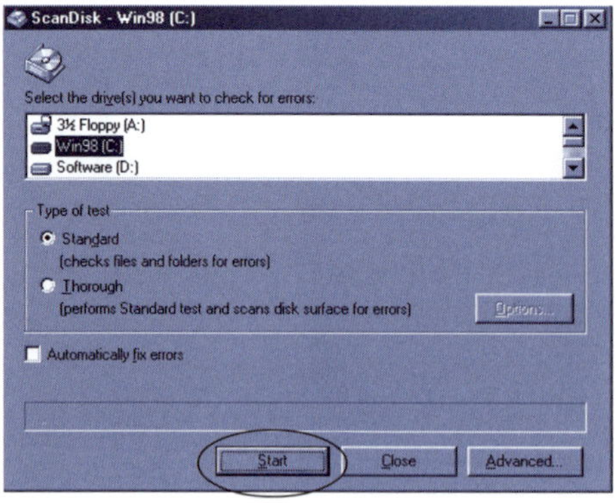

3 Select the *drives(s)* you wish to have checked and confirm the dialog box with a click on START in the Scandisk window.

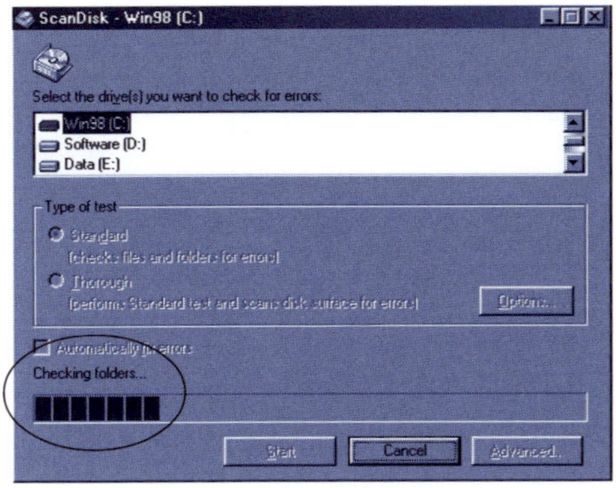

4 A progress bar shows you the progress of the hard disk checking procedure.

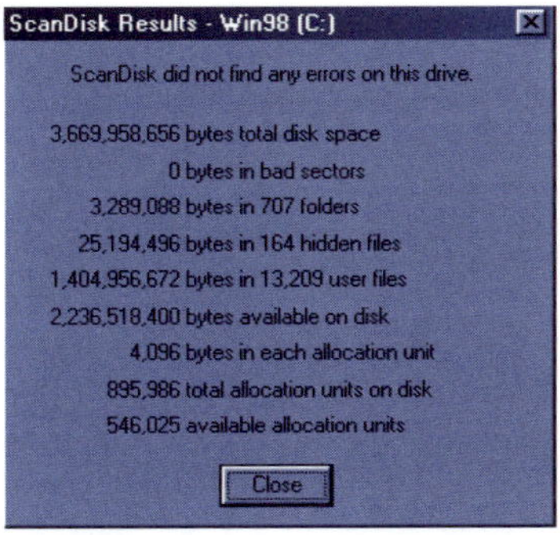

5 An error report lists the errors found, together with additional information concerning your hard disk, such as the free disk space.

4

From man to computer

What's in this chapter:

In this chapter, we will show you how to communicate with your PC. You are going to learn about all the features which differentiate the computer keyboard from a typewriter.

We will describe the function of a mouse and we will show you how a mouse works, in a step-by-step guide. In addition, you are going to learn what an interface is; how, for example, your printer is connected, and the functions of the ports on the back of your PC will be discussed.

You already know about:

You are going to learn about:

Communicating with your PC

Computer specialists have dreamt of the day when they are finally going to be able to establish natural **language communication with computer systems.** We can therefore imagine a scenario for when this dream finally comes through.

It's morning. You wake up. Still drowsy, you walk to your kitchen. All you need to wake up is a steaming cup of coffee. You know that your computer can understand your language commands, so you simply say: "Make me a coffee, please".

With your cup of coffee in your hands, you decide that you wish to read the latest electronic edition of your daily newspaper, which is already displayed on screen. So you make yourself comfortable in your armchair, and tell your computer: "Go to the next page".

Then you go to your office, and switch on your computer. The first thing you do is check your (**electronic**) **Inbox**. You see a letter from an old fellow student, who is currently spending some time abroad. You tell your computer: "Open letter from Michael". You read it and decide to reply immediately. So you **dictate** your long reply letter to your friend **to your computer,** and the letter is then mailed automatically.

You must admit: this scenario is still very much a dream. But dictating systems which can insert **complete texts** already exist. IBM has developed "VoiceType" , for example, which allows users to dictate whole texts using some specific features. Recognition of fluently spoken sentences is still a long way away, as it is too complex even for the latest computer systems.

Traditionally, you can communicate with your PC in various ways. In the following pages, you will learn to recognise and use the main **input devices** available to communicate with your computer.

Interfaces: the gate to the outside world

Follow the cable which connects your mouse to the casing of your computer. In most cases, the connecting cable goes in at the back of the case, in the plug-in socket.

Take the plug off, after manually unscrewing the securing screws. If you take the trouble to check the pins (contacts) on the mouse box, you will notice that there are exactly nine pins. Each of these pins carries **specific information,** either to the mouse or to the computer. Individual signals are specifically allocated to one pin only, so your mouse can communicate with your PC without any confusion.

This **plug-socket combination** is called an "interface". Different parts of equipment can be connected to different interfaces and your PC can thus be extended. The unit which is connected to this interface is the mouse.

It is true that there are many different interfaces, but your PC is capable of handling them all. Because every interface is equipped with a specific socket and uses a different number of pins, you **cannot make any mistake**. As a test, you can try and see whether the mouse can be plugged into a different plug on your PC.

WHAT'S THIS?

An **interface** connects external equipment with the computer using a standard hardware connection.

Every PC is equipped with the following interfaces:

1 The 9-pin serial interface
This interface is used for the mouse. Because the interface contains only nine pins, the plug is very narrow.

2 The 25-pin serial interface

The 25-pin serial interface socket is clearly larger than the 9-pin socket. This is used for the modem.

3 The 25-pin parallel interface

The parallel interface always connects the printer with the PC. Some external data files also communicate via the parallel interface.

4 The 15-pin game interface

When you connect a joystick to your computer to control games, you will find the game interface very useful.

What is the difference between these types of interface? The two **serial interfaces** are compatible with each other, and can be used for the same tasks.So, a 9-pin mouse can also be connected to the 25-pin serial interface, if a corresponding adapter is used.

Every interface can be inserted in both the "parallel" and "serial" port.

Information which is transmitted through a **serial interface** reaches the receiver only gradually. It is like a **one-lane secondary road**, where the vehicles are represented by the data. The vehicles (data) move (serially) one after the other. A serial interface is not particularly fast but it is **robust and indestructible**. It is very efficient for the transmission of small amounts of data.

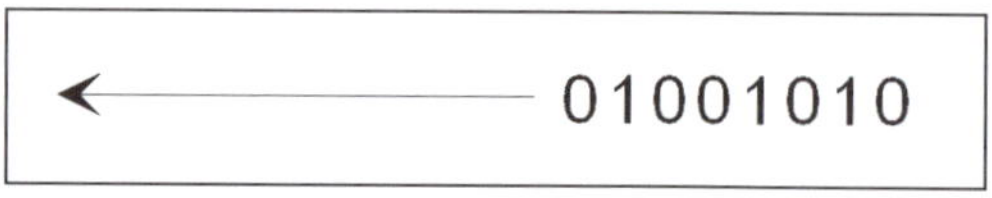

WHAT'S THIS?

The serial interface transfers only one information unit at a time. Larger amounts of data must be transferred one after the other.

WHAT'S THIS?

The **parallel standard interface** of a PC transfers eight information units simultaneously and is therefore faster than serial interfaces.

Larger amounts of data are transferred via **parallel interface**. The parallel interface on your PC, for example, extends the single track of the serial interface to more than seven. Altogether, eight data bits can be transmitted simultaneously with it, according to the transmission rate. Your printer, for example, receives several data bits at the same time, so you do not need to wait too long for your printout. Most time-critical activities are therefore run on a parallel interface.

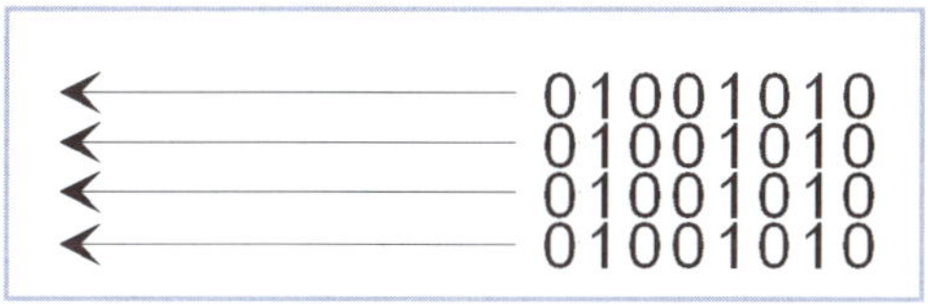

As well as printers, other items of equipment are usually connected to a parallel interface, for example **external storage devices** or **network cards** for portable computers.

Perhaps you will be surprised by the fact that a parallel interface plug has up to 25 pins, but is only capable of transferring eight data units at a time. Since only one pin is required to send one information unit, there are 17 pins spare, at least on the face of it.

What is the function of all these pins? The pins ranging from 14 to 25 are closely linked to each other. Some pins are idle and form a **"reserve"** for each project.

WHAT'S THIS?

Status signals, as well as data, are also sent by the interface. These signals transmit information about the operating state of the connected piece of equipment.

TIP

A serial data cable should not exceed 6 to 8 metres, a parallel cable should not exceed 5 metres.

WHAT'S THIS?

USB stands for Universal Serial Bus and is a new interface system, which gets around the variety of options for standards, thus reducing confusion. Windows 98 supports USB.

The remaining pins carry **status reports**, which a printer returns to the PC. This is how the PC "knows" that the active or online printer is switched off or it has run out of paper. These **status signals** are very important and are transmitted simultaneously with the live data.

The **length of a connecting cable** is of great importance for the correct trasmission of data. So, if you find that your printer prints unreadable data instead of the desired business letter, the reason may well be that the **cable is too long**. This would generate the feedback message "unavailable". To avoid such problems, cables should be as short as possible.

Windows 98 has finally put an end to the interfaces chaos: several manufacturers, such as the PC giant Siemens have designed a revolutionary system, called **USB** (Universal Serial Bus). PCs which are equipped with this system do not bother the user with technical details such as different plugs, connections or cable length.

PC cases, keyboards and monitors are now equipped with several sockets to which you can connect **arbitrary equipment**. You can connect the mouse to the keyboard or to the monitor, without any visible difference in performance. Another improvement is that now serial data transmission has become faster.

The USB also solves problems relating to drivers. The equipment connects to the USB and automatically installs the required drivers.

Other connections

When you looked for the parallel and serial ports on the back of your computer and have found them, you will also have noticed other ports – this is a good opportunity to introduce you to these briefly.

The power socket

We have already explained in the previous chapter that your PC is connected to the power supply with a **normal cable**.

The power supply regulates the voltage of the socket, used for connecting the monitor. This is an intelligent and practical way of doing it, because when you switch on your computer, the monitor is also powered up and therefore does not need to be switched on separately.

The monitor socket

A 15-pin plug is firmly screwed into a socket and has a very thick cable. This is the cable which connects the monitor and which receives information from the computer on what should be displayed. Because information transmission can be badly affected by outside interference and this can impact on the quality of the image, the cable is **protected**.

The audio jack

If your PC has an audio card, you will have discovered other sockets on the back of the computer case. Small round jacks transmit **audio signals** to a connected stereo. In addition, audio sources such as a cassette recorder or a microphone can also be connected.

Audio sockets are for stereo reception and transmission and are marked according to the standard identification protocol for audio systems, which is black (left channel) and red (right channel).

SCSI-external connections

Some PCs are equipped with a 40-pin extended SCSI external connection. We will explain SCSI in detail in another chapter. Special external equipment is connected to this connection, for example **scanners** to **import** graphics, photographs and text.

The network socket

In addition, if your PC is connected to others in a network, you will also have a network connection. Since there are many ways to create a network connection, there is no common network socket.

The online port

If you have bought an ISDN adapter or an internal modem, you will find another port on the back of your PC. It connects your computer to the telephone, for example with your ISDN connection.

The keyboard

You can use the keyboard intuitively, presumably because you remember the order of the keys from the **typewriter**.

If you have learnt to touch-type on a normal typewriter, you will have to learn new keys and key combinations. It is interesting to note that even people who type on PCs all the time, as part of their job, are unlikely to know the functions of all the keys.

The PC keyboard differs from a standard typewriter keyboard because it has a number of additional keys. It has 105 keys in total, including several **special keys to control special functions** which can in most cases be configured individually by the user.

This kind of keyboard is called the MF-II keyboard. This standard is used and adhered to by all manufacturers, and you will be able to check this, because your keyboard functions in exactly the same way on your colleague's PC.

Unfortunately, in the world of computers – and we have already witnessed this in the previous chapter – standards are not always what they are meant to be.

However, outside the PC world, there are many different types of keyboard. If you look at the MacIntosh or Amiga keyboard, you will notice that there are **considerable differences** from the way a PC keyboard is structured. Both computer keyboards show the characters keys, but all other keys are in a different order, are set up in a different way and even have different faces.

WHAT'S THIS?

MF-II keyboards have 102 keys. MF is the abbreviation of multifunction, because a PC keyboard provides more functions than a typewriter keyboard.

Look at the keyboard on your PC. The first letters on the keyboard are the **Q W E R T Y** keys, giving rises to the keyboard being known as a **QWERTY** keyboard.

European standard keyboards differ from the US standard. In the German keyboard, for example, instead of the Z there is a Y, which is why the same German keyboards are called QWERTZ keyboards. Both follow the MF-II standard keyboard parameters.

WHAT'S THIS?

Keyboards with the American character display are called **QWERTY keyboards.**

You will become familiar with all the keys on a modern keyboard and in this section we will show you how to use these.

Code pages prevent code chaos

How does your computer know whether you have connected a US standard or a German keyboard? The answer is that it doesn't know at all! If you attach a German keyboard to your PC, pressing the"Z" key produces a "Y" on the screen.

This is due to a specific reason. First of all, in the operating system, the integrated table called the "code page" contains **country-specific information**. For example, vowel mutations and the ß are included for German users, while French, Italian and Spanish users can use accented vowels instead.

WHAT'S THIS?

A code page contains country-specific information. It is loaded at the start-up of the operating system and during operation it remains in the background.

At start-up, the operating system will load the suitable code page, so that the right keyboard layout is available.

With code pages, a PC becomes extremely flexible.

Connecting to the PC

TIP

If a cable happens to be too short, you can buy a spiral extension for a few pounds in specialised shops.

TIP

If you want to work with a standard keyboard at a computer with a PS/2 connection, you must buy a suitable adapter.

Now look at the cable that connects the keyboard to the PC. A five-pin round notched plug is used and can only be inserted one way, so you cannot get it wrong. Some models show a **small white arrow** on the side of the plug pointing to the top of the plug.

Some computers are provided with sockets which are clearly too small to be used with the standard format. This is called the PS/2-keyboard socket, because IBM first used this type of socket in its PS/2 model. Usually, laptops are equipped with PS/2 keyboard sockets, to save space.

Setting up your keyboard

Under the keyboard there are two feet, which help you position the keybord so that it slopes, so that it is easier and more comfortable to work with it.

Under some keyboards there is a small switch, labelled "OT/XT". Earlier computers of the XT generation worked with a different keyboard layout which was not compatible with modern computers.

With this switch, your keyboard can be used with the old XT standard. This switch has no relevance today; it is a relic from earlier times.

We mention this switch for an essential reason: if the XT switch is in the wrong position, your PC will not recognise the keyboard. The start operation will be broken off and you will get an error message: "**keyboard fault**". Who would think that you need to look *under* the keyboard?

How to find your way around the keyboard

The main entries correspond to the keys on your keyboard. You enter your text and simple number combinations with the alpha-numeric area of the keyboard.

On the top row, you will find twelve keys, numbered F1 to F12. These are **function keys** which are subdivided into three or four blocks.

On the top left hand corner there is the [Esc] key, and on the top right side, near the **function keys**, you will find another three keys: [Print], [Scroll] lock and [Pause].

The right side of the keyboard contains the numeric key pad which corresponds to the "calculator". Every key has a double function and the key face shows these additional functions as well as the number it represents.

Between the letters and the numeric pad, you will find four arrow keys, and six other different keys.

The input block

To enter text, you will use the alpha-numeric input block. Fast typists will find it useful that the "F" and "J" keys are **recognisable to the touch**: the keys are marginally narrower on some keyboard models, or else are slightly raised. Basically, this makes orientation easier for touch-typing.

The typewriter can produce capital letters by pressing the [⇧] key together with the corresponding letter. The same function is carried out by the Shift key on the keyboard.

You use the Caps Lock key if you want to write a whole sentence in capital letters, for example a heading. A **green light** on the right side of the keyboard shows that the Caps Lock key is active. To return to the normal mode, just press the Caps Lock key again and this light will go off.

If you want the key to type a third character, just press the [Alt Gr] key and the appropriate key. The euro symbol, for example, can be produced with the combination [Alt Gr] + [4]. The copyright symbol (©) is produced with the key combination [Alt Gr]+[C].

The Enter key

The "Return" key on the typewriter corresponds to the Return or Enter key on the computer. This key is on the right hand side of the alpha-numeric block and is easy to see because it is the largest key present.

In the various computer and software documentation, both the terms Enter and Return are used. Both names identify the same key; in this book we will call it the Enter key.

The Enter key is mainly used to confirm an order to the operating system. For example, if you order your computer to delete your hard disk, the command will only be executed when you confirm it by pressing the Enter key.

The Enter key also has other functions, for example in word processing: pressing [↵] will take you to a new paragraph in the document.

The numeric pad

If you are entering a large amount of numeric data, it is easier to use the numeric pad.

It is difficult to explain why some users rarely use the keypad. One of the reasons may well be that the numeric pad supports two functions at the same time.

The **numeric keypad** also contains keys which allow you to move around on the screen. If you are working with an electronic spreadsheet, for example, you can use the arrow keys to move comfortably to the desired position.

TIP

You can recognise the current status of the [Num] key by the green light (status light) with "Num"underneath it.

You can alter the number or the navigation functions for the keys with the arrow symbols by pressing the [Num] key. If you wish to revert to the original function for that particular key, just press [Num] again.

Navigation keys

The four arrow keys which are to be found next to the **numeric keypad** on the left are used to move quickly around a document.

WHAT'S THIS?

The cursor is a flashing line which indicates where text will appear when you type.

The way **navigation keys** work and what they do is linked to the program you are using. We will introduce you to the typical uses of the navigation keys.

The Home key brings you back to the beginning of the line in word processing software.

Many spreadsheets use the Home key to move back to the beginning of the table or of the row.

The End key takes you to the end of the current line. It is the opposite of the Home key.

The Pg↑ and Pg↓ keys move your cursor up or down the screen. In this way, you can quickly view the whole of the document and correct errors.

The Ins and Del keys are not part of the navigation keys, strictly speaking, but are are positioned in the same place on the keypad. In most word processing packages, and also for entries in the operating system, the Ins key changes into the overwrite mode, which means that text you type in this mode types over previously typed text, thus replacing it.

The four arrow keys which are directly below the navigation keys are used to move the cursor. These have the same function as the arrow keys in the numeric pad.

The function keys

The **function keypad** which is positioned above the number row of the alpha-numeric block contains twelve keys. PC beginners, who have been producing their work on a typewriter before, tend to confuse the two top keyboard rows.

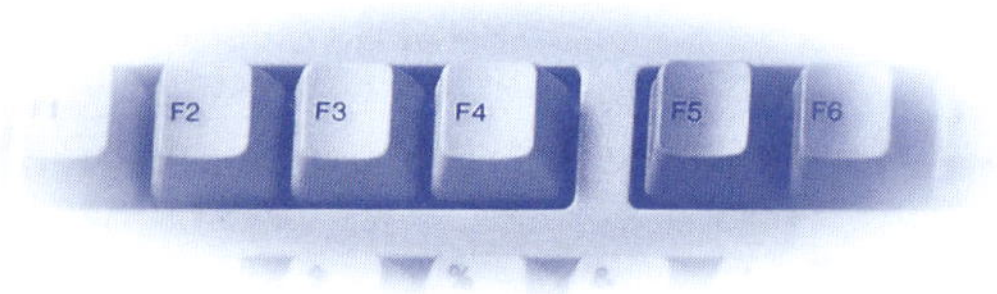

Function keys fulfil particular functions, as their name states. But what is the function of each key?

Function keys can be assigned specific functions to suit the user, as well as having their own original function. For example:

If you are writing a document in a word processing package and need to insert frequent tables in your text, you can simplify this by creating a specific function key. You can define a standard table in Microsoft Word, for example, and link it to your document with the F12 key. So, when you produce a table, Word will insert it in your document quickly, maintaining its format, whenever you press F12.

Some function keys are set up by default. Different functions can be activated depending on the **operating system** you are using. If you work in Windows 98, the Help function, which answers your questions about the program, is activated.

You will be able to learn the function of these keys by following our step-by-step guide.

The Escape key

The top left key on your keyboard is of great importance. The Escape key marked with "Esc" stops a current operation or an **execution**.

For example: if your computer asks you to confirm that you want to delete all data from your hard disk, and you want to change your mind, the [Esc] key stops the **operation**. If you have activated the print function by mistake, but do not want the current document printed, [Esc] interrupts the printout.

The Control keys

You will find the [Ctrl], [Alt] and [AltGr] keys on the same level as the space bar. There are two [Ctrl] keys, one on each side of the space bar.

We have already introduced the [AltGr] key, but which tasks do the other three keys accomplish?

"Ctrl" is the abbreviation for "**Control**". The two control keys do the same job and they are available on both sides of the keyboard for convenience.

The [Alt] key ("Alt" is short for "Alternative") has a similar function as the [Ctrl] keys. This is why the [Alt] key comes under the general label of "control keys".

When you press the Ctrl or Alt key, nothing happens. Both keys work only in combination with an alpha-numeric key. This means that, for example, if you wish to use the combination Ctrl + Home you keep the Ctrl key pressed and then press the Home key.

By using key combinations, you can execute many standard functions faster. If you are using a word processing package and want to write some text in italics, for example, you can do this with the key combination Ctrl + I.

Windows keys

Microsoft introduced a keyboard which was especially set up for Windows 95, which of course is also fully compatible with Windows 98. Although Windows 95 can be used with an MF-II keyboard, the special Microsoft keyboard has considerable advantages for the user.

With the Start key you can activate the start menu. The Start key has the same function as clicking on the Start menu button.

The second Windows key corresponds to clicking on the right mouse button. Using this key you can call up a special menu, which contains the most frequently used program functions. We will show you how the right mouse button works later in this chapter.

Both keys can be replaced by a mouse click, so it is difficult to see why the keys are there!

However, if you do a lot of work on your PC and frequently use the Start menu and the function menu opened by the right mouse button, you will appreciate these additional keys. The point is that you can carry out these actions on the keyboard without using your mouse.

Special keys

Three more special keys are above the position keys. You will rarely need to use these keys. They are a leftover from DOS and have lost their meaning in modern operating systems, such as Windows 98.

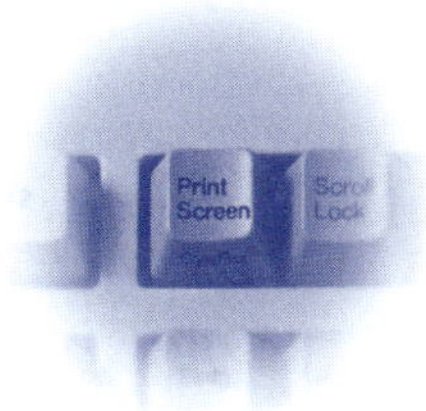

The [Print] key prints of the current screen (to give what is defined as a hard copy) in the DOS window and in DOS mode.

With the [Scroll] key you position the screen so that the navigation keys do not move the cursor, but rather scroll the text in the desired direction. A green status light confirms that the [Scroll] key is active.

The [Pause] key interrupts the operating program in the DOS mode; if you press it again, the action is resumed. This key does not affect the status of Windows 95 programs. With the key combination [Ctrl]+[Pause] some programs can be interrupted in the DOS mode.

The mouse

The **computer mouse** is the perfect complement to the keyboard. It is a **pointing device** to be used as an input device. Using the mouse buttons, you can move to any position on the screen and carry out several functions.

We will look first at what a mouse is and then at how it works.

A computer mouse consists of a **plastic case** which contains a **mobile ball** that can rotate, if the mouse is moved on a solid surface. It is important that the mouse should only be moved on a special surface, the mouse pad.

The rotation of the ball is converted into a signal. This is transmitted to the two buttons which you click, and these then relate the message to the serial interface of the computer via a cable.

The status of the serial interface is transmitted to the operating system by a special program – the **mouse driver**. The operating system projects a mouse pointer onto the screen so that you can see where you are; the position of the pointer corresponds to the movements of the mouse.

Clicking on one of the mouse buttons activates functions, such as a drop-down **menu**. Most mice have **two buttons**, but there are also mice with **three buttons**, in which case the middle one is only active in special applications, and does things such as scrolling down a screen.

What is the difference between the left and the right button?

The left mouse button is used to activate a function or to set up a command on your computer. The left button is the one that is most often used; when you read "click on..." in a manual, the instruction always refers to the left mouse button.

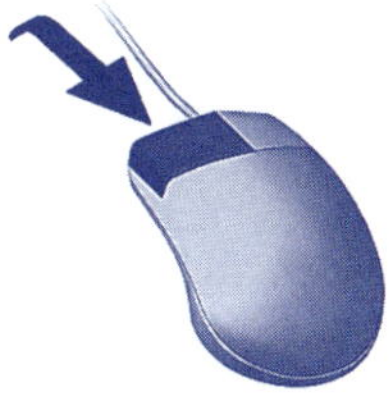

A **single click** selects an icon and activates it for a following action, such as deleting or renaming a file.

A **double click** with the left button opens the file which the mouse cursor is pointing to. The interval between the two single clicks is only a few milliseconds and most users find that they have to practise this move before they can get it right. So, remember: a single click is for selection, while a double click is for activating a file.

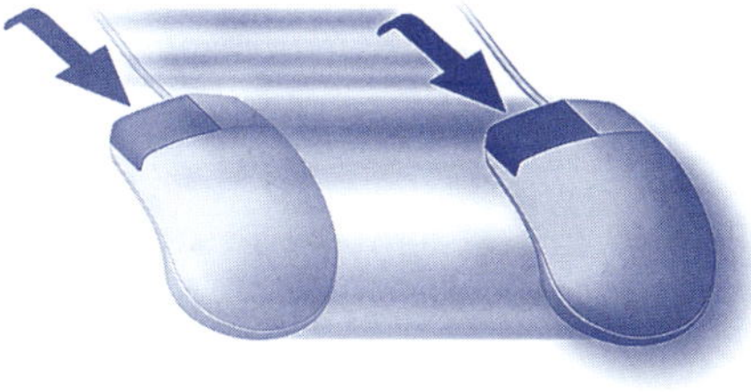

You will often notice that an icon or a piece of text can be "**dragged**" to a specific position. To move an icon with the mouse, press on the left mouse button and keep it pressed. If you move the mouse, this will "grab" the symbol with the mouse pointer so that you can move it to a new position on the screen. When you reach the desired position, release the left button of the mouse and the icon will be released as well.

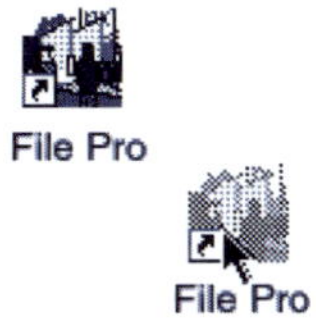

A file can be deleted in this way. The symbol of the file needs only to be dragged into the **Recycle bin**. When you drop the file in the Recycle bin, the file stays there and can be deleted from the bin. We will practise this in a later chapter.

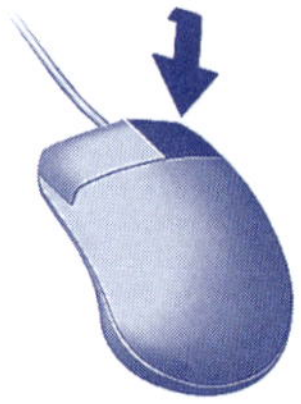

The function of the **right hand mouse** button is confined to a few selected operations. It activates a context menu which displays functions matching your specific needs in Windows.

Does your mouse have a third button? The middle mouse button is only used with special software, for example to create graphics and drawings. Special programs by the manufacturer LogiTech use the middle mouse button as a replacement for double-clicking with the left mouse button.

WHAT'S THIS?

The **drop-down menu** includes entries for the most frequently used actions appropriate to the software you are currently using.

When the mouse "hangs"

Occasionally the mouse seems to "hang" on an operation. Instead of following your movement on the mouse mat, the mouse pointer remains motionless on the screen.

The reason is that dust and other minute particles may have found their way inside the case, affecting the work of the very sensitive switches.

In this case, the ball and the inside of the buttons must be **cleaned**. This takes a couple of minutes. Turn the mouse on its back and remove the ring that keeps the ball inside the case. Take the ball out and wash it in a **mild soap solution**. The mechanism controlling the buttons can be easily recognised. Clean this with a cotton tip moistened with a little **alcohol**. After **cleaning and drying** all the elements, insert the dry ball back into the casing.

Working with keyboard and mouse

Now that you have become familiar with the functions of the special keys and you know how to handle the mouse, you can apply this knowledge to a "live" experiment.

We will take you through the functions of the mouse in the following pages with a step-by-step guide and show you how the main key combinations work in practice.

You can follow the examples working directly on your PC, if you are using the Windows 95, 98 or NT 4.0 operating systems. The functions we have introduced also work on other interfaces with the same principle, such as OS/2 and UNIX-X11.

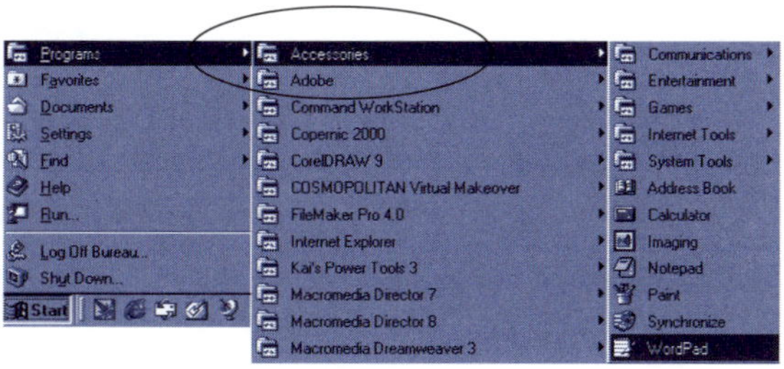

1 Click on the START button with the left mouse button and, in the open menu, move the mouse pointer to the top item, PROGRAMS. After a small delay, Windows opens a further menu on the right. Look for the entry ACCESSORIES and move the mouse pointer onto this. Another menu will appear on the right. Then, click once with the left mouse button on the entry WORDPAD.

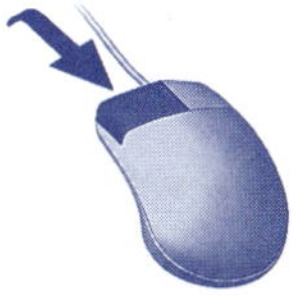

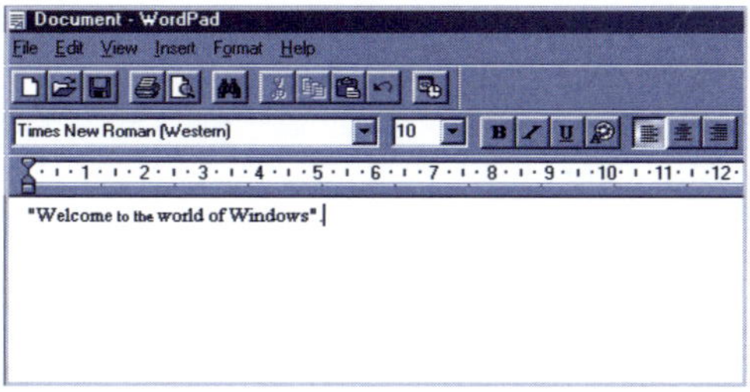

2 At first, you will see the flashing cursor on a white page. Now type the sentence: "Welcome to the world of Windows".

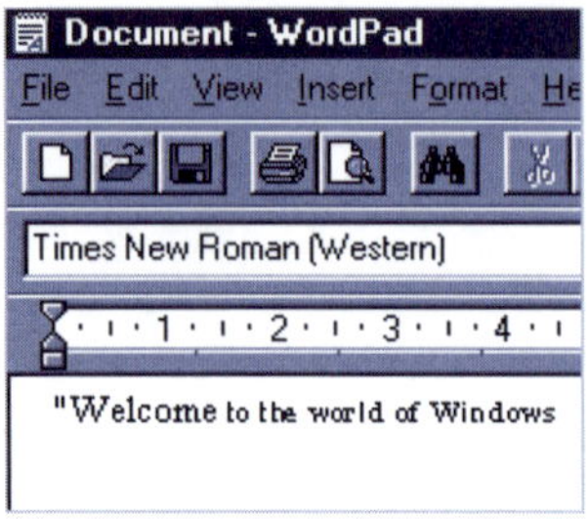

3 With the help of the arrow keys, you can now navigate within the written text. Press the left arrow button repeatedly, and move the cursor to the word "world" using the arrow keys on the numeric pad.

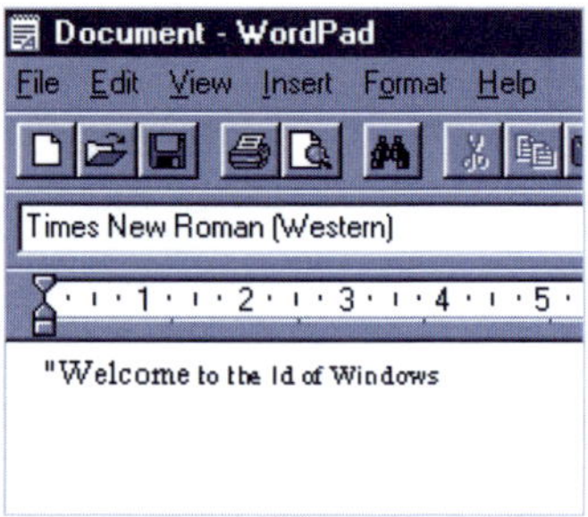

4 Delete the first three letters of the word "world". Press the Del key repeatedly until only "ld" is left.

5 Retype the text you have just deleted.

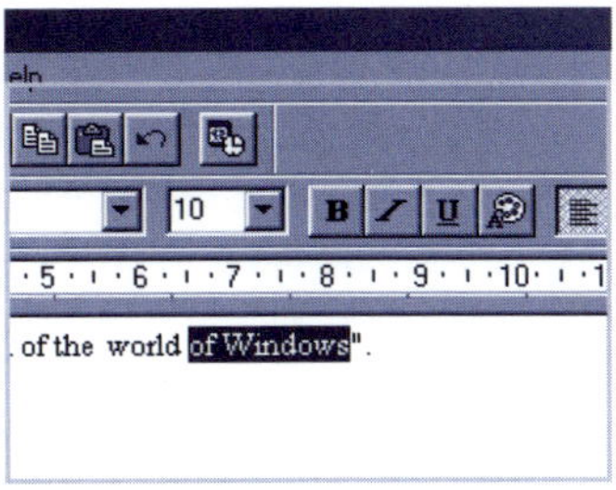

6 Now, select "of Windows" with the mouse. Click the left mouse button before the "o", keep the left mouse button pressed and move the mouse slowly to the right. The further you move to the right, the more letters are highlighted in black. When you reach the end, press the Del key to delete the highlighted part.

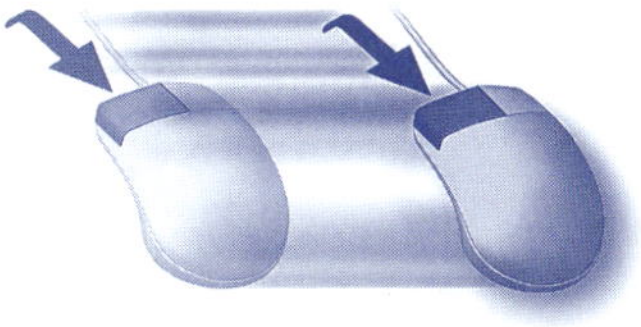

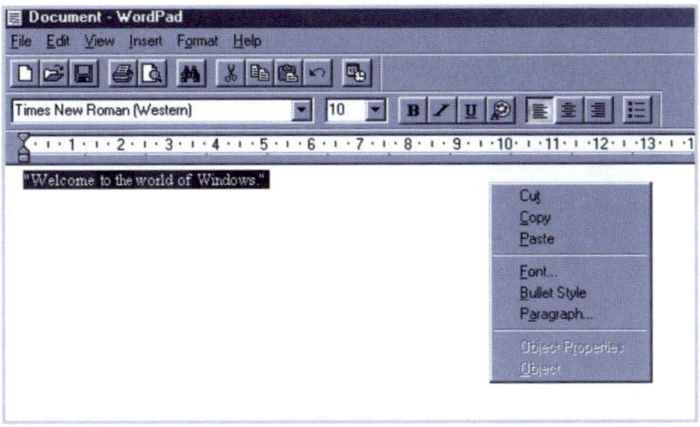

7 Now we want to change the format of the document. Select the remaining text as described in the previous step. Move the mouse pointer to any selected part, and click the right mouse button. The context menu gives you options for changing the way the text looks. Change the document font from Times New Roman to Arial.

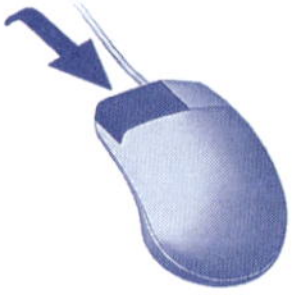

8 Now you want to change the word "world" to bold. First select the word and then click with the left mouse button on the "B" button which is above the text.

The word "world" appears clearly darker under the grey highlight. Click on "B" again to undo the bold.

9 This action is faster with a key combination. Select the word "world", if you have removed the bold in the previous step. Press the left Ctrl key together with the left ⇧. Now click on the B button and the selected text will change to bold.

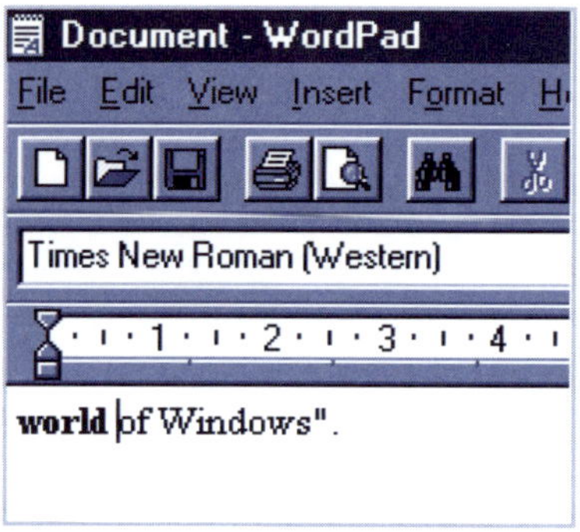

10 As a final step, we will practise using the mouse. First select the word "world". Now click once with the left mouse button on the highlighted word and keep the mouse button pressed. Move the mouse slowly to the left. A small box shows that an object (in this case your word) is "attached" to the mouse pointer. When you have put the mouse pointer before the word "Welcome", release the left mouse button.

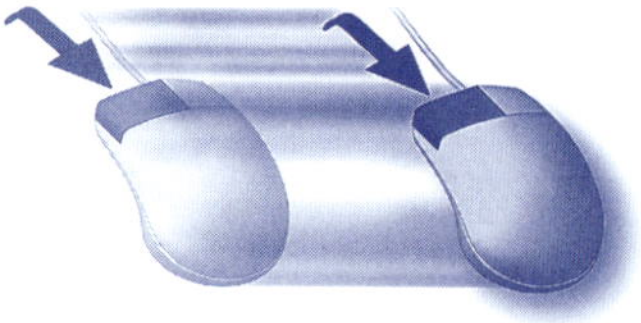

Congratulations! You have successfully completed your exercise. If you had problems with one or more steps, you should repeat the exercise or read again about the functions of the mouse and the keyboard. Remember that you can only work successfully if you know exactly how to use the basic functions of a PC.

The joystick

We have almost reached the end of this chapter. To finish, we would like to explain briefly how a joystick works. The first thing to know is that there are two different types of **joystick**.

A joystick is a type of mobile lever. The joystick is connected to the **game port** of the computer and is what you need to play games when these require the use of a joystick. The installation of a driver software is executed in this way.

Joysticks are adapted from aeroplane control levers and allow a realistic control of simulations, such as the movement of characters in games.

Each position is reported as active or not active by **digital joysticks**. But a joystick allows movements in all directions, not only **interstages**. Digital joysticks are particularly inexpensive to produce, because they only require switches to control the lever.

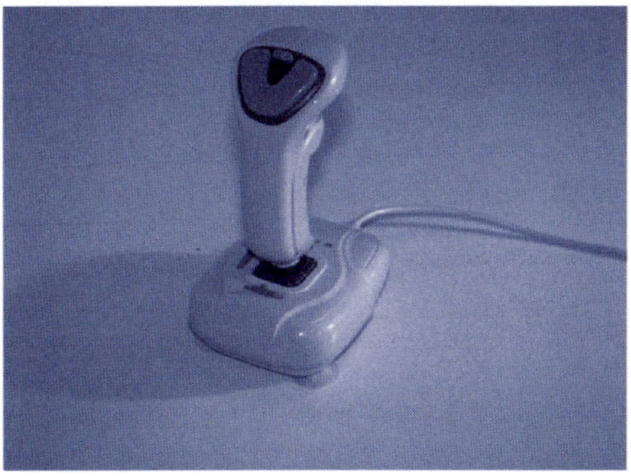

The position of the lever is controlled by sensors in **analog joysticks**. For realistic simulations an analog joystick is therefore recommended, but these are usually more expensive than digital models.

Test your knowledge

Main theme: Input devices and interfaces

You will find five tests throughout this book. By answering the questions, you can assess your learning progress and discover any gaps in your knowledge.

If you have enough time, write down the answers and compare them with the solutions at the end of the book (see page 343).

1. Which standard does a PC keyboard follow?

2. What is a code page and why is it important?

3. Which do the following keys mean?

   a) Ctrl

   b) Alt

   c) Esc

   d) Ins

   e) Home

   f) End

   g) Print

   h) Function keys

4. When experimenting in the BIOS of your PC, the Setup program asks whether you would like to save changes you have made. Although you confirm the query with "Y", the changes are not executed.

   Why is this? What can you do?

5. What is the difference between a joystick and a mouse?

6. What is a mouse driver and why must it be installed before the mouse can be used?

7. To which interface is the mouse usually connected?

8. Which four interfaces are integrated by default in a PC?

9. What is the difference between serial and parallel communication? What are the advantages of a parallel interface compared to a serial one?

10. What is the game interface for?

5 Digital documents

What's in this chapter:

This chapter shows you how to manage and save data on your PC. We are going to explain how floppy disk drives and hard disk drives work and the difference between magnetic and visual storage media.
You will then be shown how to handle folders, disk drives and documents and how to save data, as well as how to create a folder scheme.
You will learn how to write, save, sort, rename and delete documents in folders. In this way you will become familiar with basic operations.

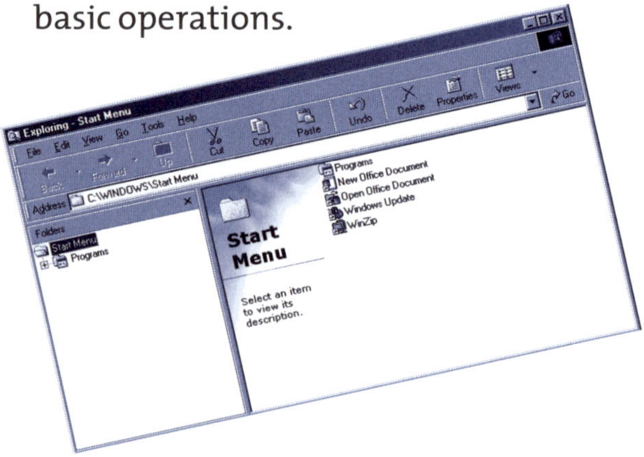

You already know about:

You are going to learn about:

The paperless office?

1980 was the year of the "**Digital Revolution**", when the attention of the mass media began to focus on personal computers.

It was then fashionable to talk about the "**paperless office**", because the computer was going to make paper documents redundant. Over twenty years later, we now know that these forecasts were too optimistic. Every office still sends letters printed on normal paper.

In fact, most players in the computer field have serious doubts as to whether the flow of paper has decreased. It appears sometimes that computers have generated a paper avalanche, with their never-ending test printouts, to check electronically stored information .

It is however true that paper-based communication has become more professional and efficient. With **standard letter templates**, which are an integral part of most word processing software, adapted for different people, writing a letter is now extremely simple. Current laser printers and ink-jet printers are very accurate and provide high quality printouts.

In addition, the software for data management and word processing has become much more user-friendly. Early programs, created by IBM in 1980, required users almost to have a degree in information technology. Today, Windows allows a **virtually intuitive** use and does not require users to have any technical knowledge at all.

Futurologists such as Brad Viennese and David Pescovitz consider the coming of the paperless office improbable, at least in the foreseeable future. The real paperless revolution has been generated by the Internet: you can submit contracts on the Internet, for example. With the electronic equivalent of your signature, the "**digital signature**", you can even sign contracts online.

This chapter will explain the relationship between magnetic media and paper. We will show you how to store documents you have created in folders and how best to organise your computer.

Saving data

The principle that allows your PC to store data is not as revolutionary as it might appear to be. If you have recorded a normal **audio cassette** before, you already know how your PC saves information: magnetic particles are gathered in a magnetic field. A hard disk contains a very large number of such **magnetisable particles** and can save the corresponding information.

WHAT'S THIS?

A hard disk is a unit which can save information, to be retrieved at any time.

Can a magnet save data? Go back to the introductory chapter of this book, where we explained the difference between analog signals and digital signals.

The main difference between the audio cassette and a computer data carrier lies here. While cassettes record sound in the form of analog signals, data carriers save the information as binary signals.

A magnetic particle corresponds to the status "1 ", while a non-magnetic particle correspond to "0". Particles are like solid layers found on a **disk** or a **tape** and are provided with a protective coating.

Permanent and temporary memory

If the information stored magnetically is retained even when the power supply is off, we call it "**permanent memory**". If you switch off your PC, the information saved on the magnetic hard disk remains unchanged. If you want to go back to the data later, the information can be loaded up by the hard disk.

WHAT'S THIS?

A **permanent memory** stores digital information, even when the power supply is turned off.

Remember the operations which run when the PC is started. The **memory chips** of the PC must read data from a read-only memory, the **ROM**. If the power supply to this memory chip is interrupted, the information contained in it is immediately **deleted**. Electronic memory is not permanent.

WHAT'S THIS?

A **temporary memory** only stores digital information so long as the power is swiched on.

The term "permanent memory" is however misleading in a way. The mini magnets are very sensitive to magnetic external influences. If you run non-magnetic particles through a magnet the digit "0" is changed into "1", with the result that the stored information is no longer correct.

Read/write head

A highly developed, miniaturised **electromagnet** moves across the data media disk. During the process of writing information, the magnet is under tension when the "1" state is to be written, while it is switched off when the "0" state is to be assigned to a particle.

CAUTION

All magnetic data carrier react strongly to magnetic and electrical fields. Keep hard disks, floppy disks and other data carriers well away from magnetic fields!

The process of reading stored information is the reverse. When the electromagnet crosses a magnetised spot, a voltage is generated and interpreted as "1". Otherwise, the head remains without tension; this state is consequently recognized as "0".

The magnet is fastened on to an **arm** which allows it to move on the hard disk. The mini magnet is called a read/write head because it is capable of both saving and loading data.

WHAT'S THIS?

The **read/write** head saves and loads information which is on the hard disk.

Tapes and disks

Early magnetic storage tapes were just like audio cassettes, and early storage units could use normal audio cassettes. Further developments worked with **proprietary formats** and used tapes which were bigger and had **more capacity**. Drives which take these magnetic tapes are called **streamers**.

WHAT'S THIS?

Drives which can read and write magnetic tapes are called streamers.

These magnetic tapes are still around and are mainly used for back-up. However, magnetic tapes have a large number of **practical disadvantages**, and this has led to the development of other types of data storage.

In any case, today's **professional data technology** still uses magnetic tapes. A high performance magnetic tape has a capacity of **48 Gigabytes** and thus can save approximately two million (!) A4 pages.

Let us look at a magnetic tape. A sequence of magnetic and non-magnetic particles is loaded onto the tape. If we want to access information which is stored at the end of the tape, the user must **rewind** the magnetic tape, an operation that may take some time. Therefore **access time** is very long compared to other data carriers.

A further disadvantage is the fact that one needs to use special hardware. If you want to save a letter written on your computer, for example, on a magnetic tape, you can only do so indirectly using a specific driver.

WHAT'S THIS?

Access time is the average period of time which lapses between accessing two different items of information.

WHAT'S THIS?

Hard disks are built with read/write heads and magnetic coated disks which can save data.

The best alternative is hard disks, which we have already discussed: the magnetic particles are no longer deposited on a tape but are copied on to a rotating plate.

The read/write head is fastened on to an arm which moves over the hard disk. With a fast rotation of the disk, specific areas can be run optionally into the magnet layer.

If we look at the element of retrieval time as a cost, the access time of a hard disk is much lower than for a magnetic tape, therefore they are better value. A further advantage is the way hard disks are built. The read/write head does not touch the interface of the magnetic layer directly – which is what happens with magnetic tapes– but floats over it **without touching it**.

An air cushion which carries the read/write head is generated by the fast rotation of the magnetic disk interface and the read/write head. Hard disks are much more wear resistant and therefore have a much longer shelf life than magnetic tapes.

WHAT'S THIS?

The much feared head crash is caused by pollution that penetrates the fixed disk system unit cover and destroys data.

The air cushion is extremely slim, thinner than a dust particle or the diameter of a human hair, for example. If any pollution penetrates the casing of the magnetic disk, the read/write head rubs it against the surface of the hard disk from time to time and destroys all data. This is very rare but much feared, known as a **head crash** and it destroys a large part of the data on the hard disk.

Modern hard disks are approximately the size of the **palm of your hand** and may go up to 50 Gbytes. Just to give you some idea, 10 Gbytes would store about 420,000 A4 pages!

The following exercise shows you how to retrieve information from your hard disks. If you work with Windows 95, 98 or NT 4.0, you can follow the instructions step by step.

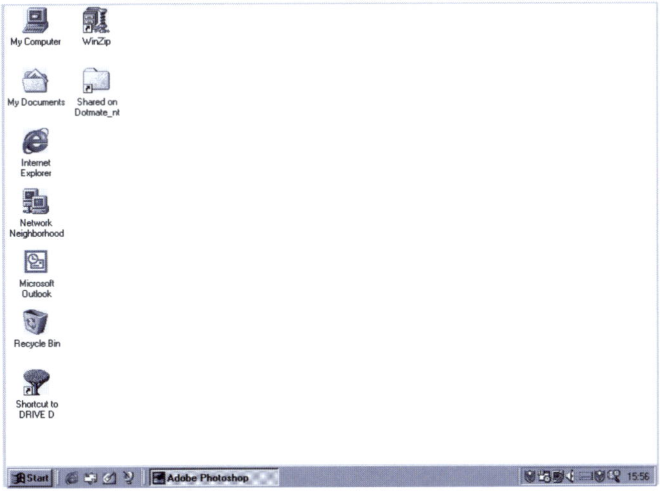

1 Start your computer up and wait until your operating system starts.

2 Double click on the My computer icon which you see at the top left corner of the screen.

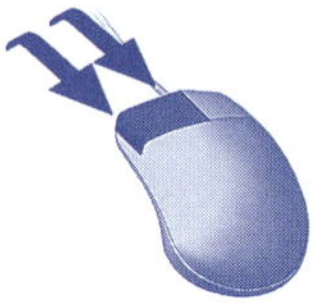

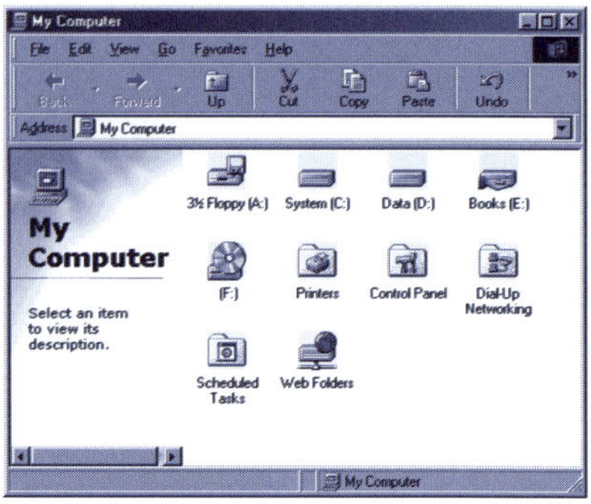

3 All data carriers represented by an icon are listed in the window.

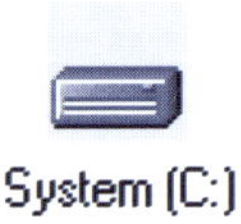

4 The C: disk drive is always the first hard disk of your computer. Hard disks are marked with special icons. If your computer has more than one hard disk, these are also listed.

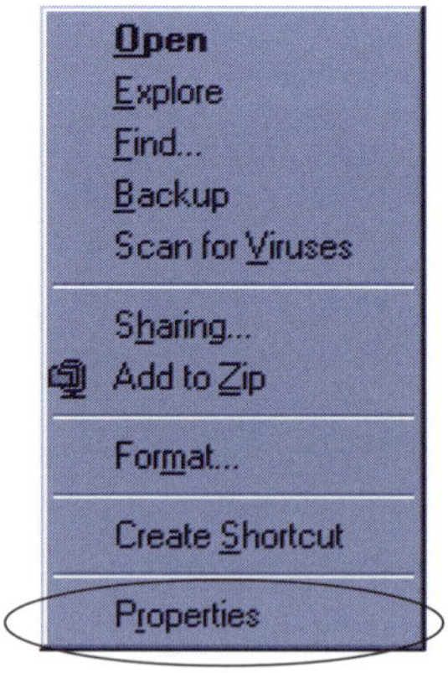

5 Move the mouse pointer on to the icon and click on it with the right mouse button. Choose the Properties entry in the context menu.

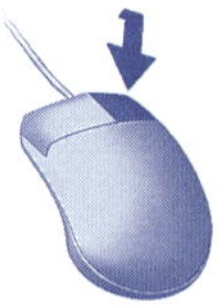

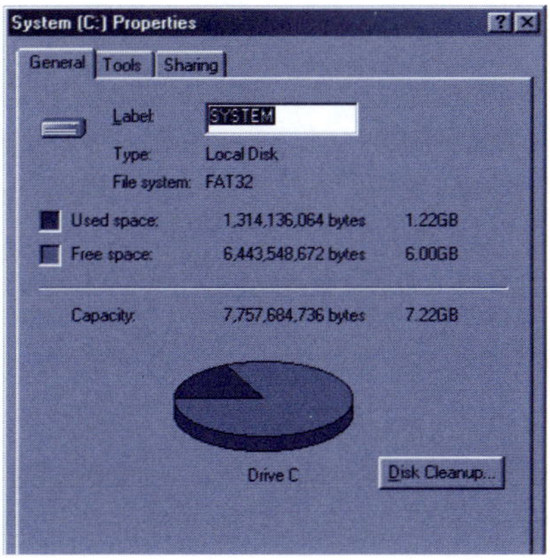

6 The window includes important data relating to your hard disk. The label reports the name of the hard disk and a pie graph illustrates the space currently occupied on this hard disk. You can see the capacity still available at a glance.

Floppy disks

Floppy disks are like hard disks. If you are prepared to waste a floppy disk, you can open it and look more closely at its insides. The grey black shiny surface contains the magnetic material and is **flexible**. They are called "**floppy disks**" from an American slang expression meaning flexible.

The read/write head, with which the information can be read and written by the floppy disk, is contained in the **floppy drive**.

Floppy disks are mechanically more robust than hard disks, but they are able to save only a small amount of data. The read/write head directly touches the reading and writing layer on the magnetic interface. This reduces the lifespan of a floppy disk considerably and produces rub offs, which let the dust collect in the disk drive case. If, when you read a floppy disk, errors appear frequently, you need to use special head cleaning disks.

For a long time, floppy disks were available in two sizes: the older 5.25" format saved up to 1.2 Mbytes (MB) of data, while the mechanically more stable 3.5" format saves up to 1.44 MB or even 2 MB. Floppy disks which can save up to 2.88 MB are also available.

If you compare the memory capacity of a floppy disk with the hard disk's capacity, the disadvantages of the floppy disks become very obvious. They can only store a small fraction of the amount of data a hard disk is capable of storing, and are comparatively far slower to use.

Currently, floppy disks are used for the day-to-day transfer of data, and in some cases they are also used to store back-up copies of **important information**. In addition, original software which you buy in computer shops used to be delivered on **floppy disk sets**. Floppy disks are today replaced by more powerful and stable data carriers such as CD-ROMs, which we will discuss later.

To preserve data saved on floppy disks for a longer period of time and avoid data loss, you will need to follow some rules when working with floppy disks:

1 Never expose floppy disks to magnetic or electrical fields.

2 Floppy disks must be stored at a standard temperature. Excessive heat or cold may affect data stability.

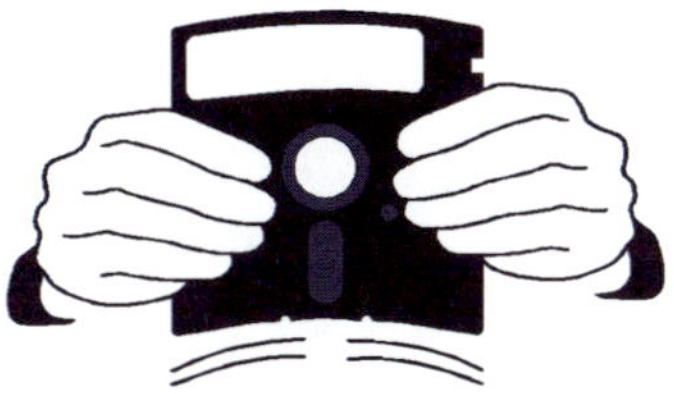

3 Do not put any heavy object on top of floppy disks and do not bend them.

4 Remove the floppy disk from the disk drive after reading or writing. Otherwise the read/write head may become damaged.

Formatting

Brand new floppy disks and hard disks consist of disks which are coated with a magnetic surface.

If you want to access the latest information saved, the surface must have an organised **structure**. The magnetic particles will be collected in the right **segment address**.

You may imagine such a structure as resembling a pie with a slice taken out of it. The single elements are small units whose surface is formed by magnetic particles.

WHAT'S THIS?

When you **format** a magnetised surface, a standardised structure is stamped on it. Disks must be formatted before they can be used to store information.

When you format a floppy disk or a hard disk, data that is already present could be lost.

While early floppy disks had to be formatted by the user before using them, today floppy disks come preformatted by the manufacturer.

Use our step-by-step guide to follow the process of formatting a floppy disk. In the example we use Windows 98; so, if you work with this operating system or with Windows 95, you can follow this exercise.

You will need a 3.5" floppy disk to do the exercise, either a new one or one whose contents you don't need any more. When formatting a data carrier, all the information present on it will be deleted!

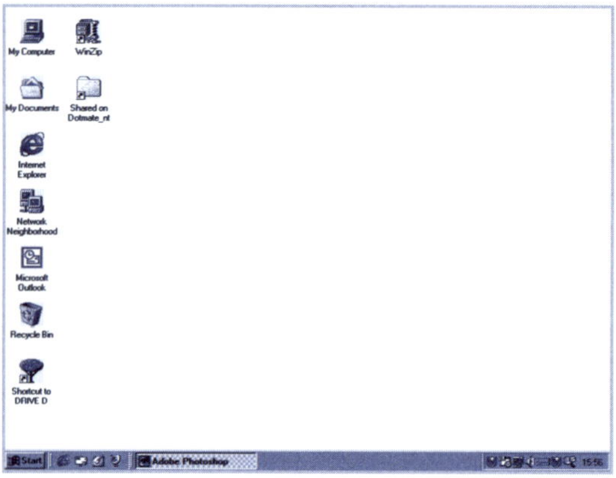

1 Start your computer and wait until Windows 95 or 98 is loaded.

2 Insert a 3.5" floppy disk into your floppy drive. The metal sliding cover must point towards the computer, with the marked side up. You will need to push the floppy disk into the drive.

3 Double-click on the MY COMPUTER icon which you find in the left upper corner of the screen.

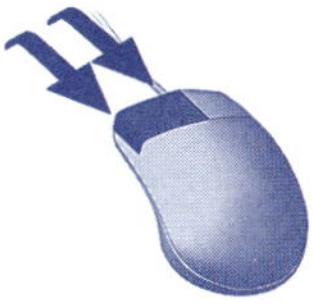

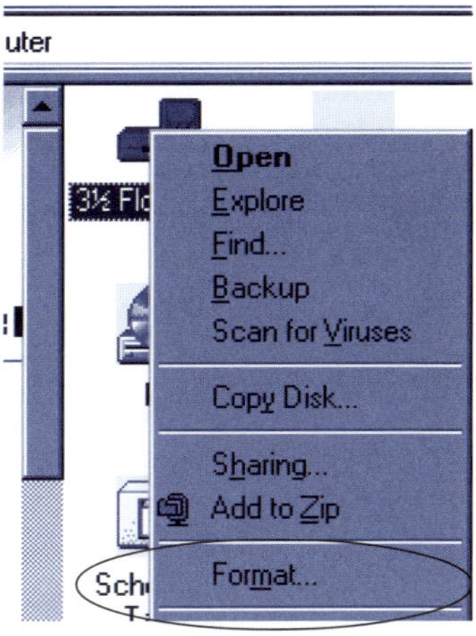

4 The *3.5"* floppy disk (A): icon represents your floppy drive. Move the mouse pointer on to the icon and click on it with the right mouse button. In the drop-down menu choose the FORMAT function.

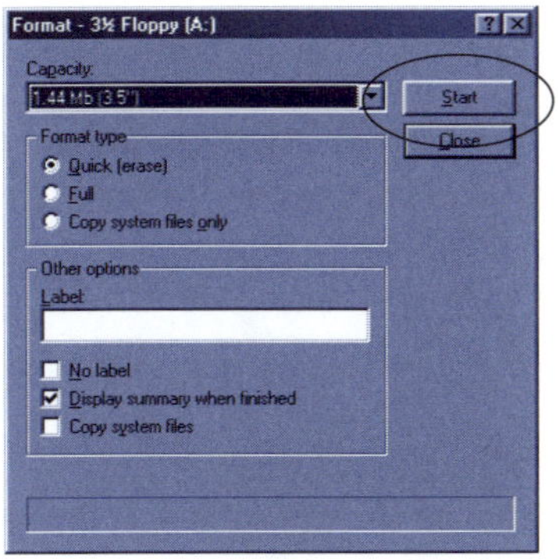

5 Leave the entries in the following window as they are, on the default format, and click on Start.

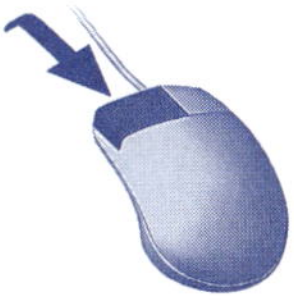

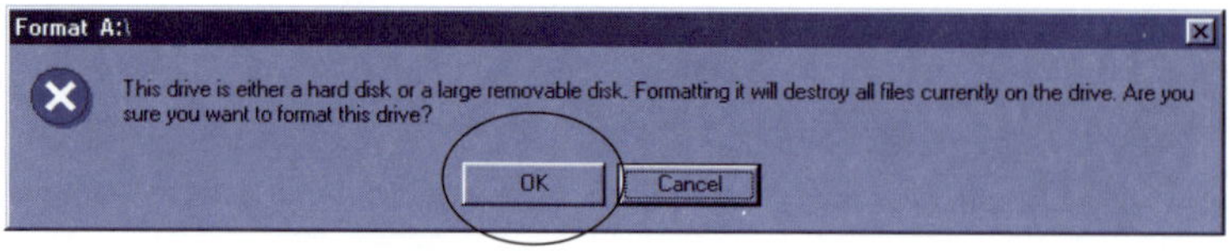

6 A warning message points out that all the data on the floppy disk will be deleted. Confirm the warning message with a click on the OK button.

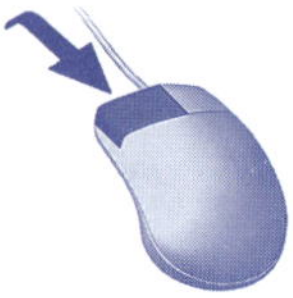

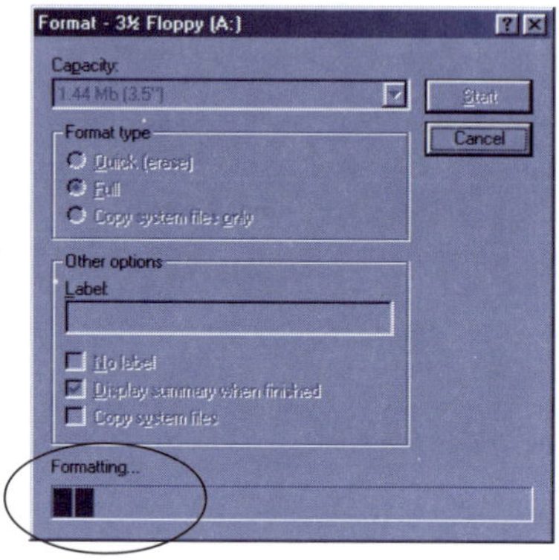

7 Now the formatting process starts; you can follow the progress in the displayed window.

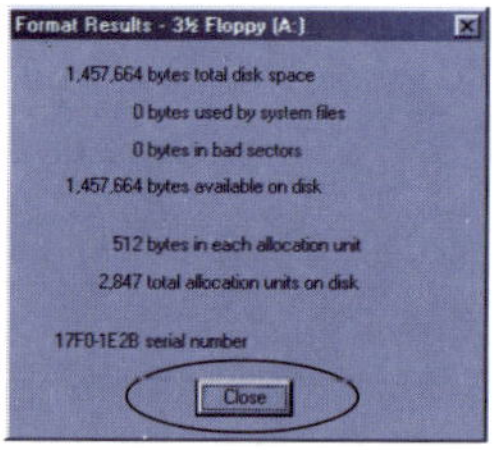

8 A report window confirms the end of the formatting operation.

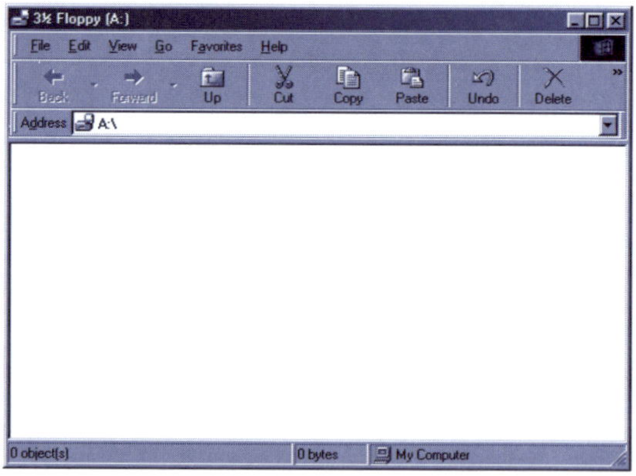

9 After formatting, double-click on the *3.5"* floppy disk (A): icon. A wider window which shows the contents of your floppy disk is displayed. Because the floppy disk has just been formatted and there are no files on the disk, the window is blank.

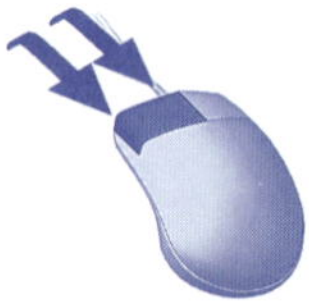

While the disk was being formatted, you may have noticed a small box in the Format Type box with the label **QuickFormat**. If you want to format a brand new preformatted floppy disk again, for example to delete all data already stored on it, you can use this function.

CD-ROMs

For a long time magnetic data storage was the only available technology. But competition to this media developed very soon: **optical** media are fast replacing **magnetic** memory.

Modern data memory uses the same **concept of light,** that is to say it uses the **reflection** on flat surfaces to save data. Innovation in audio technology storage always appears to precede and influence corresponding innovation in computer technology storage.

Conventional floppy disks are being replaced by compact disks (CD-ROMs), just as audio cassettes are being replaced by compact disks. "**CD-ROMs**" (short for Compact Disk Read Only Memory) have revolutionised digital memory technology.

We will now explain the advantages of CD-ROMs and then explain how data is saved and stored on CD-ROMs.

WHAT'S THIS?

The **CD-ROM** is – unlike hard disks and floppy disks – a memory media that operates on optical principles.

Data safety

A massive advantage is immediately obvious, compared to magnetic media. Hard disks and floppy disks can be severely affected by magnetic influences and therefore the user must take all necessary precautions against this, while CD-ROMs are much more **robust**. Although **scratches** on the **silver surface** of a CD could cause loss of data, the way CD-ROMs work and the way they store data is fairly simple.

Capacity

Software programs, used to be delivered on floppy disks, but now most are provided on CD-ROMs, because these have a much larger capacity than floppy disks: 650 MB, to 700 MB. The trend for **multimedia presentations** has fostered the switch to an optical storage medium, because graphics, video and audio data cannot be accommodated in a simple floppy disk.

Price

The very reasonable price of blank CD-ROMs makes it possible for most people to use CD-ROMS. No other media can match the CD-ROM for value for money, in terms of cost versus capacity. The low price of external CD-ROM drives and the fact that all new computers have an internal CD-ROM drive reduces the cost of CD-ROM technology.

However, there are two disadvantages in CD-ROM technology, which make using CDs impossible for some purposes. First of all, modern CD-ROM drives are subject to the speed of the hard disk. Another clear disadvantage is that data can be read by a CD-ROM drive, but not written. You will need special equipment, a **CD-ROM burner** (see later), to write to a CD-ROM.

WHAT'S THIS?

Standard CD-ROM drives can only read CD-ROMs. To write data on to a CD, you will need a **CD-ROM burner,** also called a CD-ROM writer.

To work with CD-ROMs, follow these instructions.

1 Do not expose CD-ROMs to direct sunlight. The disk may bend and become useless.

2 Never touch the surface with fingers. Grease and sweat leave marks which may cause problems for the PC in reading the CD.

3 Store the CD-ROM in its jewel case. This will prevent dust from being deposited on its surface.

4 Mark the top side only of the CD-ROM with a soft pen or a soft felt-tip pen, not a biro or pencil.

How optical media save and read

If magnetic particles are present, optical media cannot work with tensions produced by a magnetic field.

"**Miniature mirrors**" take on the task of the magnet particle on CD-ROMs. If the bundled laser meets this mirror, it is reflected. Such a reflection can be caught by a structure, the same way as light refraction, and interpreted as "1".

The surface of the silver CD-ROM contains grooves which are called "pits". When the laser meets these pits, it "swallows" the pit and interprets the missing signals as "0". Now you can understand why a fingerprint mark causes chaos: if the laser beam meets a greasy spot, it will no longer be able to reflect and will therefore read the message as "0", which would be the wrong interpretation.

To put as much information as possible on to a specific area, the laser must have as small a diameter as possible; it must be carefully "focused". In practice, you need a laser beam which reflects the CD-ROM surface. The laser beam does not react to very low intensity and as a consequence it will not touch the surface. Since the sampling method is carried out without touching the surface, the CD-ROM drive cannot be damaged.

When burning (or writing) data to a CD-ROM, grooves must be impressed on the CD. Since this operation requires a higher energy from the laser beam, you will need to use a purpose-built CD-ROM burner burn the pits on to the CD.

CD-ROMs do not need to be formatted. Their different way of saving data does not require a standardised structure to be created, which is what is required by magnetic media.

CD burners or writers

With the help of a CD burner, you can produce CD-ROMs yourself. Using a powerful laser beam, a data pattern is burnt on an "empty" CD-ROM (i.e. a "blank CD") which can then be read by any CD-ROM drive. CD burners are suitable for saving data for archive purposes, for example, photo collections and to save large amount of data.

It is interesting to note that you cannot only write data on to your CDs, but you can also record high quality sound CDs.

CD-RW

The CD-ReWritable (or CD-RW for short) can be used several times. Its contents can be deleted about 1,000 times, and the CD-RW can be written to again and again; this considerably reduces the cost of storing data .

A CD-RW is about ten times more expensive than a standard blank CD; to play and burn this type of CD, you will need a special CD-RW burner.

DVD – the "new darling" of the optical media

The "Digital Versatile Disk" or DVD, is the newest form of optical media. A DVD-driver can store up to 7 GB of data.

Because of its capacity limitations, CD-ROMs are often restricted in what they can be used for. With 650 or even 700 MB, a single unit seldom provides sufficient memory capacity; some multimedia applications, which take up a lot of memory, are already delivered on several CD-ROMs.

The DVD originates from video, which also sees its future in the digital storage of data. Originally, the DVD was produced as a better alternative to the video cassette.

A single-sided DVD can store up to 4.7 GB, and this capacity is doubled on double-sided disks, so the DVD's capacity is clearly superior to that of the CD-ROM. The DVD is also a better option in terms of the problems created by the large number of standards currently on the market: there are approximately eight main standards for CD-RWs, while there are only three for DVDs, so, compatibility is another important advantage for DVDs.

The DVD suits video technology perfectly. The standard DVD video will be able to record complete movies on removable media and provide clear, bright pictures. The DVD-RAM can work like a hard disk and DVD-ROM equipment is connected like CD-ROM drives.

The future of DVD and CD-ROMs

People ideally want a system that can read both CD-ROMs and DVDs. Otherwise the two systems will be in competition with each other and the DVD is likely to win the battle because it is more widely used and has a larger distribution.

To allow users of both systems to use CD-ROMs and DVDs with a single piece of equipment, R&D departments of large manufacturers have designed a special laser. This can read both CDs with wavelengths in the red frequency domain and DVDs with wavelengths in the blue frequency.

That's why Hewlett-Packard works with disk drives that can not only read but also write both to DVDs and CD-RWs. Equipment with two lasers, one for DVDs and one for CDs, are currently under development.

Troubleshooting

Do not be frightened: we are not going to ask you to take a screwdriver and unscrew the hard disk or other hardware.

Troubleshooting is how you can solve small problems with your floppy disks or the hard disk. Windows 95, 98 and NT 4.0 have built-in **programs** which automatically check hard disk errors and immediately clear small defects.

For example, when you save or retrieve data, you may find that an application program does not close a document correctly. This operation leaves a track on the hard disk and causes corrupted files. These errors are considered to be **logical defects,** because the mechanics or electronics of the hard disk have not been damaged, only the file structure.

A **test program** recognises these bad structures and corrects them. You should use maintenance programs regularly to prevent problems from occurring. Prevention is better than cure, therefore you should run the test software as a matter of routine at least every couple of weeks.

The following step-by-step guide will show you how you can carry out small repairs, using the Scandisk utility in Windows 98.

1 Start your computer and wait until Windows 98 is loaded.

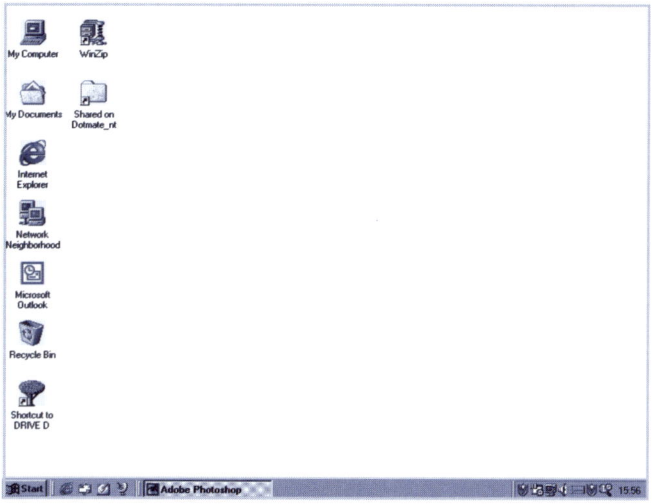

2 Double click on the MY COMPUTER icon.

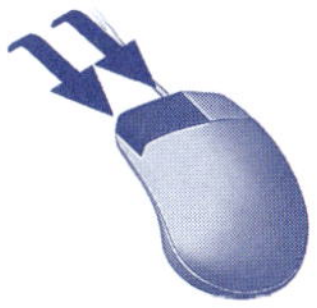

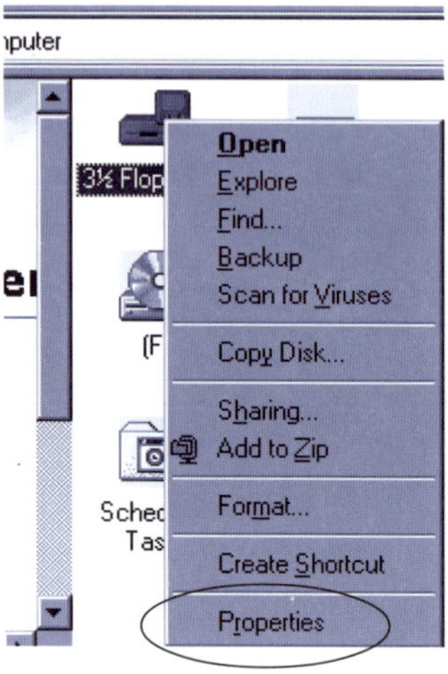

3 Position the mouse pointer on the icon of the drive you would like to check and press the right mouse button. Choose the *Properties* entry in the drop-down menu.

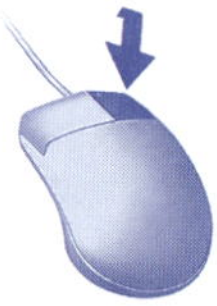

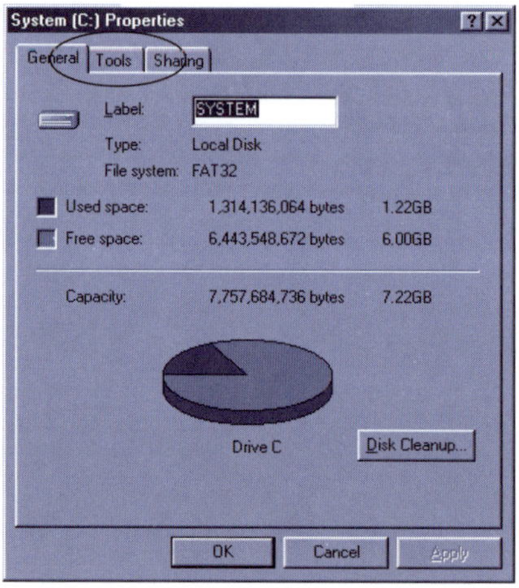

4 We have already introduced you to this window. Click on the TOOLS tab.

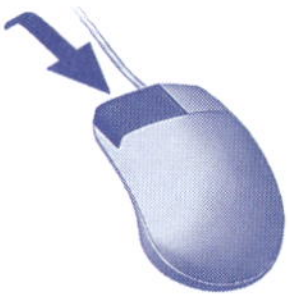

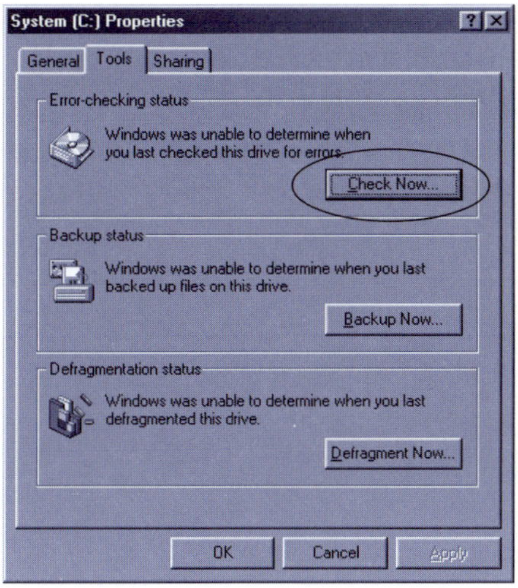

5 You can see the heading "Error-checking status" in the upper part of the window. Confirm this operation by clicking on the CHECK NOW button.

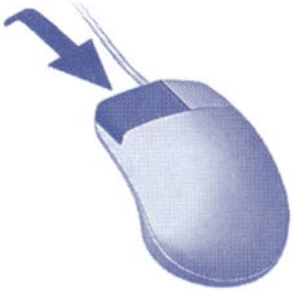

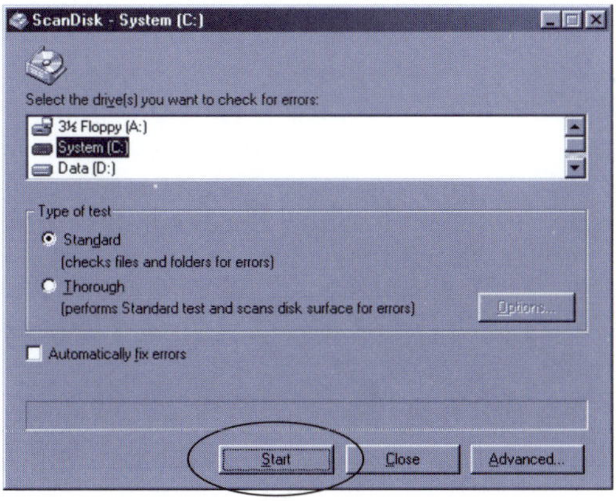

6 Confirm the following dialog box without altering any of the settings.

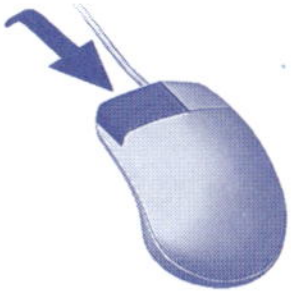

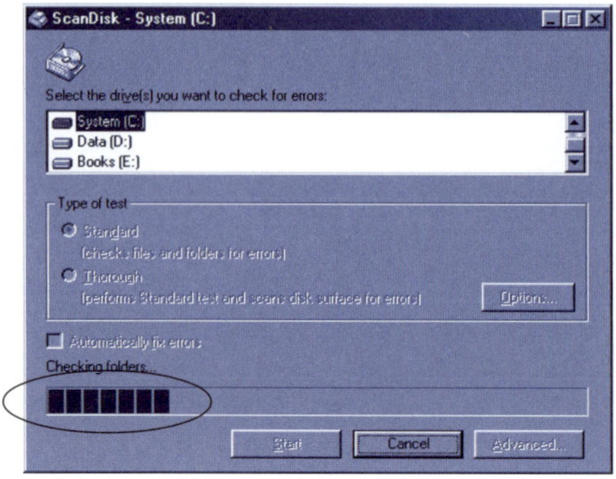

7 The checking of the hard disk or the floppy disk now starts. During the course of the check, a progress status bar is displayed which shows the areas being checked.

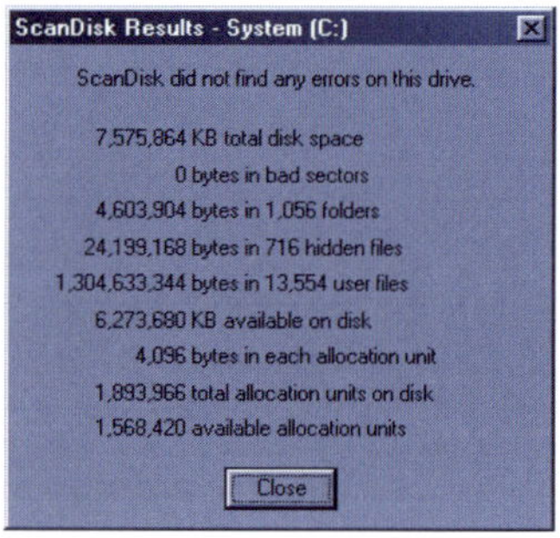

8 At the end of the checking process, a summary of results is displayed, which tells you if errors were found and if they have been fixed.

Defragmenting your hard drive

From time to time, you need to tidy up your desk or go through your working files. If you fail to organise your documents into separate piles, there will be chaos: your invoices will disappear under a pile of advertising mail, and how will you find them again if they are in the wrong place?

The same thing applies to your computer. You create text documents with your word processor program and store these on the hard disk. If at any time you want to access them again, you will have to search for them, which can be time-consuming.

You need to do some housekeeping and clearing up as part of your routine. Parts of files ("fragments") are collected together properly and therefore sorted when you defragment your disk drive. Your PC can then access data faster, because it does not need to search for files: instead of searching for parts of files and picking up individual parts that need to be put together, it can open the sorted fragments as a whole unit.

It is the same in your office. If you store documents for a project in different files, when you are asked to find all the individual papers, you will waste time searching through the various files. But if you have filed all papers belonging to the project in a single folder, the information is quickly available.

Organising data on your hard disk is very fast. Small hard disks are organised in about 10 minutes, big ones require about 30 minutes, dependending, of course, on the condition of the hard disk.

If you feel that retrieving information is taking longer than usual, it is time to tidy up your computer. You should clean your hard disk **at least once a month**, and if you use your computer frequently, you should clean it more often.

The following step-by-step guide shows you how to tidy up your hard disk using the Window 98 program called **Defrag**. Defrag was installed on your PC when the operating system was installed and is thus available as a standard.

CAUTION

If you use an external program to clean your hard disk, be careful that it is fully compatible with Windows 95. Incompatible software can destroy data on your hard disk!

1 In My Computer, click with the right mouse button on the icon of the hard disk which you want to tidy up. Select the *Properties* entry in the drop-down menu.

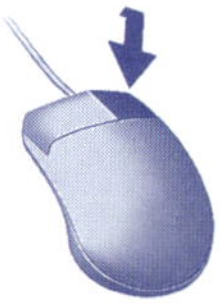

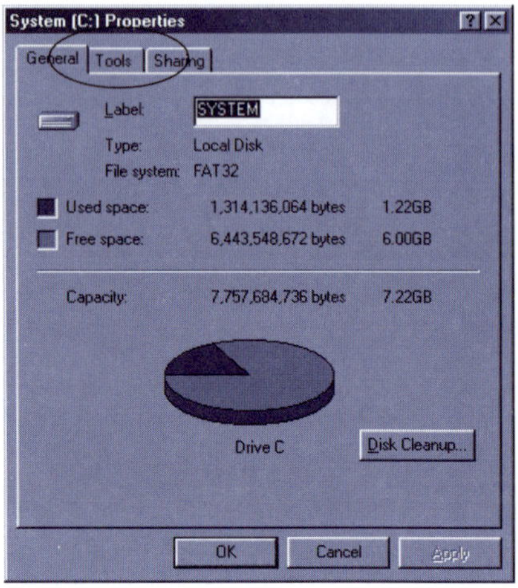

2 The window that opens is already known to you. Click on the Tools tab.

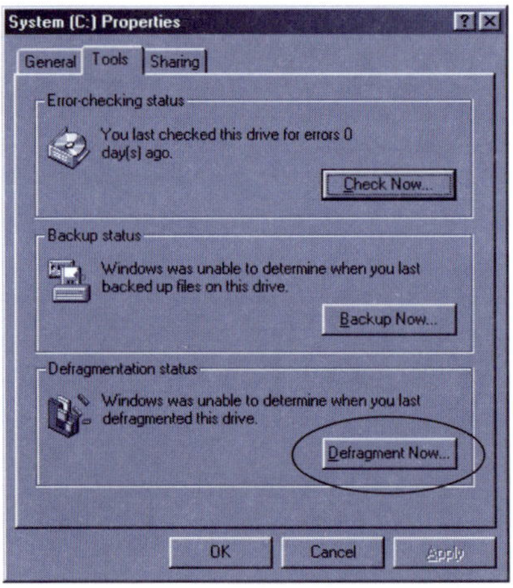

3 Choose the defragmentation routine, by clicking on the Defragment Now button. You will also be told how long it has been since the last defragmentation operation was carried out.

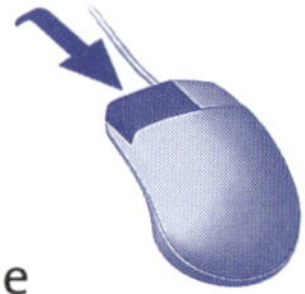

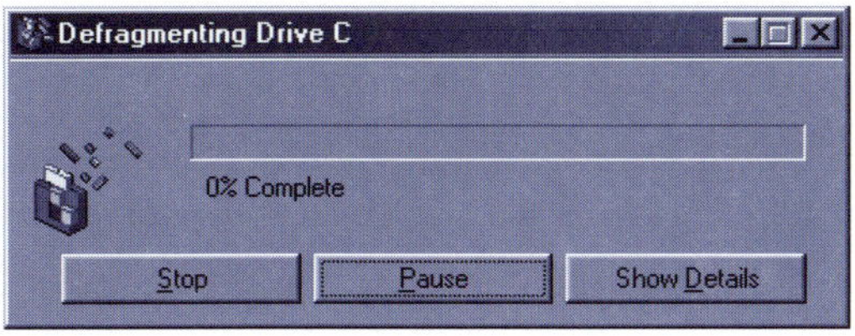

4 The above window reports the status of the fragmenting operation in progress. The above operation has not begun.

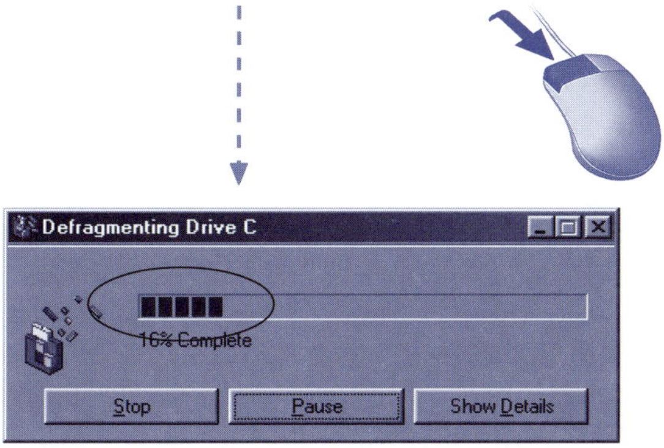

5 The defragmentation process can be followed on the progress bar.

The data structure of your computer

The rest of this chapter will show you how information is structured in your computer.

Our example, in the section on hard disks, has shown that about 420,000 A4 pages can be saved on a 10 GB hard disk. If your home or office PC has, say, 2 GB, 84,000 pages of text can be stored. You can imagine that such a large amount of data requires an efficient and well organised structure.

Let us look at how your real office, or the room you work in, is organised, before we go on to the filing system in your PC. The designers of PC drives learned their lessons from real life, so the file structure principle will be familiar to you.

The following table gives you an overview of how an office and a computer work.

Your office	**Your computer**
You work at a desk which is the "centre" of your office.	The **Desktop** in your PC corresponds to the desk; it also has a central function.
In your office, you can find cabinets containing folders.	**Data carriers** (such as folders or hard disks) contain data.
Cabinets contain folders with paper documents grouped by subject matter.	Data carriers contain **folders,** which are documents in a digital format.
Individual **documents** are the smallest unit of information in your office.	**Electronic documents (files)** are the smallest units which can be saved to your disk.
The waste paper bin contains all the documents you no longer need.	File discarded documents in **the Recycle Bin.**

In the next few pages, we will show you how to use the various features.

The Desktop: a virtual desk

It is easy even for new users to understand the function of the desktop you find in Windows 98.

The Windows concept sees the desktop as the **central coordination** place of your activities. It is called Desktop because of the relationship between the Windows desktop and your desk.

WHAT'S THIS?

The desktop is the central interface of your PC and corresponds to your real life desk.

The icons you see displayed after the start can be thought of as objects, that you have placed on your desk. These objects can be an application program such as Word for Windows, or a document you have created.

The second edition of Windows 98 offers an extended Active Desktop. This is interactively connected with programs, files and the Internet.

You can put personal data on the Desktop. If you frequently access data from the floppy disk, for example, you can put the floppy disk drive on the desktop. The following step-by-step guide shows you how to move an icon on to the desktop.

1 Switch on your computer and wait until Windows 95, 98, or NT 4.0 is loaded.

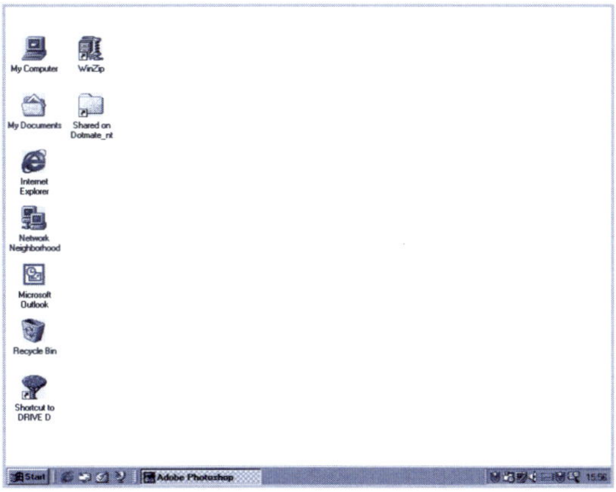

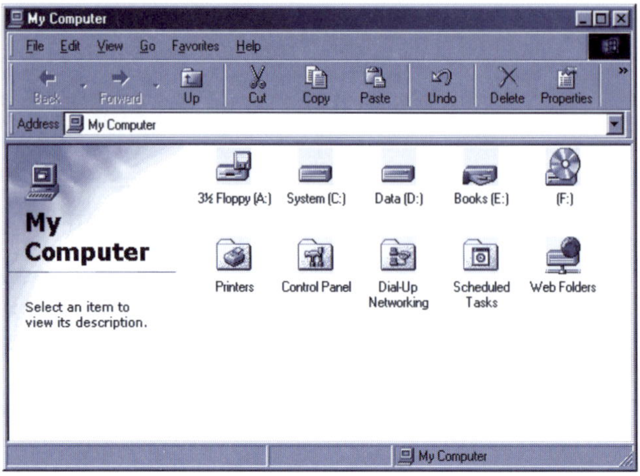

2 Double click on the MY COMPUTER icon. A window opens.

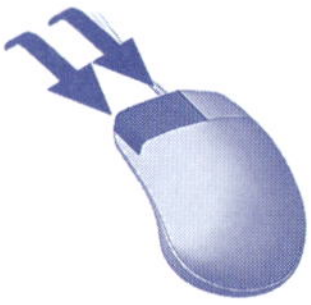

3 Click with the left mouse button on the 3.5" floppy disk (A:) icon and keep the left button pressed. The floppy disk icon becomes "attached" to the mouse pointer and can be moved.

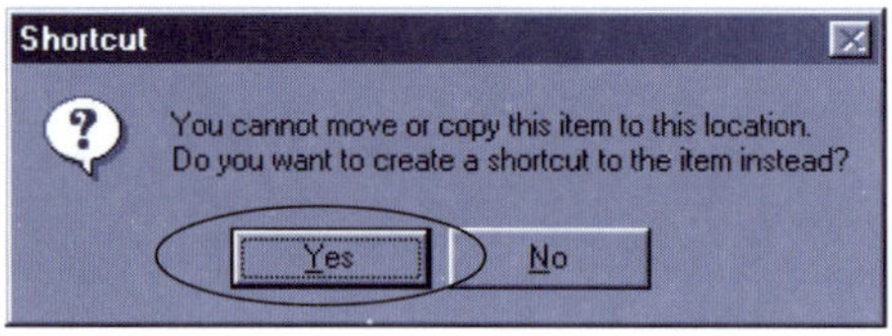

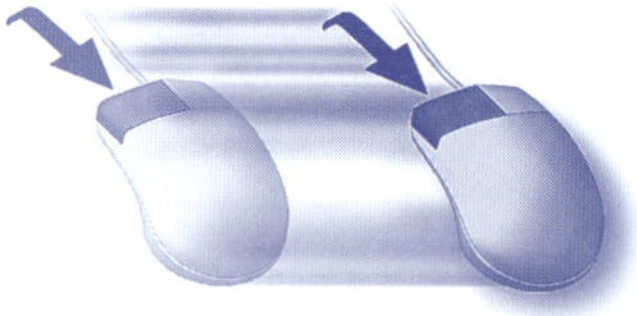

4 Place the icon on the desktop in a free space and release the left button. Confirm the dialog box with a click on YES.

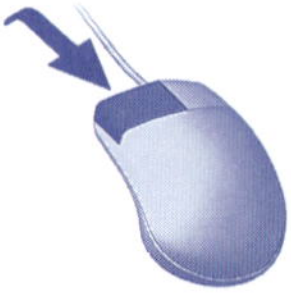

5 The new icon is now on the Desktop and is called *Shortcut to 3.5"FLOPPY (A:)*.

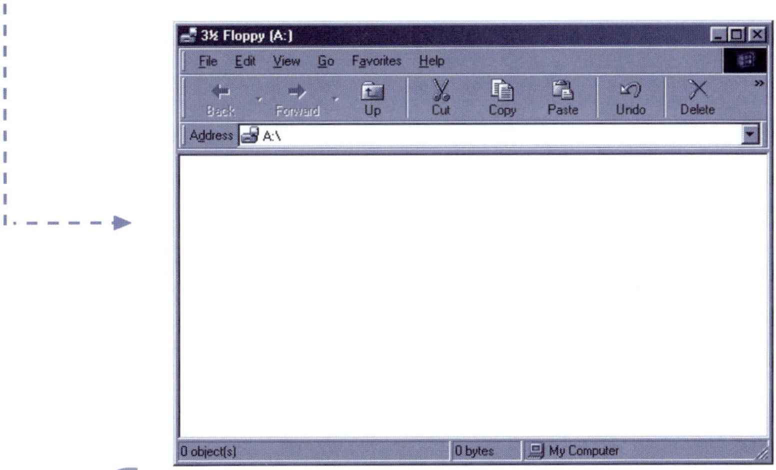

6 Finally, check whether the icon works correctly. Insert a floppy disk (possibly with data on it) into disk drive A: and double-click on the new icon. The contents of the floppy disk will be displayed.

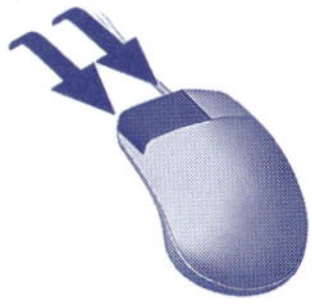

In this way you can put any objects you like on your virtual desk. If you want to practise how to move objects again, you can drag your hard disk or the CD-ROM drive on the desktop, following the same procedure.

In step four, you confirmed that a Shortcut has been created; your new icon is called "Shortcut to...".

If you click on the SHORTCUT TO... icon, this click corresponds to a click on the floppy disks icon in the My Computer window. But if you rename the shortcut, the primary icon will not be changed.

WHAT'S THIS?

A Shortcut is a reference to the original icon.

The Recycle Bin

You will probably have noticed the **Recycle Bin**. Put objects you no longer need here, then they can be **deleted** with the recycle bin function. If you inadvertently throw a file you still need into the Recycle Bin, you can restore the file the same way you would with a normal waste basket. If the Recycle Bin is emptied, all files in it are **permanently deleted**.

The following step-by-step guide will show you how to use the Recycle Bin. We use Windows 95, 98 or NT 4.0 as an example; you will also find a corresponding function under Mac OS/2 and the graphic UNIX interface.

In the following exercise, we will move the Shortcut we have created in the previous step-by-step guide to the Recycle Bin.

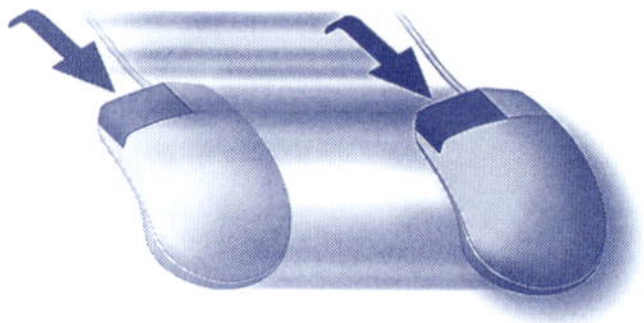

1 Click with the left mouse button on the Shortcut icon we have just created for the *3.5"* floppy disk (A:) and keep the button pressed.

2 Move the mouse, keeping the left button pressed on to the Recycle Bin icon. The icon is attached to the mouse pointer. Then release the mouse button when the Recycle Bin icon goes dark; this shows that you are pointing to it.

3 The Shortcut has disappeared from the desktop. You will now see some crumpled paper in the Recycle Bin icon; a visual hint that it contains files.

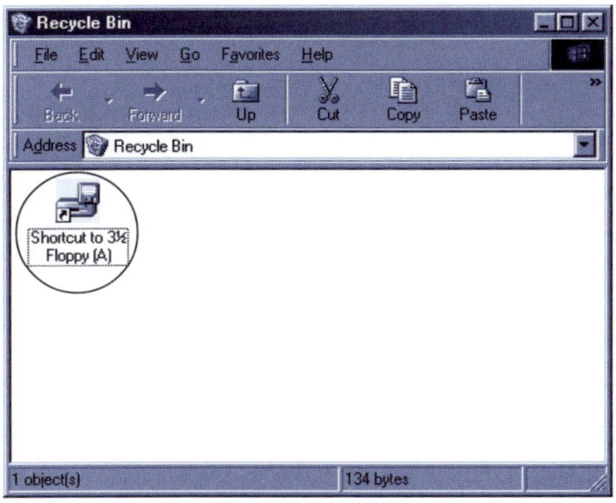

4 Double-click on the Recycle Bin icon; the upper entry is *Shortcut to...* click on the File menu and choose the Restore entry. The deleted file is restored and its icon is put back on the Desktop.

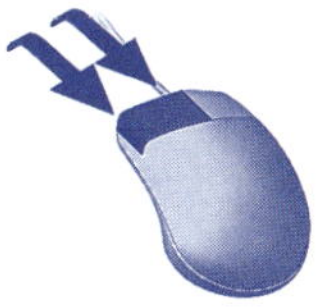

5 Throw the Shortcut into the Recycle Bin again and right-click on the Recycle Bin. Choose the EMPTY RECYCLE BIN entry in the drop-down menu.

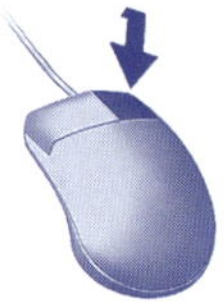

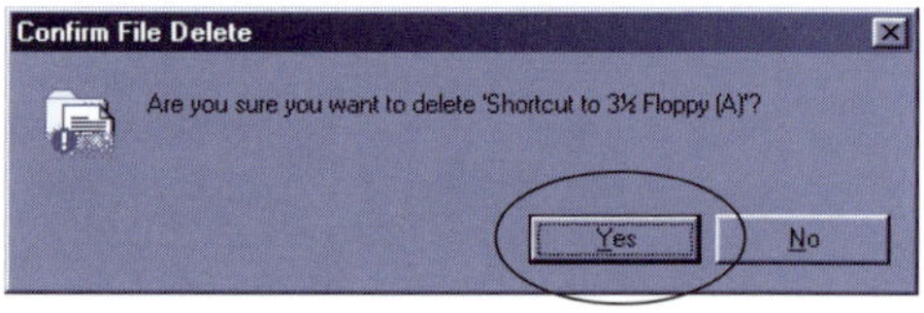

6 A warning message tells you that the documents contained in the Recycle Bin are to be deleted permanently. Click on YES to confirm that this is OK.

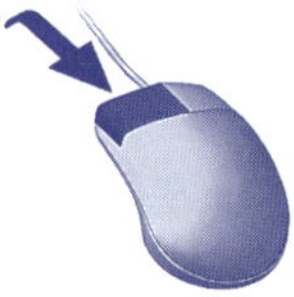

7 The Recycle Bin icon has changed: an empty Recycle Bin shows that it no longer contains data.

TIP

You can put data in the Recycle Bin in other ways, not only by dragging the icon to the Recycle Bin icon. Files are also put in to the Recycle Bin when you use the Delete function.

It is important at this point to mention a possible risk when you use the Recycle Bin. We are going to use a real life example, to explain this problem.

An employee of an engineering office works with **sensitive** and **confidential** documents which contain the construction plans of a scientific measuring piece of equipment. He works on his PC during the day, and saves the secret documents on a floppy disk which he puts into the company safe. He deletes the original documents from the hard disk on the PC with the Recycle Bin function.

A commercial spy could easily use this opportunity to rebuild the contents of the **Recycle Bin** and sell the confidential information to the competition.

Therefore, if you work with sensitive information, always remember to empty the Recycle Bin after you have placed documents into it!

WHAT'S THIS?

A **file manager** manages the data structure of a computer.

File Manager

There are software programs for managing the data structure of a computer, just like an office manager would run an office. All manufacturers of a graphic operating system equip their product with **file managers**.

The file manager of Windows 3.x used to be called "file manager". It is now called "Explorer" in Windows 95, 98 and NT 4.0.

TIP

Explorer is an independent program which allows data manipulation. It is not the same as the Windows 95/98 desktop and for this reason should not be confused with it.

We will show you how to work with Explorer, the replacement for previous file managers, in the following step-by-step guide. You will learn how to work with files and folders in later exercises. If you work with Windows 95, 98 or NT 4.0, you will be able to follow the examples below.

1 Click with the right mouse button on the START button in the bottom left-hand corner of the Windows screen. Choose EXPLORE in the Start menu.

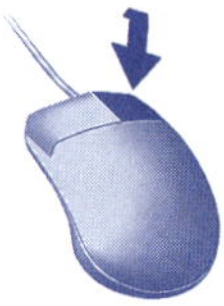

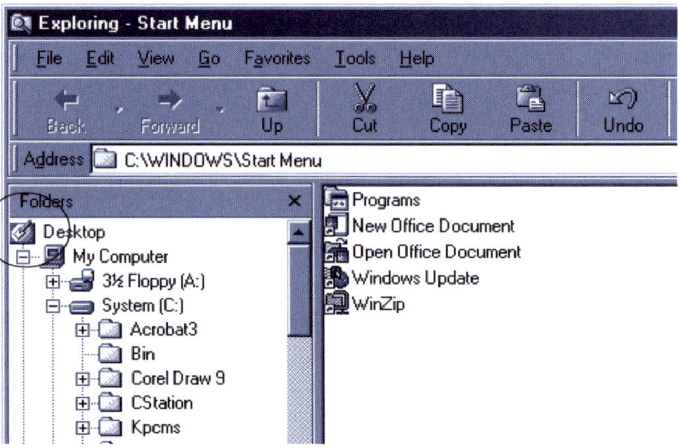

2 Click on the left part of the Explorer window (*Folders*) on the topmost entry *Desktop*. If the entry is not visible, use the scroll bar on the right margin of the window to find it.

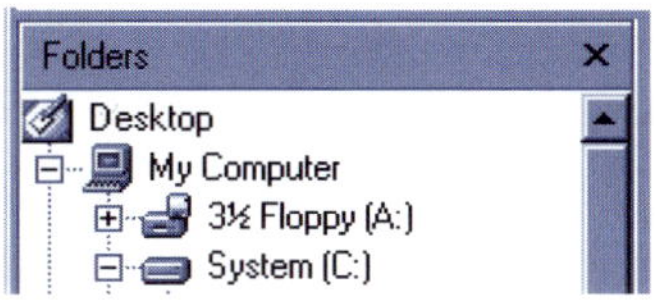

3 You will see various hierarchical levels. The *Desktop* is the topmost level; the related icon shows a desk.

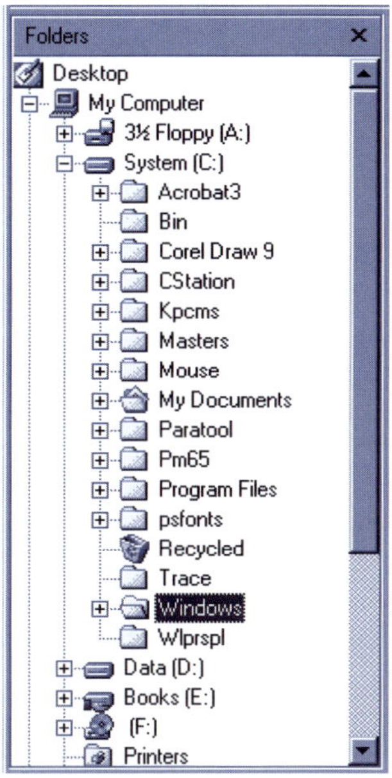

4 The objects which are currently on the Desktop are the second level. You will see the entry *My Computer* and, further down the list, the *Recycle Bin*.

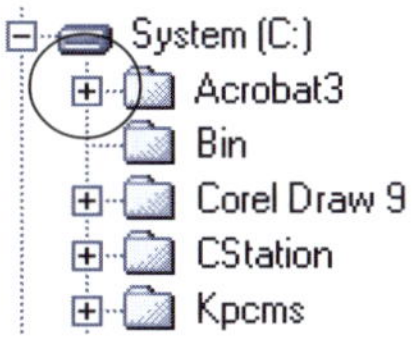

5 Lower levels can be displayed by clicking on the "+" symbol of the related branch. Subordinate levels will become visible; the respective contents are listed on the right side of the Explorer window. Click on My Computer. The subordinate levels are the disk drives.

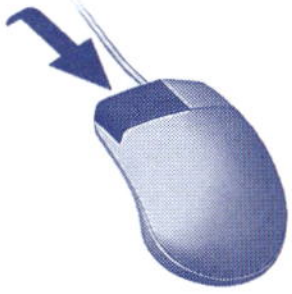

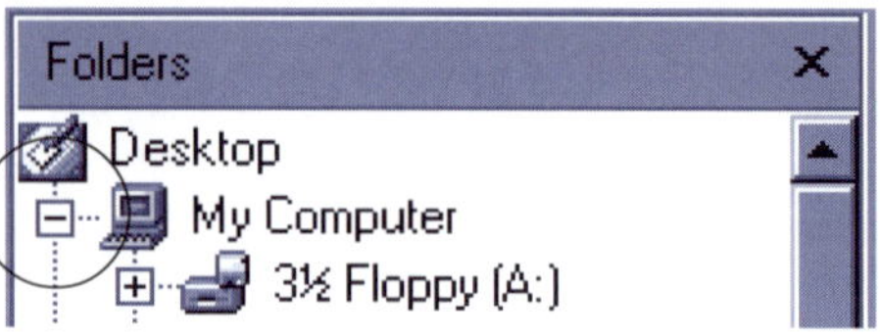

6 You can compact the levels any time by clicking on the "-" symbol. Leave the *My Computer* level by clicking on the minus sign in front of it. The displayed disk drive icons disappear.

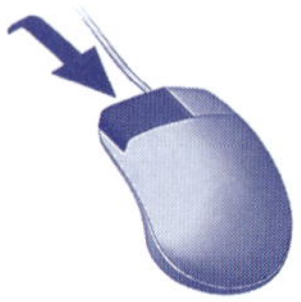

Designating disk drives

You know that disk drives are represented by a letter followed by a **colon**.

Do you remember when we created the shortcut for the floppy disk drive in the previous exercise? The name you can see in "My Computer " is 3.5" Floppy (**A**:); the hard disk is also represented by the letter **C**:.

The CD-ROM drive and all other drives which you find in "My Computer"are also prefixed with a letter. This "drive letter" identifies each drive present in your system. A **colon** always follows the letter.

For example, if you copy a file from the hard disk on to a floppy disk using the mouse, and then move it into the hard disk icon, in computer language this operation will be called "copying file X from drive A: to drive C:".

> **WHAT'S THIS?**
>
> Each disk drive of your computer is assigned a **drive letter,** for drives where data can be read and written. A letter may therefore be assigned only once within a computer system.

This conventional way of naming drives is very common and does not only apply to Windows 98. It originates from early computer history, when disk drives were also identified by a drive letter.

The letters A: and B: are reserved for **floppy disks**, so you can work with a maximum of two floppy disks in a computer. Your PC probably is equipped with only one disk drive, so you will not use the label B:.

TIP

Some computer systems are an exception and work with a completely different syntax. However, these are special systems with which you will not normally work.

The other letters can be assigned in different ways. C: is usually the **label assigned** to the hard disk of your computer, but if you use more than one hard disk or your only hard disk is subdivided, you will use the labels D:, E: and so on.

Your **CD-ROM drive** is assigned the next free label, usually the letter that follows the ones assigned to the floppy disk and hard disk drives.

If your computer is part of a computer network, you can use more letters to name the different parts, so that you can assign labels to a maximum of 26 disk drives (according to the letters of the alphabet) on your computer.

Folders and files

My Computer is just a folder, although it is a special one. The drives of your computer and the printer driver are contained in this folder, for example.

You already know how to use a folder. A **double click** on the folder icon **opens** the folder. The folder is closed when you **close the window**.

Folders used to be described as "Directories". DOS versions also use the "Directory" definition. Since Microsoft brought out Windows 95, the new concept of a Folder has become a standard for the industry. This concept is also applied in Windows 98.

You can put many folders on your hard disk. The great advantage of this structure lies in the possibility of creating subfolders in **different hierarchies**.

You can therefore create folders in a very flexible way. In this section, we will show you two typical folder structures, so you can create a folder structure which corresponds to your individual needs.

1st example

The two folders in the first example are named Company information and Personal Data to describe the contents of the respective folder. Let's have a look at the other folders contained in the main folder, Company Data. The first level folders are Receipts, Invoices, Account and Other Correspondence".

On a third level, other subfolders could be created. In the Receipts folder, for example, there are four other subfolders named Bills I-98 up to Bills IV-98.

> **TIP**
> Whenever possible, try to name folders according to their contents, so that you can easily remember them.

Within these folders, documents can be organised in such a way that they can immediately be found when you need them. For example, if an accountant happens to be searching for invoices issued in the second quarter of 1998, he will intuitively search information in the Company information/Invoices/Invoices II-98 folder. This is why you should always assign clearly recognisable names that you will remember!

2nd example

In the second example, the **Customer information** folder is not sorted according to the correspondence category but according to client names. The sublevels are named Annunziato, Mitton and Watkinson. In the third level, folders are organised according to categories, as follows.

Folder Names

Folders names can contain up to 256 characters. Vowel permutations and some special characters such as hyphens can be used; other special characters such as colon or quotation marks are reserved for the operating system and therefore cannot be used to name files.

A typical folder name would contain a maximum of 15 characters and indicate the contents of the folder. So, for example, instead of naming your folder **Invoices 3**, you should name it **Inv. May-July**.

The following step-by-step guide shows you how to create, rename and delete folders up to the third level. If you work with Windows 95, 98 or NT 4.0, you can follow the steps directly.

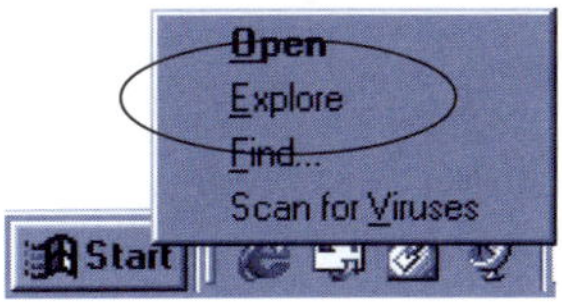

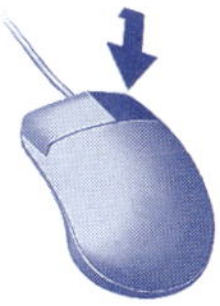

1 Click with the right mouse button on the START menu button and select the EXPLORE entry in the drop-down menu.

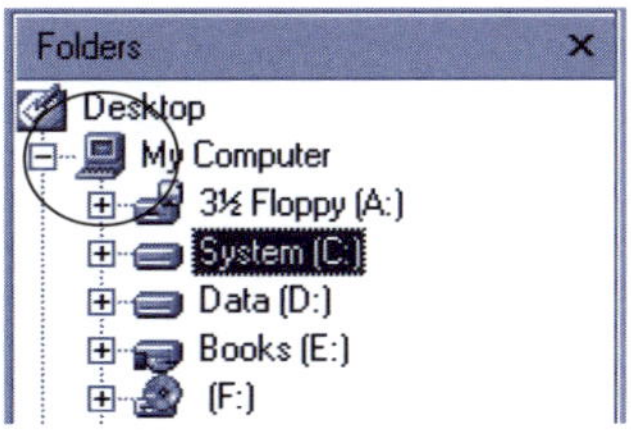

2 Open the *My Computer* folder by clicking on the preceding "+" sign.

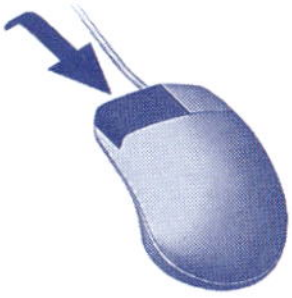

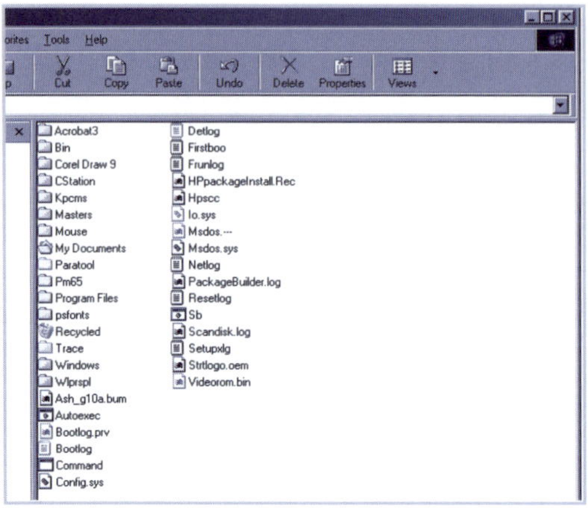

3 Choose your hard disk by clicking on *hard disk C:*. The entry is highlighted in blue and all available folders are shown on the right of the screen.

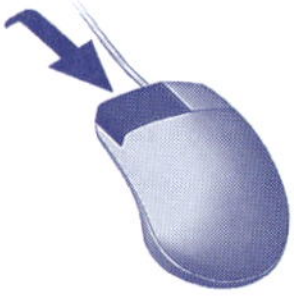

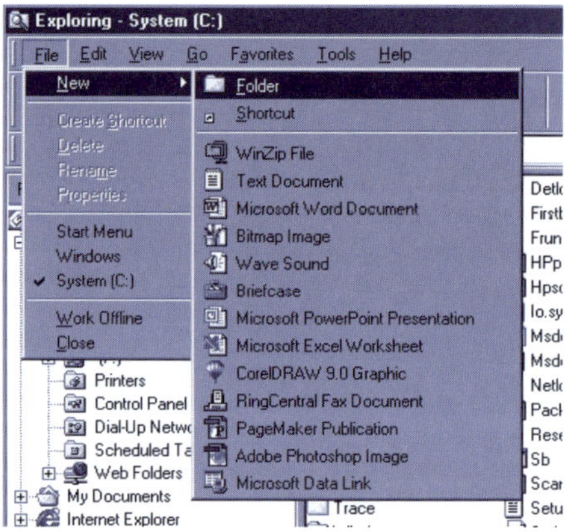

4 As a first step, we will define a new main folder and name it Company Information. Click on FILE in the MENU bar and choose NEW.

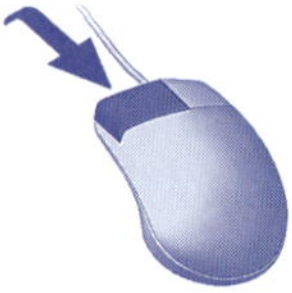

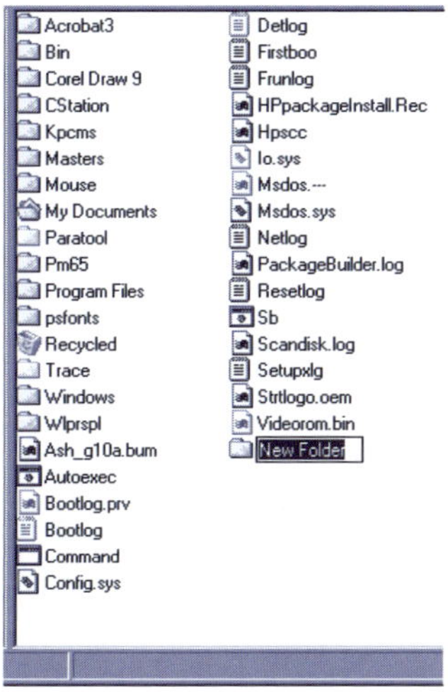

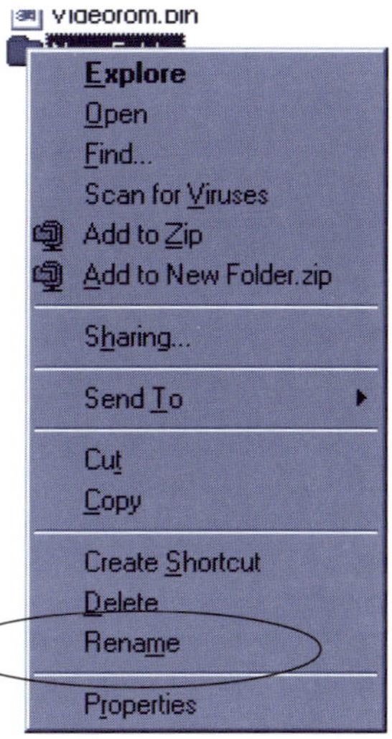

5 Click on the topmost entry to create a NEW FOLDER. A New Folder icon named *New Folder* appears on the right of the screen. Confirm the name by pressing Enter.

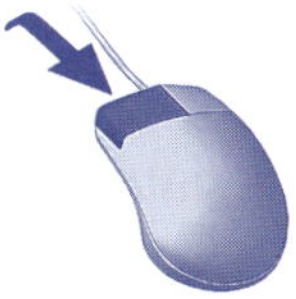

6 The next step is to rename the new folder. Click with the right mouse button on the folder and choose RENAME. Type Company Information as the name of the new folder and confirm it with Return.

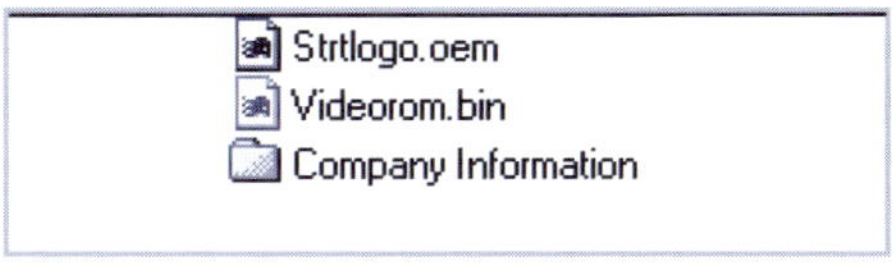

7 The Company Information folder now moves to the left side of the Explorer window.

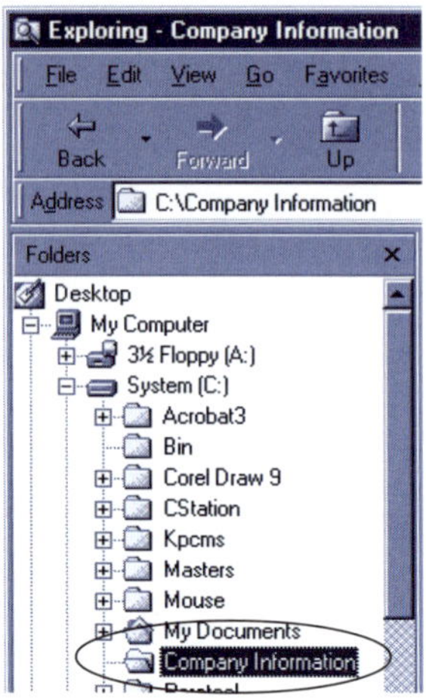

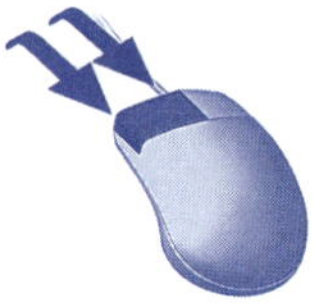

8 To define further subfolders, you must select the higher folder in the hierarchy. Now click with the left mouse button on the Company Information folder.

9 Choose FILE/NEW/FOLDER again and create a folder named Account. Now, when you click on the Company Information folder, the Account folder should be displayed on the right hand side window of the Company Information folder.

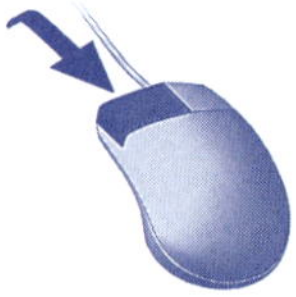

10 Define a third subfolder which will be inserted below the Account folder and give it the name Annunziato.

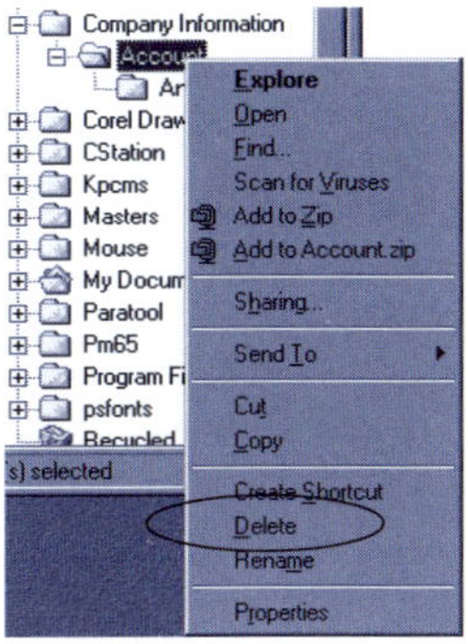

11 To complete this exercise, we are going to delete the folder Account and the subfolder Annunziato. Click with the right mouse button on the Account folder and choose DELETE.

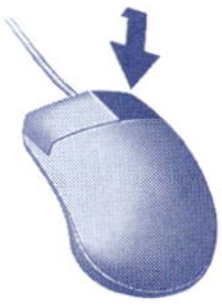

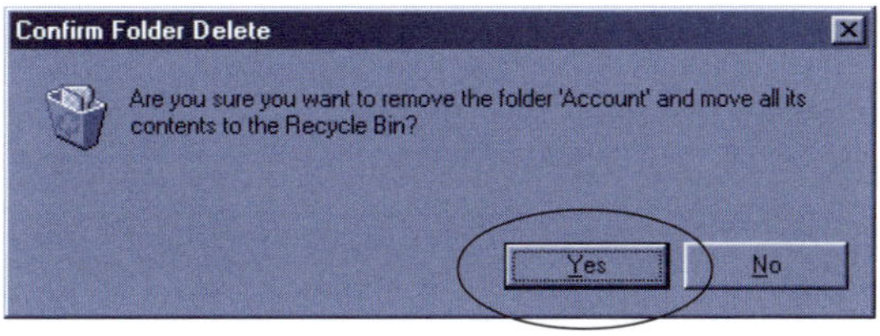

12 Confirm the warning message that warns you that the chosen folder and its contents are now going to be deleted.

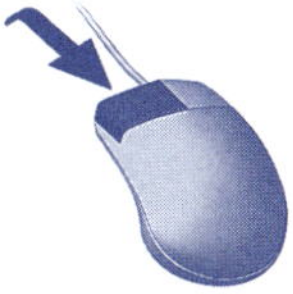

Now you know the basic operations needed for creating and moving folders. On this basis, you can now define your own structure for saving files during your work.

TIP

You can rename a folder faster by clicking twice on it, leaving a short interval between the two clicks. The folder is highlighted in blue and can now be renamed.

Files

While a **Folder** is simply a container, a useful organising tool, files contain actual information.

A file can contain an **executable program**, for example Word for Windows. Windows 98, for example, stores the operating system's internal information as files. For this reason, files form the central basis of the information process.

Files are electronic documents created using a word processor or a graphics program, for example, and then saved on a drive.

Files are the **smallest units of information** in a computer.

File names

Early versions of DOS and Windows could only assign file names which contained a maximum of eight characters. But most users found that eight characters were not enough in practice. At the time, UNIX, OS/2, Apple Macintosh and various other operating systems could already work with longer file names.

Being restricted to eight characters meant that a proper **description** of the file content was often impossible. Imagine that you have written several letters to Mr Mitton. You had a number of possibilities for naming these files:

MITTON1

LETTMITT

LTMITTON

LMITTON1

It is obvious that these word combinations are not particularly meaningful and you could have problems when you want to access the file again later. What was the content of "MITTON1"? How do you name the second letter to Mr Mitton? "LETTMITT" is already assigned. Which is the most recent letter? And the additional problem which restricts your choice is that some characters you may want to use can cause system problems, so they are forbidden.

With Windows 95, 98 and NT 4.0, the Windows operating system had to solve this issue. File names can now contain a maximum of **256 characters**, which means users can now create fully descriptive file names. So, for example, the letter to Mr Mitton could be named:

"Invitation to Mr Mitton for the meeting of 25-11-99"

The extended file name system is also case-sensitive, which means it can use **upper** and **lower case** letters. Special characters such as **commas**, **dots** or **hyphens** can now be used.

CAUTION

If you install software in Windows 98 which was developed for earlier Windows versions, files and folders cannot be renamed with the new 256 character conversion. In this case, you can only use file names with a maximum of eight characters.

File extensions

It has always been possible to extend the eight character file name by using **three supplementary characters.** This original system was known as the "**8+3 system**".

These three extra characters were called "**file extensions**", and are used to specify the file type. The three characters are conventionally separated from the file name by a dot. Therefore, for example, the letter to Mr Mitton could be named:

MITTON1.TXT

MITTON1.DOC

MITTON1.XYZ

The extension "**.txt**" refers to a **text** file. A software application recognises this ending and decides whether the file can be read. You can edit a text file using a word processor, but not a graphics program.

The following table lists some file extensions and the description of their meaning. You will find an extensive overview of the most commonly used file extensions at the end of the book.

File extension	**Type**
TXT	Text file
DOC	Word Text file
GIF	Graphic file
XLS	Microsoft Excel spreadsheet
DBF	Database
HTML	Internet text (Hyper Text Markup Language)

The following step-by-step guide will show you how to save a file on your hard disk. We will create a test document, then we will save it with the appropriate name into a new folder.

1 Create a new folder on your hard disk C: with the help of Explorer and call it Text. We will save the test document to this folder when ready.

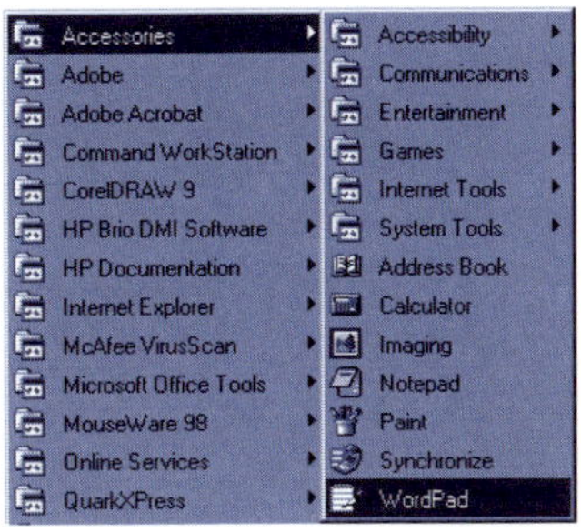

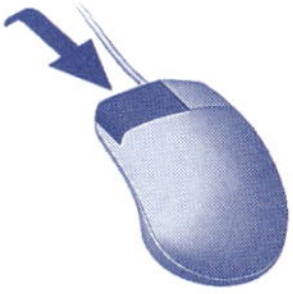

2 Click on the START menu button and choose PROGRAMS. Click on ACCESSORIES and select WORDPAD.

3 Now key in some words.

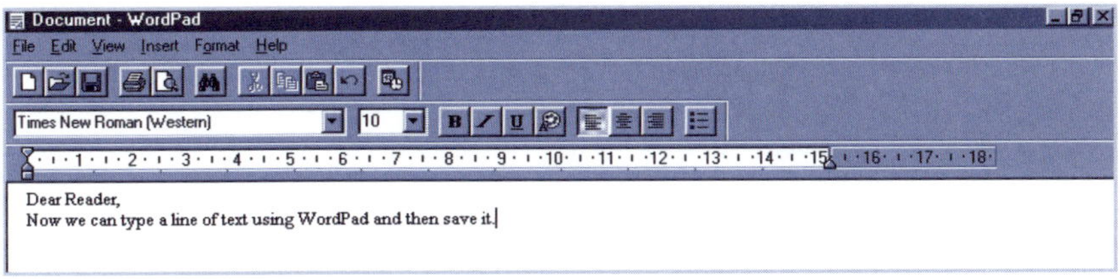

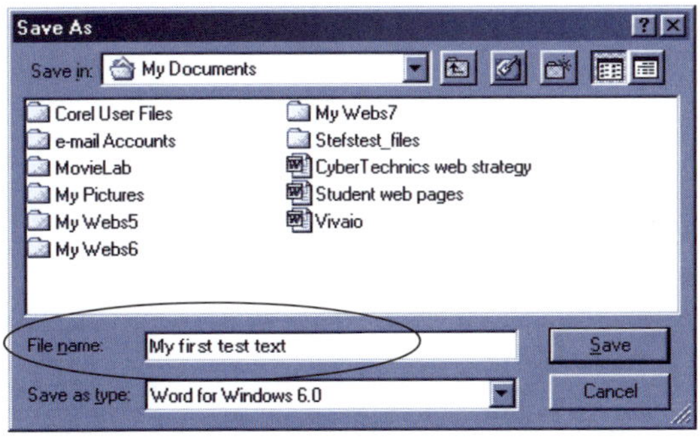

4 Choose the SAVE AS option in the drop-down File menu. The *Save As* window opens and asks you to enter the file name in the *File name* field. Click with the mouse on *My Documents* and type in the name "My first test text".

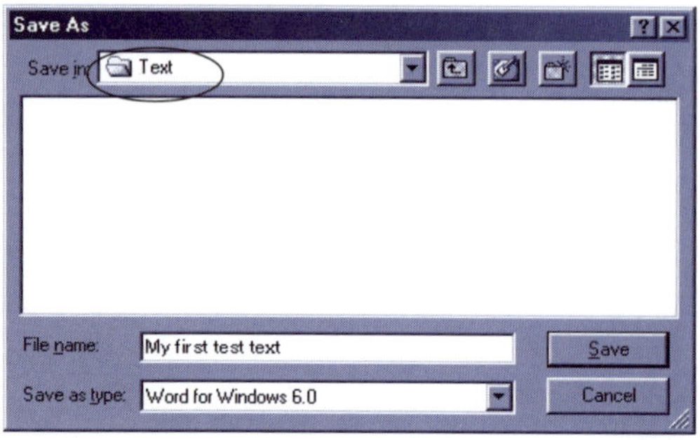

5 Now click on My Computer and choose your hard disk C:. You will now find the Text folder listed. Open this by double-clicking on it.

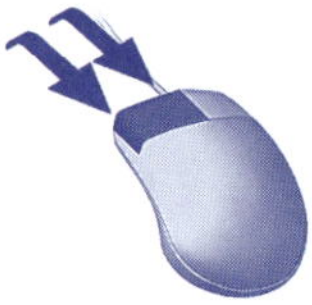

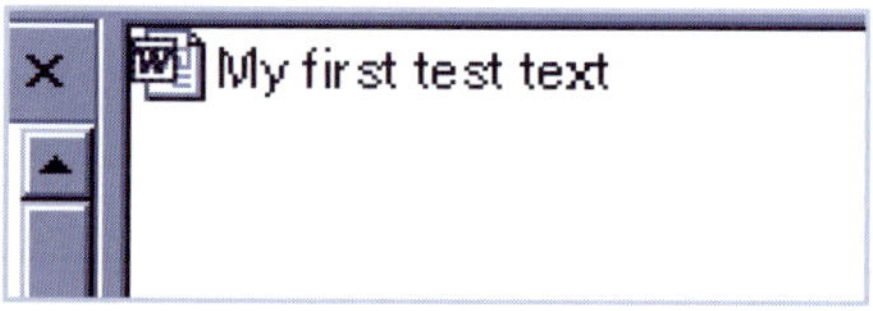

6 You can save files into the Text folder by clicking on Save. The file is now displayed as part of the Text folder in the right hand side of the screen.

Wildcards

The file name system **recognises** "**wildcards**" that you can use when searching for a saved file.

This sounds complicated, but in practice it is very helpful and you will probably use the system quite often. The following example will show you why wildcards are so important when doing a **file search,** and will explain what wildcards are actually for.

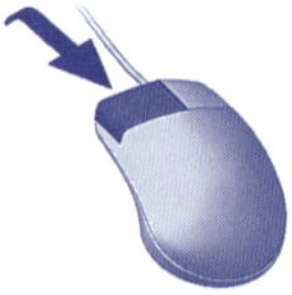

If, for example, you have saved a file with the name "**ANNUNZIATO**", but you cannot remember the exact spelling of this name, you can still search for this file. You can search in such a way that your PC will recognise the spelling "**ANNUZIATO**" or "**ANNUNZEATO**" and "**ANNUNZUATO**".

WHAT'S THIS?

The **Wildcard** "?" (question mark) replaces any character in a character string.

To do this replace some characters with a wildcard. If you set up your search to find all files with the name "**ANNUNZ??TO**", you will be shown a list which takes into consideration a number of spellings of this name. You can see that the question mark replaces any letter and could be used anywhere within the name. The file search parameters could be "**A?????????**", in which case you will have a list of all the file names starting with an "A" and followed by the appropriate number of characters.

WHAT'S THIS?

The **Wildcard** "*" (star) replaces a long string of characters.

However, the file system recognises another extension "*". The star replaces a long character string. The selection "A*", for example, would find all file names which start with an "A", regardless of their length.

Finding files

Most operating systems give you the option of finding your files on **various drives**. This is important if you have saved a file, and you cannot remember the name of the folder where you saved it.

You could open each folder and check, but this would take up a lot of time and is a tedious task. This is what computers are good at, so leave it to your PC to find it instead!

Early operating systems usually required users to enter the specific path to be able to find a file; modern systems, however, are able to find a file on the basis of a **search string**.

The following step-by-step guide will show you how the Find function of Windows 95, 98 and NT 4.0 works. This procedure works with other operating systems as well. As an example, we will search for the "My first test text" file.

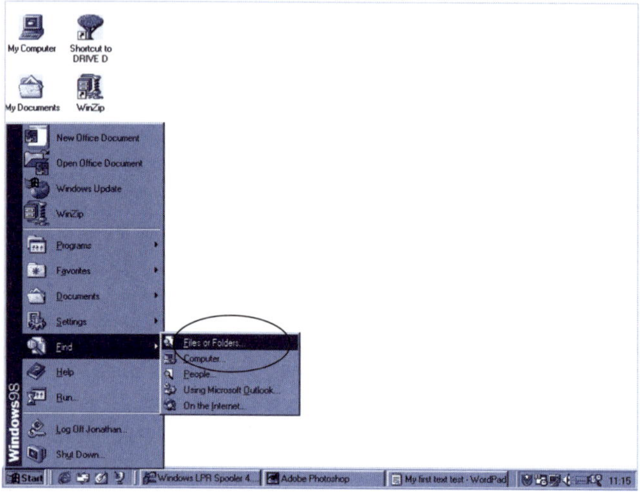

1 Click on the Start menu button and choose the Find command. Then click on Files or Folders....

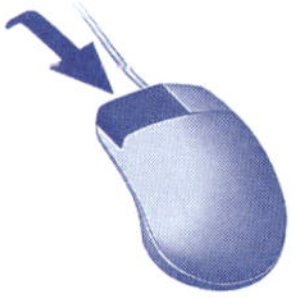

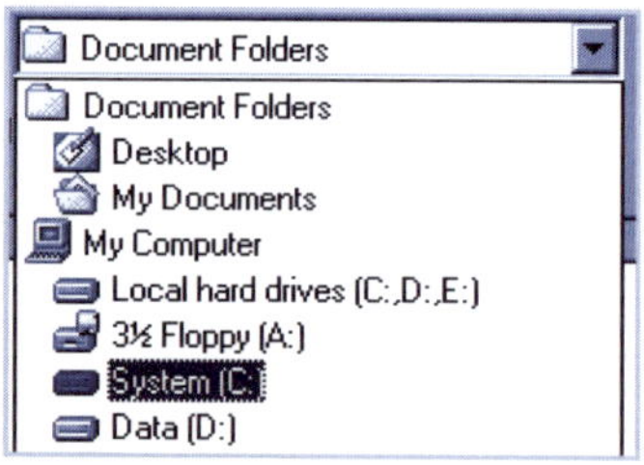

2 The window allows you to search for specific files on the different drives of your system. You can also search the floppy drive or your CD-ROM drive.

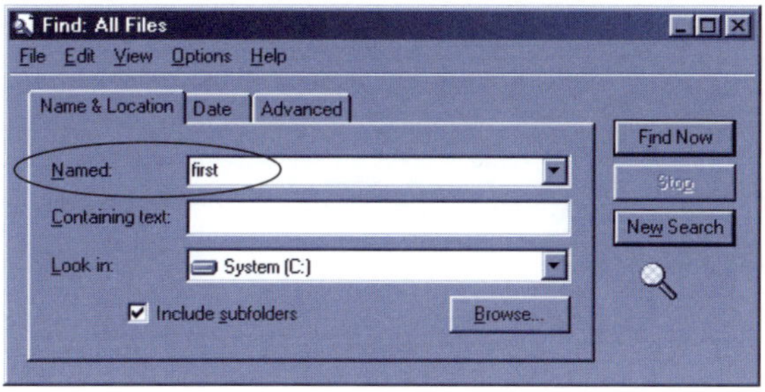

3 In the *Named* field of this window, enter the word "First", (one of the words in the file name "My first test text").

4 Click on FIND NOW to start the search.

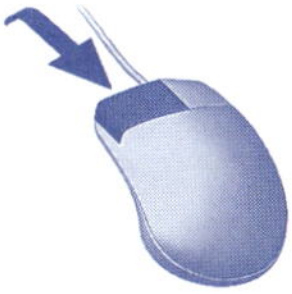

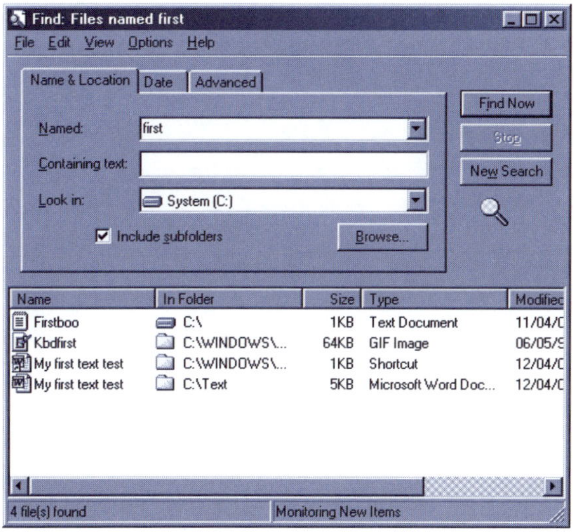

5 After a few seconds, the computer will find some files and will list them in the Results area of the Find dialog box. You will also be told in which folder each file is stored.

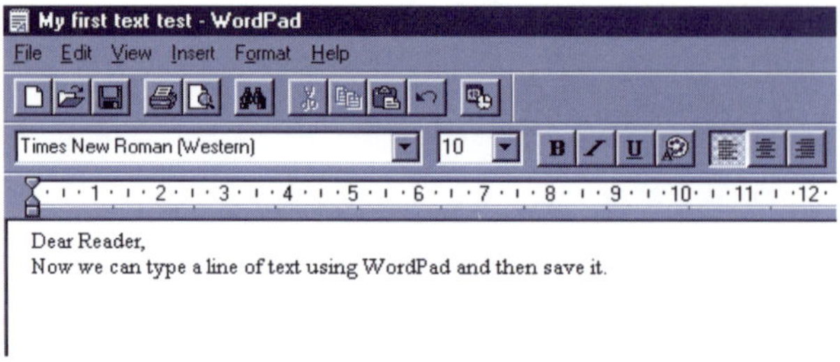

6 You can look at the contents of the file by clicking twice on the file in the *Find* dialog box. The appropriate application, in our case WordPad, is launched and the document loaded.

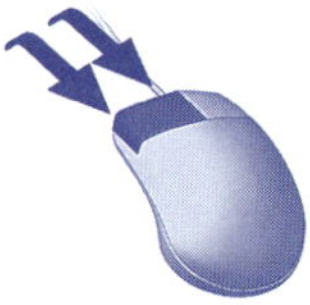

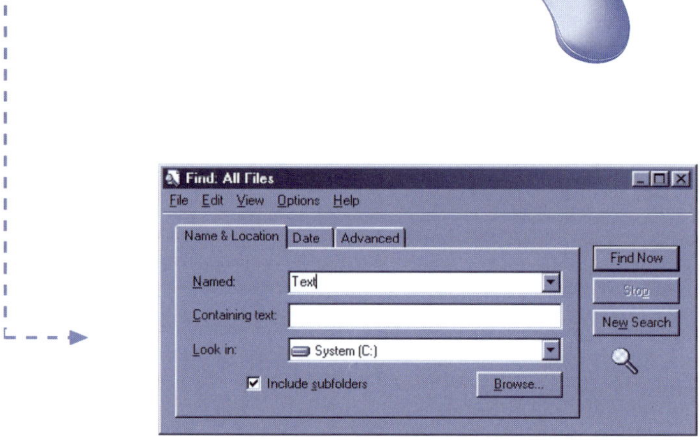

7 To practice, you can search for the Text Folder using a suitable search term.

Moving files

Eventually, you will want to move documents to different folders. In Windows, this operation is called "Drag & Drop".

WHAT'S THIS?

Drag & Drop describes a mouse operation to move files or folders to new locations.

For example, spreadsheet calculations for the next financial year can be moved using the drag & drop procedure, so you can create and save your spreadsheet in this year's folder and then move it to next year's.

The following step-by-step guide shows you how to move the sample document saved in the Text folder on the Desktop into a different folder.

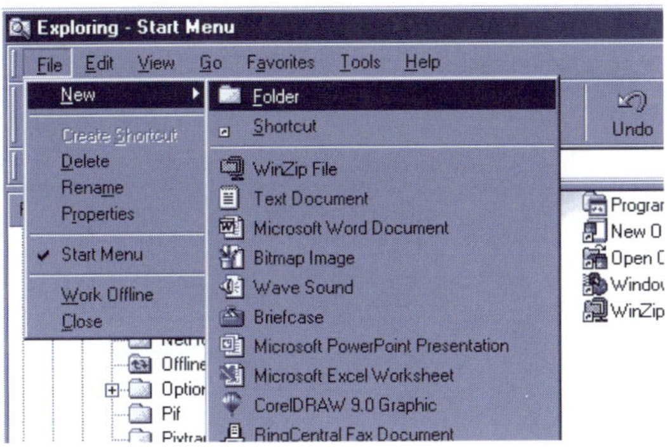

1 Put a new folder on your hard disk C: and name it *Filing 1999*.

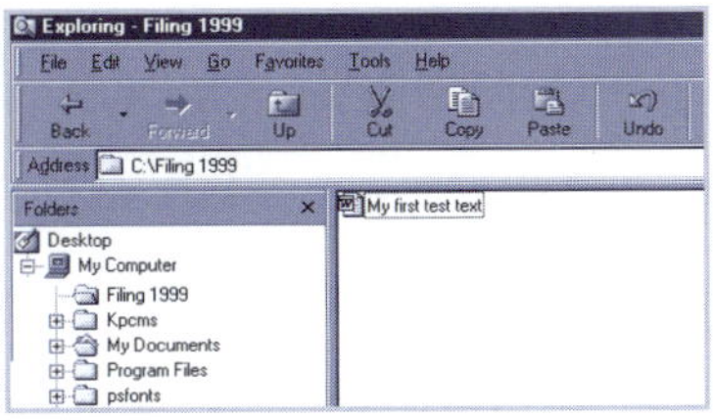

2 Open Explorer and you will see the summary of contents in the Filing 1999 folder. This includes the document *My first test text*.

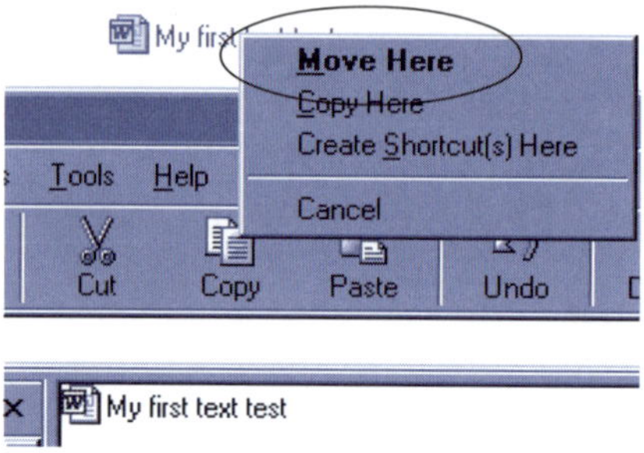

3 Click with the right mouse button on the file icon and keep the button pressed. Now move the icon attached to the mouse pointer to a free space on the Desktop. If you release the mouse button now, a drop-down menu opens. Select MOVE HERE.

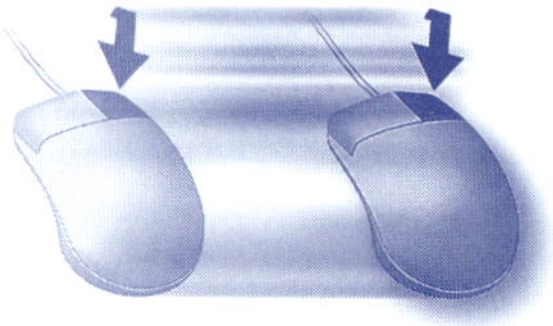

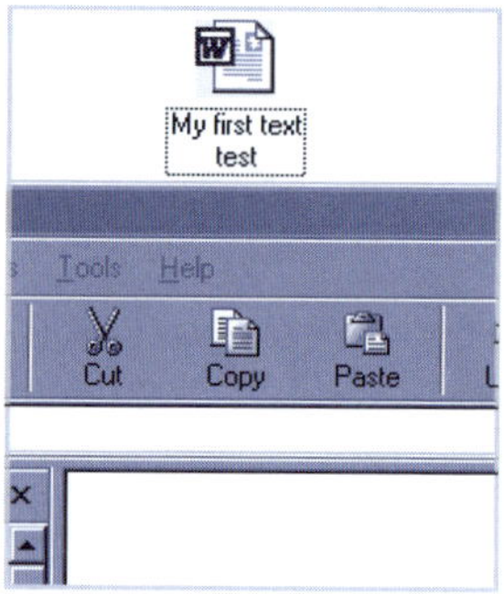

4 In this way, the icon you were dragging is put down on the desktop and is deleted from the original Filing 1999 folder.

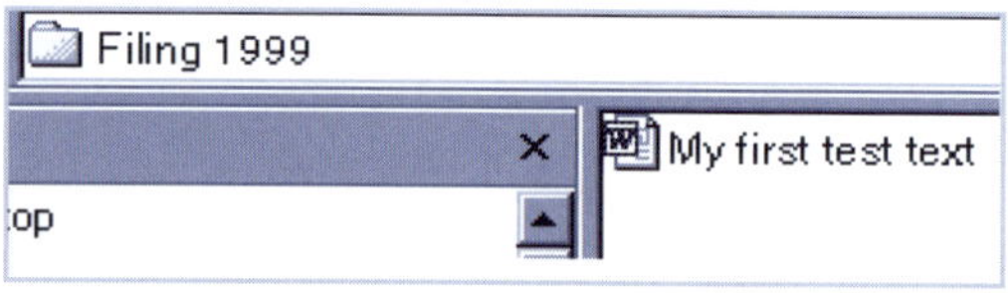

5 Select the new folder named *Filing 1999* in Explorer. Drag the file icon. The icon disappears from the Desktop and is placed in the Folder instead.

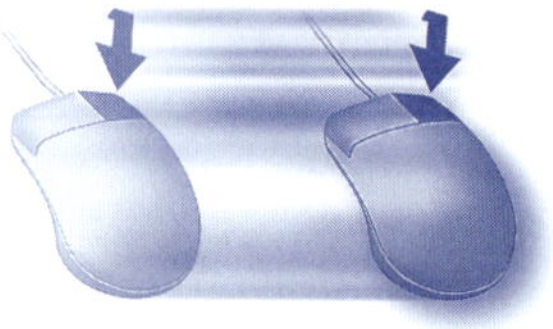

You can move files without having to move them on the Desktop. To do this, open a second Explorer window and position it parallel to the first. Files or whole folders can be moved now between the windows.

Creating shortcuts or copying?

The last important tip we would like to give you, at the end of this chapter on handling files, concerns the difference between **copying** and **creating shortcuts**.

In the previous step-by-step guide you learned not only how to move objects attached to the mouse pointer, but also how to copy and create a shortcut. We have already explained what a shortcut is.

While a shortcut represents a **reference** to a file, if you choose "Create a copy", you will create a second copy of the file, totally independent from the original one, and you can place it into a different position.

If you amend the original file, the shortcut is also adapted, but a copied file will not be automatically updated. Sometimes this is not a good idea, if you are working with several different copies of the same document. You may have difficulty identifying which copy is the most recent and which is an old version. Therefore, you should always **create a shortcut** to a current file and make a copy only occasionally, for example as a back-up.

6 How does your computer work?

What's in this chapter:

We will now show you the tasks a computer can perform and tell you why man is superior to computers.
We are going to explain what a processor is and why there are several generations of processors. We will also show you the relationship between clock frequency and speed and describe the function of the Bus system as the data transportation "freeway". To conclude, we will introduce you to the language of the PC, which is made up of bits and bytes.

You already know about:

You are going to learn about:

It may not be intelligent but it is incredibly fast

Can you calculate million of numbers in a second? You are unlikely to be able to, but a computer can. Its electronic computing brain seems to be a true all-rounder. In a flash, it can calculate square roots from any number, logarithms, sine and tangents from anything you want, can subtract, add and multiply in a fraction of a second.

So, you think the computer is actually the genius it would appear to be? We have already explained that the computer has serious problems when faced with decoding "language", for example.

But it also has many other failures in completing tasks: no computer can decode handwriting with high precision. While you can read a handwritten letter without effort, a PC, even with all its expensive electronic tools, would have serious difficulties decoding it.

Perhaps you have already seen the following sentence; if you have never seen it before, read it carefully to understand its meaning:

If a fly flies behind flies, flies fly in front of a fly.

The word "flies" is used three times, as a plural noun and as a verb. The word "fly" is also used three times, as a singular noun and as a verb. You may need to read the sentence three or four times before you can really grasp its meaning. But a sentence such as this one would create an insoluble problem for a computer. The English language grammar check, for example, is available on PC, but is still full of mistakes.

The translation of texts into a different language, such as German into English, for example, is a substantial effort for a PC. Even reasonably efficient translation software programs always require human editing.

The real issue is this: computers do not have a mind, and the human intellect will always put men on a higher level than their electronic helpers. The creative activities man is capable of gives him a predominant and unrivalled position when compared with computers.

Routine activities, however, which can be executed by following instructions, can be carried out faster by computers than by man. So, using computers to carry out these types of activities is an advantage. This kind of clear sequences of operational schemes, aimed at carrying out operations and calculations, are called "algorithms" or "computer routines".

WHAT'S THIS?

An **algorithm** or computer **routine** executed by a computer is a list of specific orders and computing steps.

All the efforts of computer engineers are aimed at equipping computers with a degree of intelligence. Admittedly, this discipline, which is called "artificial intelligence", has had some astonishing results. But computers' ability is in no way comparable to the neural intelligence of man.

You may have followed the famous chess event of May 1997. The IBM high-performance computer "Deep Blue" managed to beat the chess world's champion and master Kasparov. After only ten minutes, the Grand Master faced checkmate.

This event appeared to onlookers as the triumph of engineering over man. But if you look at it more closely, "Deep Blue" had simply calculated an algorithm. He calculated all possible following moves of the world's chess champion and executed the resulting optimum moves at an inconceivable speed.

But what is surprising is that an immensely powerful multi-million dollar computer was needed to beat a man.

In this chapter, we will describe how a computer works and we will explain bits and bytes.

The processor

The processor, which forms the central unit of every computer, is like a brain configured for arithmetic operations. These processors are present in various types of equipment, where you would never have guessed the existence of a computing chip.

About 80 per cent of processors perform their tasks in non-computing equipment, for example washing machines, lawnmowers, electrical toothbrushes, television sets, stereos, petrol pumps and so on.

The word "computer" comes from "to compute" meaning "to calculate". The only thing a processor knows how to do is execute any type of calculation at an incredibly fast pace. The processor is usually called "CPU" for short.

Until now, we have spoken of computers as being "incredibly" and "hugely" fast. This may have created some misunderstandings and an idealistic image of computing speed, so we need to introduce the concept of "MIPS".

WHAT'S THIS?

The **CPU** (central processing unit) is the central unit of every computer. It executes calculations and sequences of operations following specific coordinates and parameters.

The MIPS value defines how many single addition and subtraction instructions the processor of the computer can execute per second. Particularly powerful computers can add or subtract up to 100 million numbers per second. How long would this operation take you?

WHAT'S THIS?

MIPS is the abbreviation for "Million Instructions Per Second" and provides a parameter for the processing speed of a computer.

The MIPS value is misleading, though: it is wrong to use it as the only way to measure the total performance of a computer, as the following example shows:

If our 100-MIPS processor receives data from a slow module which does not deliver data at the speed required to achieve the declared calculation speed, the processor must insert waiting time, that is an "internal loop", and its speed is limited by this. However, there are technological remedies to the slowing down activity of internal loops, so that sequences of operations in the PC are kept as efficient as possible.

WHAT'S THIS?

Wait states (which are really "internal loops") slow down the CPU and reduce effective processing capacity.

Different CPU generations

The difference between the various generations of processors is in their internal structure and construction. Usually, a new processor generation involves a considerable increase in cost, compared to the previous generation, but it provides an extension of the application area.

The reason why there have been several processor generations is the need for more powerful components, so that data could be handled faster. Older PCs are fitted with slower and smaller hard disks, compared to modern Pentium PCs, which are equipped with expensive hard disks with a much larger capacity and speed.

Intel, the processor market leader, introduced new processors at varying intervals during the last few years, and these are taken as the parameters for the various generations. The CPUs produced by other manufacturers are always compatible with the corresponding Intel models.

The first PC processor was introduced in 1979. Its name was XT, which stands for Extended Technology. In comparison with modern processors, its processing performance was ridiculously low: a Pentium processor calculates about 200 times faster!

In 1982, three years later, the XT had already been superseded by the AT. This abreviation stands for Advanced Technology and PCs with this new processor cost no more than the previous generation. In 1986, the next generation was introduced by Intel, the 386 processor; in 1989 came its successor, the 486.

Many modern PCs are equipped with a Pentium processor. The change in naming policy, from numbers to words, was for legal reasons: because of the immense success of this type of processor, Intel's competitors produced very similar CPUs. Such processors are described as "clones" and, obviously, they are competition for the manufacturers of the original chip.

American law decided that number combinations such as the logical sequential name of the processor, 586, could not be legally protected under the copyright law. Every processor manufacturer would have therefore been able to name their processor 586s, for example. So the Intel marketing strategy team decided to opt for a name that could be copyrighted, hence the name "Pentium".

WHAT'S THIS?

Clones are post-structures of original processors which use the same engineering and are compatible with the original one.

Perhaps you have a Pentium MMX. This means that your computer has the ability to handle online and graphics programs, which usually make special demands on the processor, because the MMX processor is equipped with special multimedia handling technology.

The Pentium II, another fifth generation processor, is an extended Pentium processor which derives from the original Intel processor but is equipped with a higher processing power. The original Pentium Pro is no longer a serious contender in the current computer performance race.

WHAT'S THIS?

MMX is an abbreviation for Multimedia Extension and is a special part in the processor responsible for handling the fast graphic files of multimedia programs.

The new super-processor is called Pentium III and is currently the best processor for PCs. Even the competition would see the Pentium III as a high end processor.

What to buy: only the best?

A leading processor designer working at Intel has made the following comparison: "If the car industry had gone through the same type of development as computer technology, a Rolls Royce today would cost approximately the same as a packet of cigarettes and would be the size of a postage stamp."

This statement goes a long way to explaining why many users are so unsure of what to choose when they need to buy a computer. Of course, you could listen to the advice of your computer dealer and buy the most expensive top of the range computer, but you know that in six months' time your expensive model will become a middle range model and would probably cost half the price you paid for it.

For the average user, it is sensible to choose a high end PC. The price–performance ratio is very favourable when considering a Pentium III, because any future increase in speed is very unlikely to be directly proportional to an increase in cost.

Today, you would be well advised to choose an average computer equipped with a Pentium processor. A 486 processor would not be able to cope with an operating system such as Windows 98, and would be incredibly slow, because of the need for wait states.

Clock frequency: the measure of speed

A processor needs an accurate time basis to set up calculations at exactly defined intervals.

The principle used by the PC corresponds to the time measurement of a quartz clock: a crystal goes through a specific number of vibrations within a specified time. The measure for this time basis is the clock frequency, which is indicated in megahertz, shortened to MHz.

Therefore, it can safely be stated that the higher the clock frequency, the more powerful the PC is.

WHAT'S THIS?

The clock **frequency** of a PC is indicated in megahertz (MHz) and is a measure of the system speed.

How fast does an average computer work today? While the user of early PCs had to be satisfied with a clock frequency of only 8 MHz, the crystal time of modern computers can reach 800 MHz.

You can check the clock frequency of your PC by looking at its case. The LED display on the case shows the clock speed of your computer.

Unfortunately, this indication is not very reliable, because it does not consider the clock frequency of the processor. The indication provided by the computer manufacturer is more reliable.

The following step-by-step guide will show you how to find out the clock speed of your computer, if you work with Windows NT 4.0.

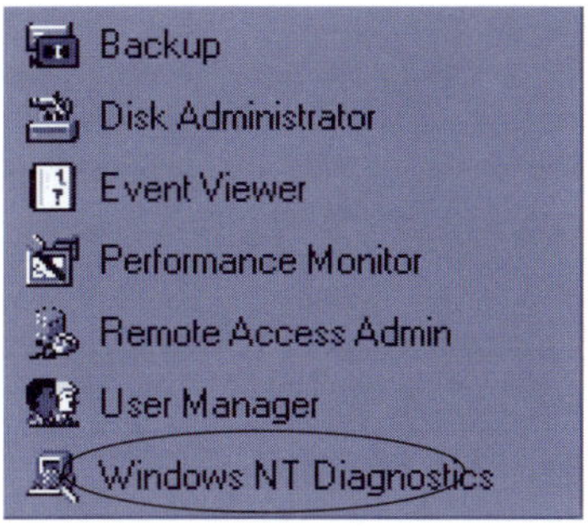

1 Click on the START menu button and choose PROGRAMS and ADMINISTRATION (General). Then click on WINDOWS NT DIAGNOSTICS.

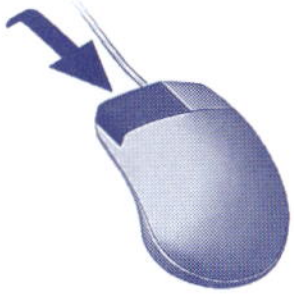

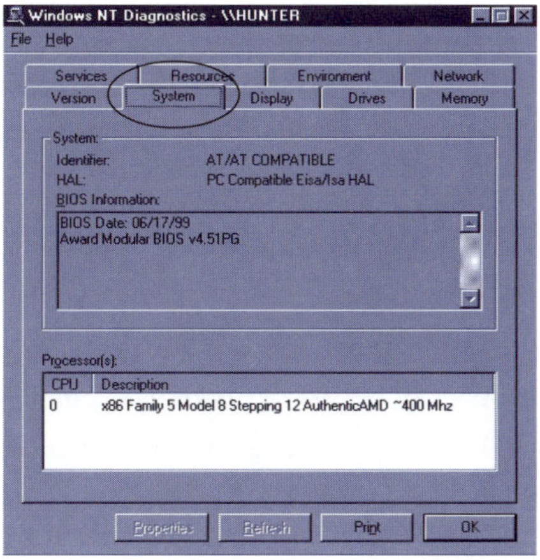

2 Choose the SYSTEM tab.

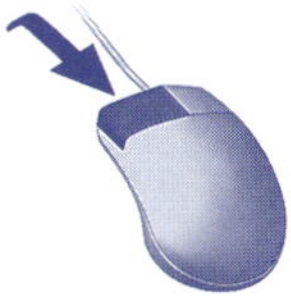

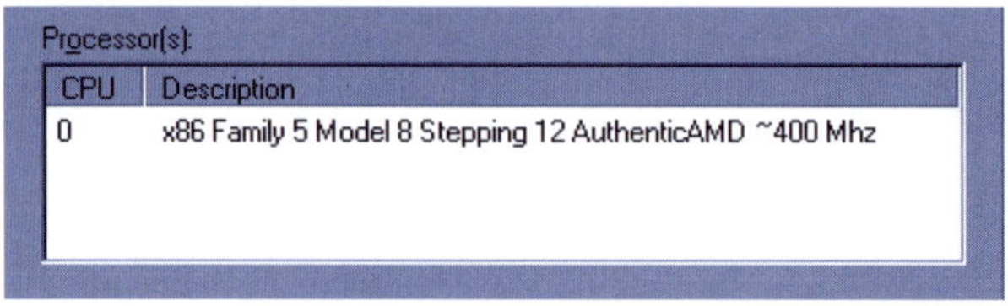

3 In the bottom part of the open window, you will find a Processor(s) label. The last numeric string ends with Mhz and represents the clock frequency of your processor.

The bus system for data transfer

Perhaps you wonder how data to be calculated reach the processor and how the outcome of the calculations is sent to your printer or to the screen.

Obviously, the processor must be equipped with a transport system – comparable to a data highway – which sends data to the hard disk, the CD-ROM drive, monitor, printer, mouse and all other components.

The way a bus system handles data transfer is complex. Think of the effort which is required to transport data with a clock frequency of perhaps 66 or 133 MHz!

WHAT'S THIS?

The data transfer system of a computer is called the **bus system**.

The following step-by-step guide gives you an idea of how computers operate and shows you how the bus system works.

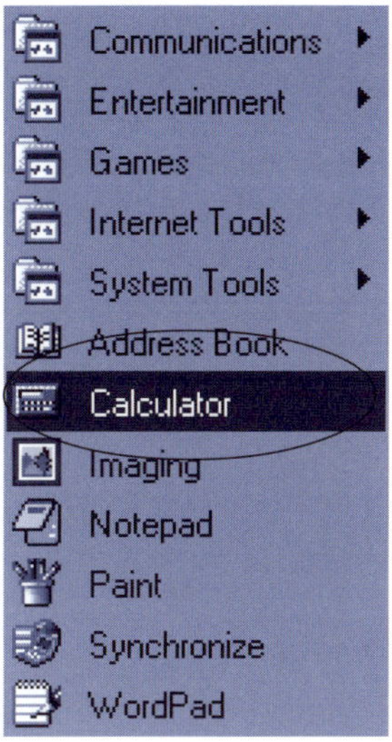

1 Click on the START menu button and choose PROGRAMS and then ACCESSORIES. Click on the CALCULATOR entry.

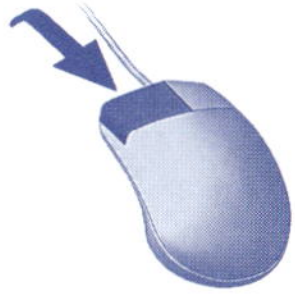

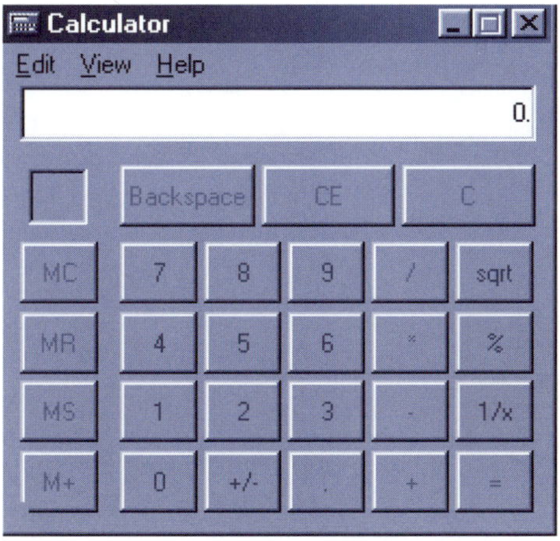

2 The Windows calculator will appear on the Desktop. Ask it to calculate the square root of 1024.

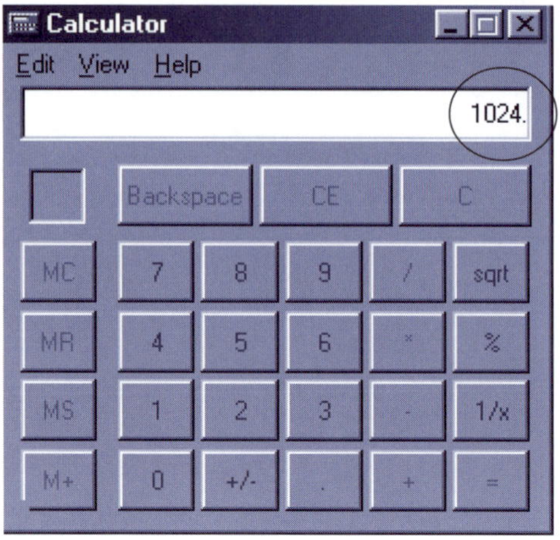

3 Enter 1024 with the keyboard or the mouse, and press the square root calculation key, sqrt.

4 Windows 98 recognises your input and your mouse click and sends the command "calculate the square root of the number 1024" to the Bus system. At this point, you wonder whether the processor has sufficient processing resources.

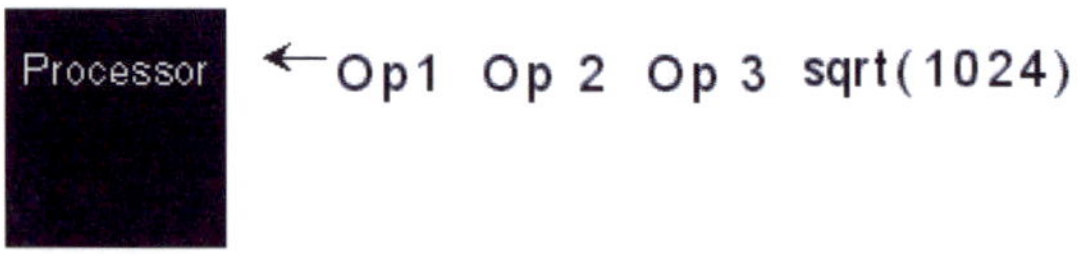

5 The command sets in motion a string of processing operations, preset by the processor.

6 The processor calculates the result by following a number of processing steps and it decides that the answer is 32.

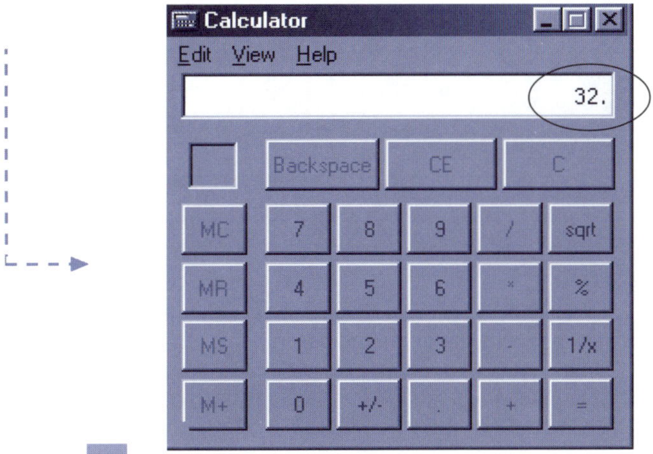

7 The bus system then feeds the result back to the graphics card, and displays it in the calculator. Only a fraction of a second has elapsed between pressing the sqrt button and the result appearing on screen!

There are different types of bus systems. Older systems worked with an architecture called ISA which stands for Industrial Standard Architecture.

WHAT'S THIS?

PCI is the abbreviation for Peripheral Component Interconnect, the current standard bus system.

This bus system is not really suitable for modern computers because of its considerable disadvantages, as well as a low transmission rate. The bus architecture used today by default is called PCI and is produced by Siemens.

Several components and peripherals, which communicate with the processor, are connected to the PCI bus. The printer and the mouse, the monitor and expansion modules, which will be discussed in another chapter, are also indirectly connected to the PCI bus.

The PCI differs from other high data transfer systems because of its properties. If you want to add expansion components to your PC, you need a technically experienced user or sometimes even an expert.

WHAT'S THIS?

Plug & Play (or PnP for short) is a standard in the Windows environment that allows users to add extra peripherals to their PC.

PCI is Plug & Play compatible, so you can extend your PC by simply plugging in the additional module and then switching it on to extend your PC properties.

In the next chapter, we will show you which extended properties are useful for your personal needs.

The motherboard

What is a bus system, in physical terms? Several track conductors connect the single components to each other, such as the processor and the hard disk.

WHAT'S THIS?

The **bus system** sits on the main board; the essential steering and controlling functions of a PC are resident in the motherboard.

The track conductors are positioned on a supporting platform. The functions of this main board, or motherboard, include data transfer and various other coordinating functions. Calculation and control units, as well as the processor, are located on the main board.

In order to be able to fit as many track conductors as possible on a small area – computers are becoming smaller and smaller – the electrical tracks are transferred not only to the interface but also to deeper layers of the motherboard.

Because track conductors are as fine as a single hair, they can go through small electrical charges and thus make expensive boards useless.

CAUTION

Treat computer boards with track conductors extremely carefully and do not expose them to electrical charges!

In the previous chapters, we have already introduced you to some of the essential elements which are located on the motherboard.

The motherboard includes:

- The processor
- The BIOS
- The timing generator and the internal real time watch
- The control unit of the hard disks, floppy disk and CD-ROM drives
- The interfaces
- The main memory
- The Bus system

Bits and bytes

Earlier we saw why a computer uses the binary system.

We are now going to explain in more detail how your computer works with the binary system. This is really important, because the whole of the computer world is based on this system which, at first sight, is alien to most people.

The bit

The smallest information unit which a computer can process is a **bit**. A bit can accept the state of "0" and "1" and thus can be represented as a magnetic particle on the hard disk or as electrical "In/Out" information.

> **WHAT'S THIS?**
>
> The **bit** (short for Binary Digit) is the smallest information unit in data technology. It is the basic element of the computer binary system.

Ask yourself how many different information strings can be represented using only these two numbers. You will probably answer "Two, zero and one!".

Basically, what happens is that, if the binary system is not efficient, with only these two states, "0" and "1", you cannot transfer large chunks of information.

However, if only two bits are used, more information can be transferred. You may already know that there are four different states which can be used, as shown here:

```
1.Bit: 1 1 0 0
2.Bit: 1 0 1 0
```

With just one additional bit – a three-bit system – you can represent eight items of information:

```
1. Bit: 1 1 1 1 0 0 0 0

2. Bit: 0 0 0 0 1 1 1 1

3. Bit: 1 1 0 0 1 1 0 0

4. Bit: 0 1 0 1 0 1 0 1
```

Now, if you assign a character to each of these bit combinations shown in a vertical row, you will be able to represent 16 states.

A four-bit system can represent 16 data items, a five-bit system can represent 32 data items. Because in standard communication we use 26 letters and 10 numbers (altogether, 36 units), a six-bit system (which gives 64 representable characters) should be sufficient.

However, computers use eight bits at once, to represent 256 data items.

The byte

We have stated that 256 different characters can be represented with the 8-bit system. You can distinguish between upper and lower case letters; moreover, there are enough information units to represent specific characters used in different languages.

The computer groups these 8-bits into a new unit, the **byte**.

The following sequence shows how your computer converts a character into a binary sequence and back again before outputting it.

WHAT'S THIS?

A **byte** is another unit in computer engineering. It consists of eight bits. The byte is the smallest information unit to represent a number or a letter.

9

1 Use the keyboard to enter the number "9" which your computer will add to the number "2", which has already been entered.

11101010
+
10010011

2 The computer converts the number to a binary number and submits it to the Bus system which passes the information on.

10010101

3 The processor receives both numbers for calculation in the binary format and gives the result back in binary form to the Bus system.

11

4 Before releasing the information, the calculated binary number is translated into the decimal format: 11.

The ASCII code

You already know that a decimal number is assigned to each binary 0-1 combination. But which decimal number corresponds to the binary number "1001011"?

Just imagine what would happen if each manufacturer used a different correspondence system: you would type an "A" on the keyboard, but your word processing program would interpret this as an "H", the hard disk would save it as a "U" and the printer would print it as an "R".

Obviously, we need a defined structure which assigns a binary number to a decimal number or another character logically and systematically. A system which executes this operation is the ASCII coding procedure for the computer.

Two other code procedures are ISO and EBCDIC, but these are less common than ASCII.

WHAT'S THAT?

ASCII is the abbreviation for American Standard Code for Information Interchange and represents a code procedure which assigns a decimal number or a character to each binary combination.

Because the ASCII code was originally based on the English language, early versions did not cater for special characters used by other languages. The first ASCII code contains 7 bits, the new version, Extended ASCII, now has 8 bits, and it includes special characters. ANSI is an ASCII expansion under Windows. It extends ASCII to colours and special functions (such as flickering images).

TIP

Occasionally, you may find that, if you are writing in a non-English language, accented letters or non-English characters are not printed or represented on the monitor correctly, especially with older or special software. This is because such software only provides the simple 7-bit ASCII code or works with an 8-bit which does not comply with the Extended ASCII standard.

Test your knowledge

Main theme: Memory and storage

This second test deals with hard drives and floppy disks and how data and files are structured. You will find the answers at the back of the book.

1. Explain the difference between folders, files and disk drives.

2. What does Drag & Drop mean?

3. Explain the main advantages of hard disks versus floppy disks.

4. What is a "head crash" and why is it so dangerous?

5. What does "formatting" mean and why do CD-ROMs not need to be formatted?

6. Explain the function of a streamer. Why is a magnetic tape very slow at retrieving data?

7. How much faster is a 100 MHz Pentium than a 50 MHz Pentium ?

8. Describe the difference between a bit and a byte.

9. What does the abbreviation ASCII stand for and why is this standard so important?

10. List at least five components present on the motherboard.

7 Printing

What's in this chapter:

In this chapter we will explain which types of printers are suitable for different purposes and applications. You will also learn about the difference between laser, needle and ink-jet printers, and learn what a plotter is.
We will show you the difference between parallel and serial printers and discuss how printing signals are fed back to the PC.
Finally, we will print a test document and check the resulting printout.

You already know about:

You are going to learn about:

Computer and paper: are they inseparably connected?

One of the main tasks in electronic data processing development was the efficient administration of large amounts of data. Users no longer need to look for reams of paper in cabinets full of folders, but can now request a document by simply sending a command to their computer.

When you work with your computer, you will soon realise (or maybe you have already noticed) that computers and paper are inseparably linked to each other.

In previous chapters, we have already established that computers have caused an increase in the amount of **paper** used. It has been agreed that the "paperless office" is just a pipe dream and will remain so for a long time. It is typical that a page of typed information is usually printed out on paper between ten and twenty times.

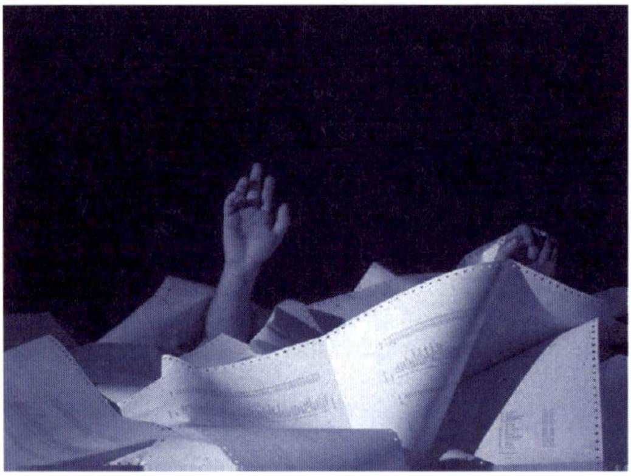

One reason for this may be that, since presumably not all your business partners have a computer, the only way to communicate with them is by means of a paper document.

Another reason is that printed information is not only used for communication purposes, but also for archive purposes; it is very difficult to replace printed paper with electronic storage media, because the advantage with printouts is that they are readable independently from the hardware used.

The printer is a tool which has developed with the computer, like many other computer-related tools. The following pages will provide you with a brief history of the development of printer technology. Later on, we will introduce current printer models, so that you have up-to-date and appropriate knowledge when you next decide to buy a printer.

Early printers

When computer were first built, early printers were like their immediate predecessors, **typewriters**. Instead of nimble fingers that diligently entered text and numbers, the computer was able to communicate via a simple interface with the typewriter and place strings of data on paper.

These printers were called **daisy-wheel printers** because they printed characters using a daisy wheel. If you wanted to use one of these now, you would find it impossible to print graphics, because daisy-wheel printers are not flexible enough and they are very slow.

WHAT'S THIS?

Daisy-wheel printers work like typewriters, but they are no longer used.

The next generation of printers used thin metal needles, instead of characters. You are familiar with the principle behind the workings of your digital watch, which displays numbers as LEDs. Dot-matrix printers worked in the same way, generating characters with 7 to 36 dots.

WHAT'S THIS?

Dot-matrix printers use metal pins to produce characters using combinations of single dots.

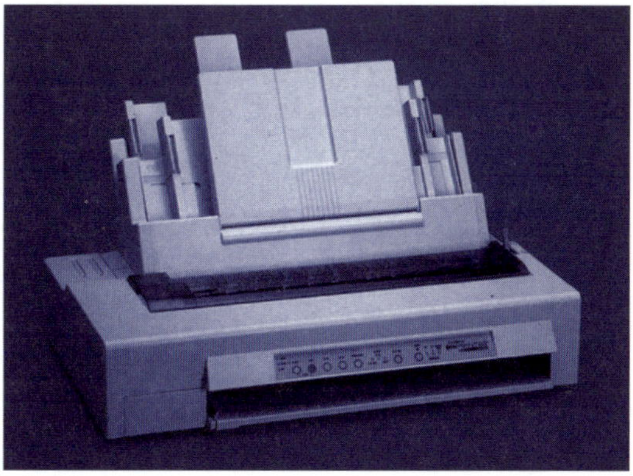

Characters printed by a dot-matrix printers were coarse and jagged because the dots were visible with the naked eye. The concept of quality printing was not even considered; at the time, the term used was "NLQ printers".

> **WHAT'S THIS?**
>
> **NLQ** is an abbreviation for "Near Letter Quality".

The best that customers could expect, when producing advertising material and important documents, was "letter quality". If today you are offered a second-hand NLQ printer, do not even touch it!

Dot-matrix printers were better than previous ones because they could actually print graphics. Because single needles could print specific areas on the paper page, they were able to print black and white images.

A further disadvantage of dot-matrix printers was that they were extremely noisy. The sound of the pressure of ten or twenty metal pins was so annoying that users could even buy ear plugs to protect themselves from the noise.

However, dot-matrix printers have some advantages. They are hard-wearing, cheap and relatively fast, and therefore are a cheap alternative for occasional use and for domestic use. Because they are based on the impact-printing principle, dot-matrix printers can work with self-carbon paper and can print on preprinted forms (such as transfer forms, tax returns). Therefore, dot-matrix printers are still used industrially.

> **WHAT'S THIS?**
>
> **Impact printers** produce characters by the mechanical process of colour assignment used by a colour carrier, for example the ribbon.

Daisy wheel and dot-matrix printers are typical impact printers.

Ink-jet printers

The most popular printer today is undoubtedly the **ink-jet printer**. The simple concept underlying the design of these printers combines a reasonable price with good print quality.

The print head consists of 24 to 48, or more, nozzles arranged geometrically, which can control the deposit of the ink in the form of small droplets. The single nozzles are called steering wheel electronics.

With this kind of printer, which deposits ink on to the paper, printouts tend to be **blurred**. Although printer manufacturers have improved the performance of these printers considerably, ink-jet printers are currently only occasionally used to print envelopes or address labels, for example.

WHAT'S THIS?

Ink-jet printers use ink droplets instead of metal pins used by a dot-matrix printer. Individual characters are produced from the combination of single dots.

The main problem is that large black areas can generate blotches on the sheet of paper, because the ink can be damp.

In order to try and solve this problem, Hewlett-Packard started to manufacture ink-jet printers which use a special power-based ink. Printouts produced with this ink appear much more even.

Laser printers

Laser printers, which work just like a photocopier, are the latest success in terms of advanced technology. Laser printers are far superior to any previous printing technology, especially if you need to print graphics; they are also perfect for printing text documents.

WHAT'S THIS?

Laser printers combine characters from colour particles, generated by toners. They work like a photocopier and produce high-quality printouts.

Because of their reasonable price, laser printers are also used by non-professional users. A clear disadvantage is their high maintenance costs. As well as consumables, such as **toners** and special **print heads**, the drum must also be replaced regularly and this may become expensive. The cost of 80 gsm A4 laser paper is about £4 for 1000 sheets.

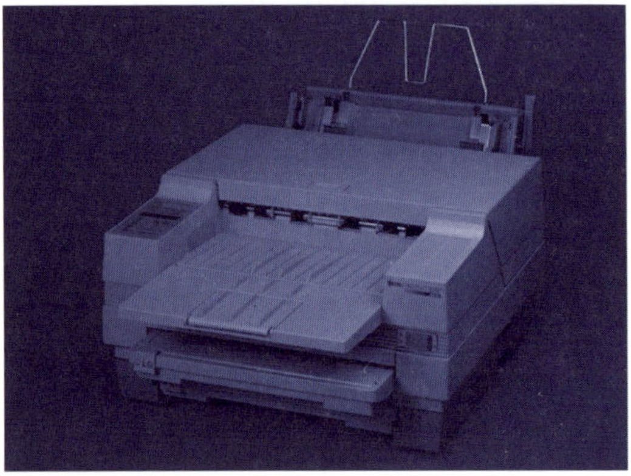

Laser and ink-jet printers are non-impact printers, because they do not need any mechanical contact with the paper sheet they are printing. It is therefore impossible to use them to print multiple copies on carbon paper and preprinted forms.

Other types of printers

Thermal transfer printers

The thermal transfer printer was used some years ago exclusively for special applications, but it had some advantages.

The print head consists of heatable fields which detach a special varnish from an inking ribbon. This varnish is absorbed by the underlying paper, producing a sharp impression. As well as printing on paper, it is also possible to print on transparencies, labels and even textile fabrics.

Thermal transfer printers are only really suitable in cases when users require a high-quality printout in low quantity. The price of an A4 colour printout may be £3 to £4, which is expensive, but justified by the photo quality of the colours.

Plotters

Plotters are not printers. A controller and steering wheel mechanism moves coloured ink cartridges in a horizontal and vertical direction on the sheet of paper which remains still. The vertical and horizontal movement of the cartridges allows complex graphics to be reproduced when the colour tracings touch the paper.

Plotters sizes range from A4 paper to A1 or even A0. Plotters are mainly used professionally by architects or engineers.

Serial or parallel?

All PC printers work with a **parallel port**. But they can also work with a serial interface; when we introduced the concept of interfaces, we explained that serial interfaces are slower than parallel ones.

While a serial printer is capable of printing short texts reasonably fast, it becomes extremely slow when printing graphics. Therefore, it is always better to use the parallel interface; printer manufacturers have recognised the advantages of using a parallel interface, so serial printers have become fairly rare.

An extended parallel port standard, based on Centronics technology, was developed in order to be able to send data from PCs to printers faster. This interface, called **EPP**, allows enhanced data transfer; if both the computer and the printer are equipped with this port, you would be able to enjoy a higher transmission rate.

WHAT'S THIS?

EPP is an abbreviation for Enhanced Parallel Port and it refers to an extended parallel interface, which sends information to the printer at a faster pace.

ECP (Enhanced Capabilities Port) is a development of EPP. It doubles the data transfer rate. ECPs are installed on almost all new computers and today are used for faster printing and scanning.

Status signals

In Chapter 4, we introduced the parallel interface. We explained that some of the pins at the end of the leads carry printers' **status signals**.

For example, the printer can send a message to the PC stating that it has run out of paper. The PC tells you that this is the case and invites you to insert more paper.

WHAT'S THIS?

With the **on-line signal,** the printer informs the computer that the printer is ready to print.

An important status signal which you should be aware of is the **on-line signal**. If this signal is active, the printer reports it is ready for printing. Your printer may be equipped with an on-line button. If you press it during printing, printing is temporarily interrupted.

Printer resolution – the measure of quality

All printers build documents or graphics from single dots; a dot-matrix printer uses metal pins, an ink-jet printer uses ink droplets and a laser printer uses toner particles.

Imagine that you need to create a specific graphic from a number of small dots. You will obviously group **dots as close together as possible** to obtain a visible printed image. If there are large gaps between dots, when the graphic is printed, individual dots are immediately recognisable and you lose track of the overall picture, because the printout image appears irregular and unfocused.

Printer manufacturers have therefore designed their printers so that they are capable of placing as many dots as possible on a specific print area.

WHAT'S THIS?

dpi is the abbreviation for dots per inch and this is the measure of printer resolution.

The number of "dots per inch" (dpi) is a measure of a printer's resolution and, as a result, of print quality. Therefore, **print quality** is related to the number of dots the printer can place within an inch. The higher the dpi, the higher the quality of output.

The number of dots a modern printer can produce per inch is showed in the following table:

Print resolution statistics

Print type	Resolution
9-dot-matrix printer	150 dpi
24-dot-matrix printer	300 dpi
Ink-jet printer	300–700 dpi
Laser printer	300–1,200 dpi
Professional reprographics	1,200–4,000 dpi

Colour printers

Up to fairly recently, colour printers were prohibitively expensive for average users and dot-matrix printers were able to produce reasonable print results. Since then, manufacturers have started producing inexpensive colour printers.

Many users are happy with black and white printers. If you need **colour printing**, however, a color ink-jet printer would probably do the job. They work with ink droplets which produce millions of colours.

Most colour ink-jet printers have a **twin-chamber system**. The first chamber in the cartridge contains black ink, and the second chamber contains cyan, magenta and yellow ink. This system is known as CMYK and it is able to produce up to 16.7 million different colours by mixing these inks.

The big disadvantage of **twin-chamber technology** is clear when you need to change the cartridge. Since the three primary colours are all contained in the same physical unit, you will need to replace the complete cartridge when one primary colour is empty, although the others may still be full. Therefore, many manufacturers now provide a four-chamber system, so that single primary colours can be replaced individually, thus saving money.

The main technical problem to be addressed during development of colour print technology was **matching** colours between the image on screen and its output. We will see in another chapter that your monitor combines colours using a completely different system. To convert a specific colour combination from your screen to a combination that can be matched by your colour printer requires a complex algorithm; such an algorithm is present in the form of a printer driver specific to that printer.

Currently, colour laser printers are very popular, but they are still more expensive than colour ink-jet printers, since they cost around £4,500.

Printer language

Different printer technologies involve different standards. Printers follow standards that are to a certain extent compatible.

WHAT'S THAT?

A **generic printer driver** processes ASCII fonts and is therefore supported by all printers, independent of printer technology.

Many users are surprised when, after connecting their printer to the parallel interface, it outputs gobbledygook on paper.

All printers are at least capable of working with **ASCII,** which we have already discussed. This means they have a **generic printer driver**, which works with all printers.

TIP

Consider that only simple ASCII text can be printed in generic printout mode. Graphics and special character are not sent to paper correctly!

So, before you go back to your computer shop to complain that your printer is not working properly, you should set up the generic printer driver on Windows 95 or 98 and then try to output a simple text document.

The following step-by-step guide shows you how to set up a generic printer in Windows 98 and print a test page. All other operating systems also offer a generic driver whose installation, however, differs between systems.

1 Click on the My Computer icon. You will find an icon named Printers.

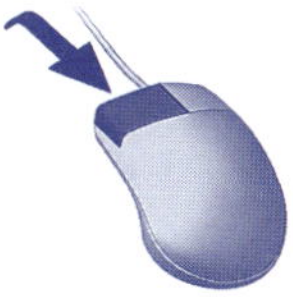

2 Double-click on the PRINTERS icon. If printers were already set up in your system, you will find further icons, one for each printer. Choose *Add Printer* with a double click on the icon.

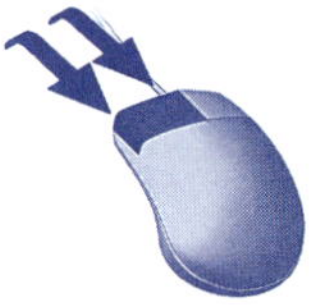

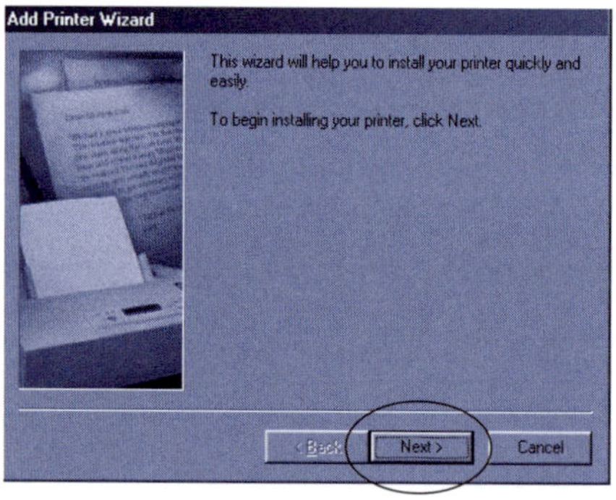

3 A Printer Wizard will help you with the installation of your printer. Click on NEXT.

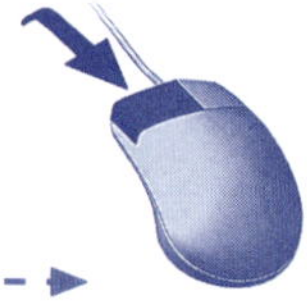

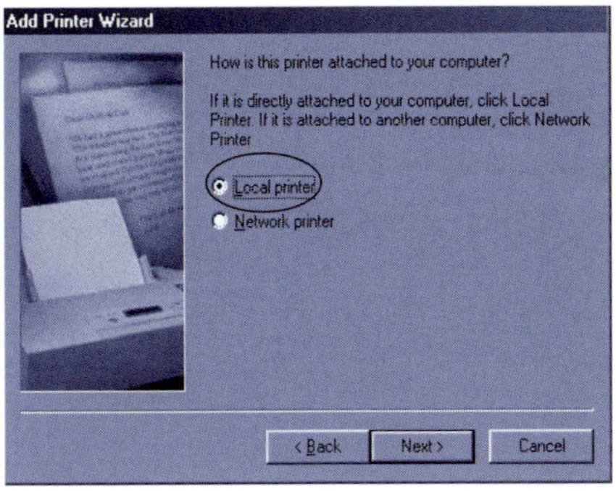

4 In the next window, select the *Local printer* radio button.

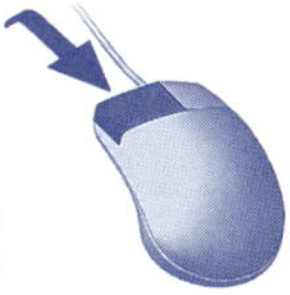

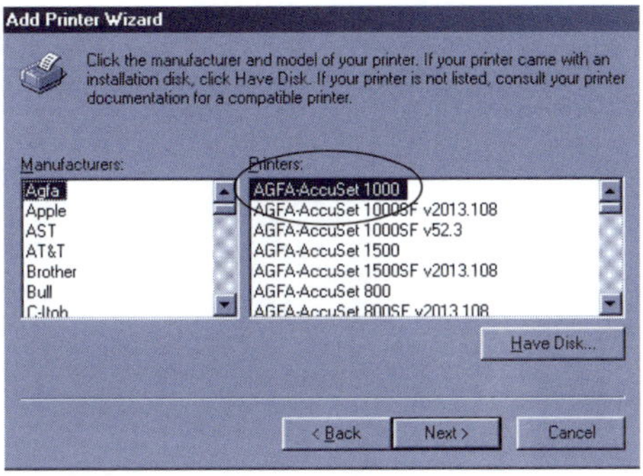

5 You will choose the printer type in the next window. First, select the manufacturer of the printer you wish to install. In the right side of the window, Windows 98 lists all the printers from each manufacturer for you to choose.

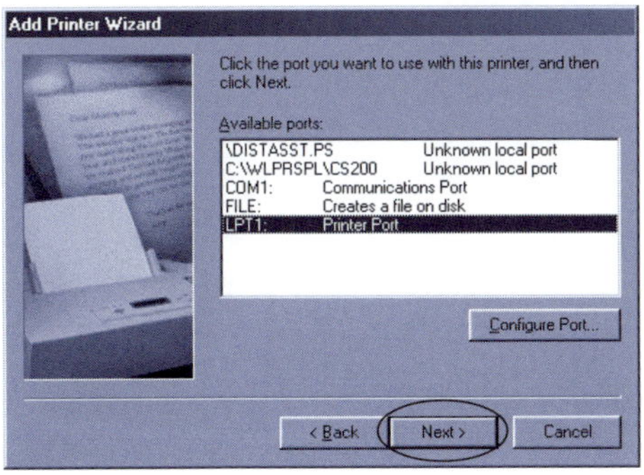

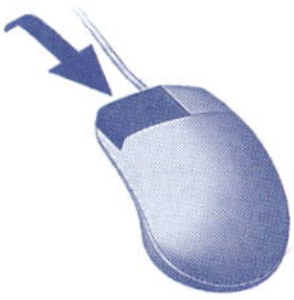

6 Click on NEXT, choose LPT1 as printer output and confirm with NEXT.

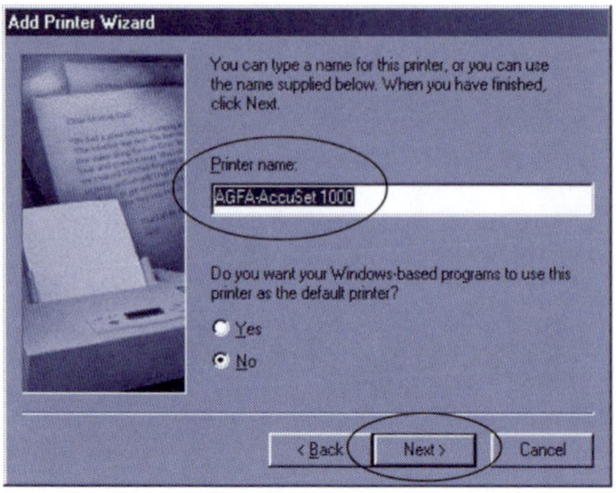

7 Use the name of your new printer and confirm by clicking on NEXT.

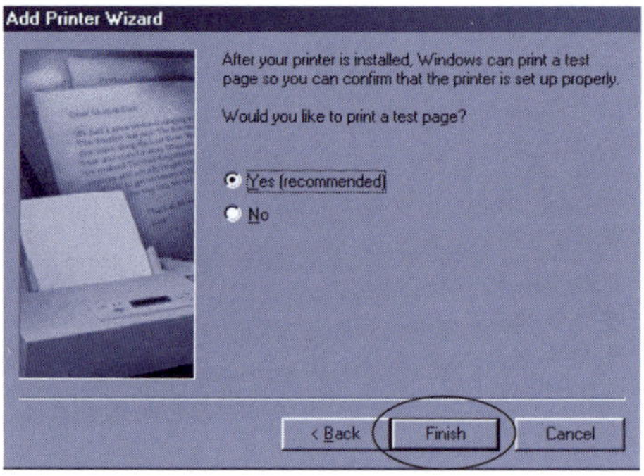

8 At the end of this process, Windows 98 asks you whether you wish to print a test page. If your printer is not switched on, turn it on and insert paper. When you click on FINISH, Windows will print a single-sided text document. If the text is readable, you have connected the printer to your PC correctly.

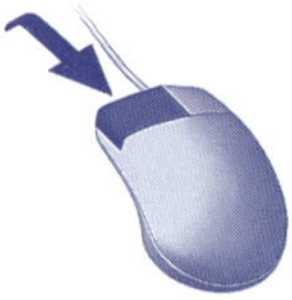

What happens if your printer prints gobbledygook? If you wish to print graphics and different characters which are not defined by the ASCII code, your printer must be equipped with a "printer standard language".

WHAT'S THIS?

Printer language or printer standard language enables a printer to print data based on the ASCII code using the printer's utilities. Printer language is also described as Emulation.

Printer manufacturers use their own **printer language**, to "communicate" with their printer models. A printer driver is installed in the operating system to access the application programs and to output printouts.

These underlying standards were programmed by well known manufacturers and are recognised by all printers by special programming. For this reason, you will find that Windows 98 has a printer list of probably a thousand models, even though the basic driver is only marginally different.

The following list will provide some explanations for a better understanding of printer language:

The Epson code

The printer manufacturer **Epson** developed a printer language for dot-matrix printers and called this ESCP, Epson Standard Code for Printers. Most dot-matrix printers and some ink-jet and laser printers still use this code.

The desk-jet driver

One of the forerunners in this field was the leading printer manufacturer Hewlett-Packard which produced ink-jet and laser printers. Their standards influenced printer markets for a long period of time. They established the general code for ink-jet printers. At present, most of the competition still adopts the HP Desk-jet standard.

The laser driver

Hewlett-Packard has also established a standard for laser printers. Behind the name HP Laserjet hides a universal laser printer language which is understood by many laser printers.

PostScript

Adobe has now created a professional standard by devising a printer language called PostScript, and integrating this language into high-quality high-end printers.

Postscript means "after printout". The principle is very advanced when compared to other techniques, but it requires expensive hardware. The printer is provided with a certain level of "intelligence" and can carry out complex processing work while printing. In this way, printing is faster and the computer is available for other tasks at the same time.

Installing a printer driver

If you want your printer to work at its optimum level, you will need to install a printer driver. When you purchased your printer, you will have received a set of floppy disks or a CD-ROM to go with your printer; these contain the apropriate printer driver.

You can also use standard printer drivers provided by your operating system.

CAUTION

If possible, you should use the floppy disk or CD-ROM provided by the manufacturer. The drivers contained here are always more up-to-date than the drivers of the operating system and often offer functions which standard drivers do not have.

Installing any printer driver uses the same procedure as the one described before. This can be applied to the installation of a completely new printer driver. The following step-by-step guide will again take you through the installation of a specific new printer driver.

If you work with Windows 95 or 98, you can follow the installation as it is described, but the procedure also applies if you have already installed your printer or you have already configured the printing area. Use the CD-ROM for Windows Installation or the floppy disk set provided by the manufacturer.

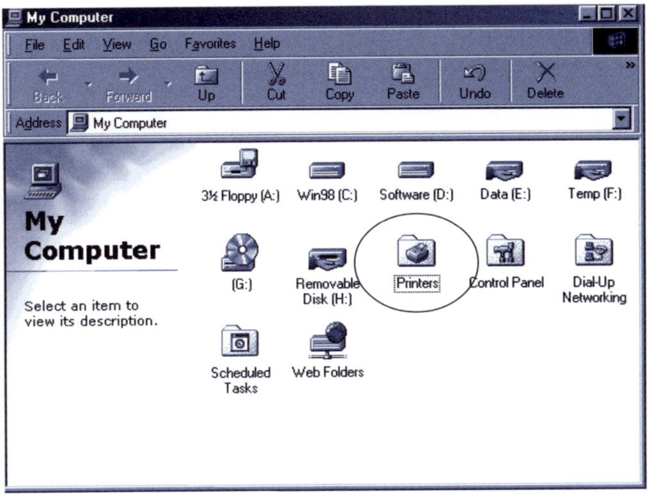

1 Double-click on MY COMPUTER icon and then select PRINTERS.

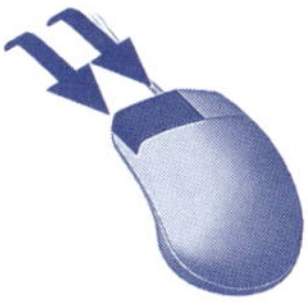

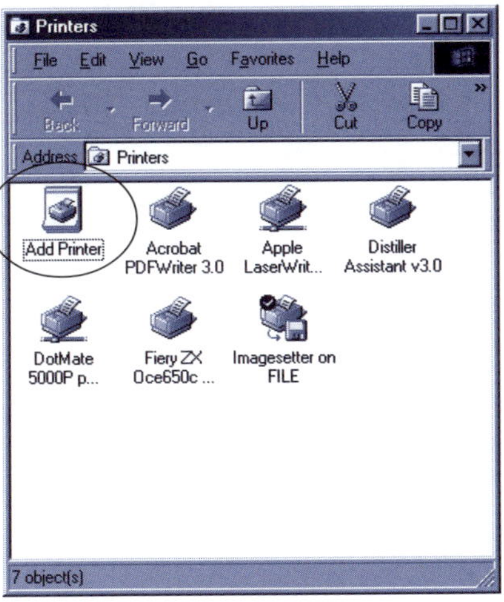

2 Click on *Add Printer* to install a new printer. The generic printer already installed is also shown in this window.

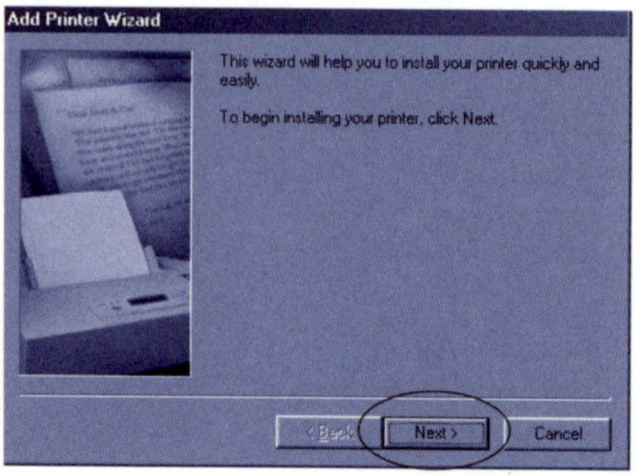

3 Confirm the welcome message of the Printer Wizard with a click on NEXT.

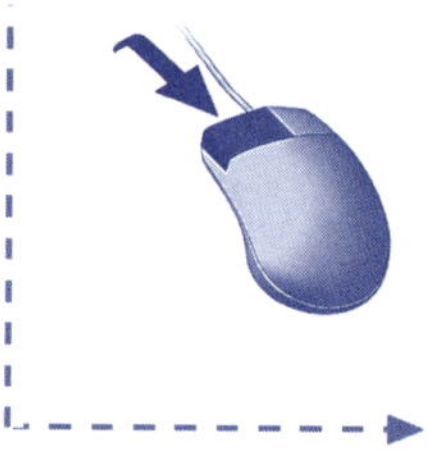

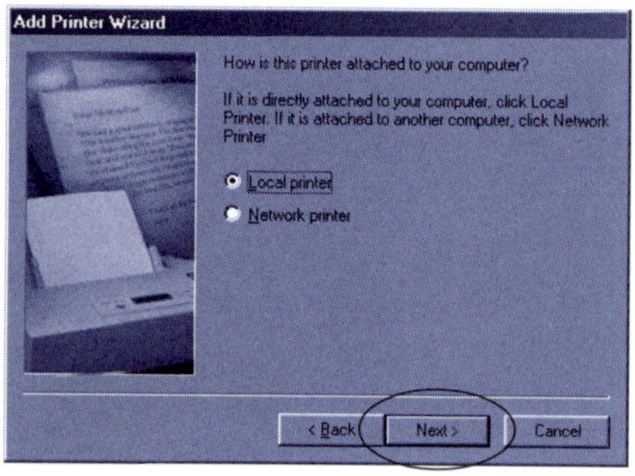

4 Select *Local printers* and confirm the following window with NEXT.

5 If you want to use the set of floppies or the CD-ROM provided by the printer manufacturer, go straight to step 7.

If you do not have a set of floppies or a CD-ROM, in the Manufacturers list on the left (which is in alphabetical order), choose the name of the manufacturer of your printer, for example "Apple".

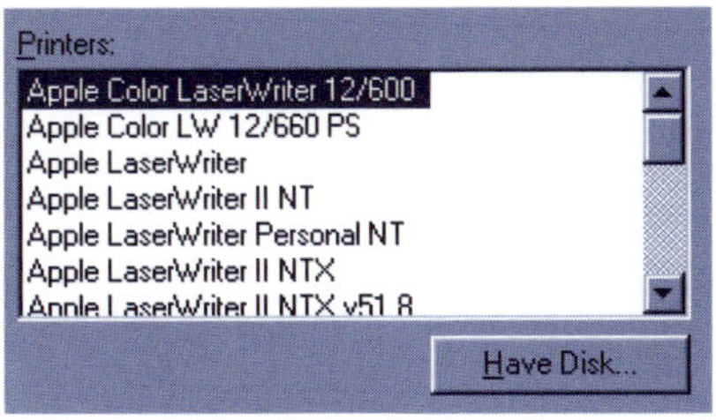

6 Select the printer model in the right side of the window, for example "Apple Color LaserWriter". If your printer is not listed here, you will find additional support at the end of this step-by-step guide.

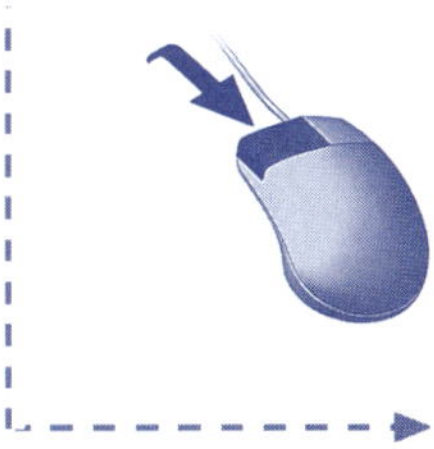

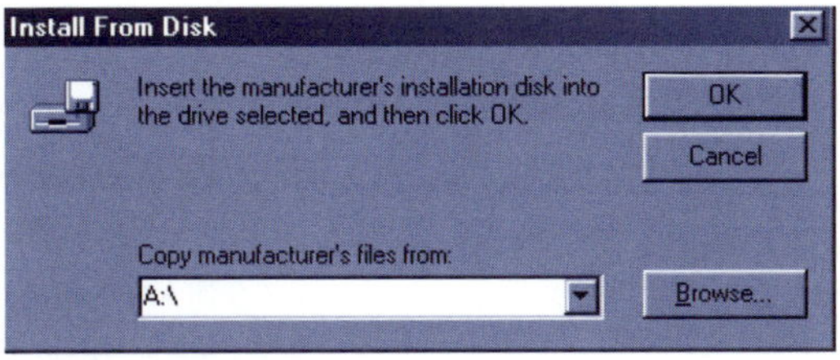

7 When the Install from Disk dialog box appears, insert the first installation disk. Click on OK. All drivers saved on the floppy disk are listed now. Click on the driver of your model and then choose NEXT.

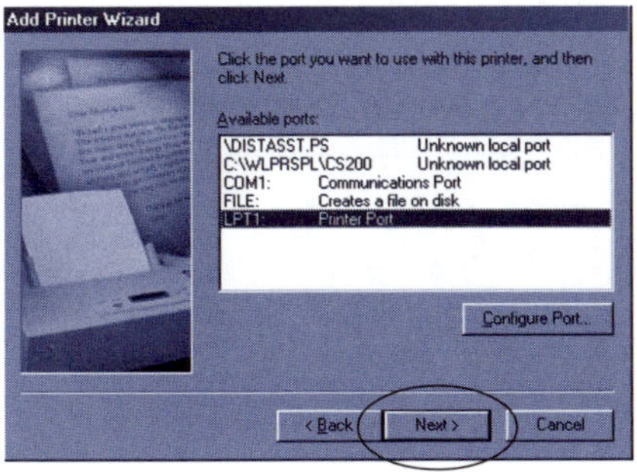

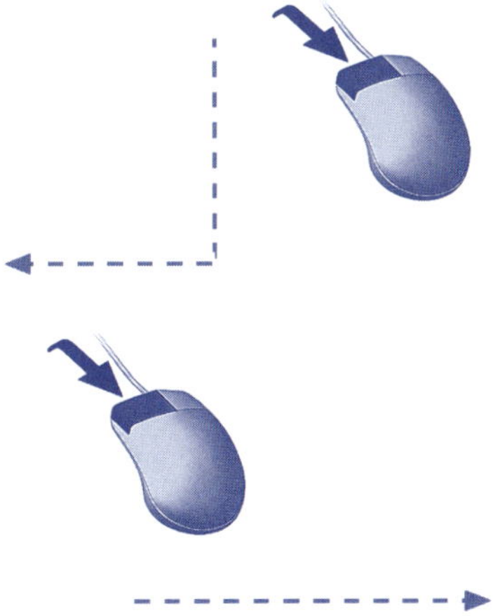

8 Select LPT1 as your printer port and click on NEXT.

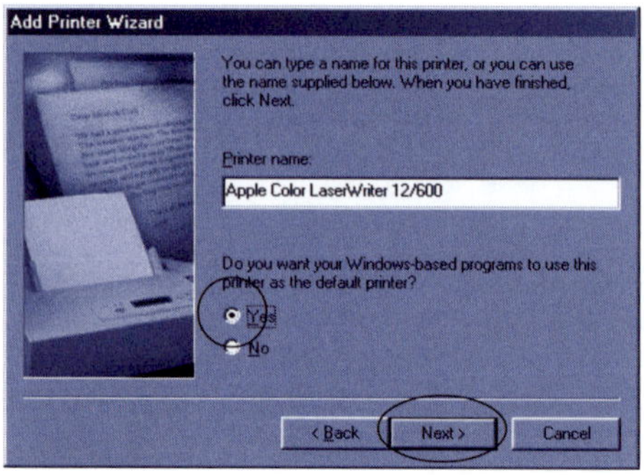

9 You can either type the name of your printer or keep the default name in the appropriate field. Select the *Yes* radio button, so Windows will use the new printer as the default printer. Confirm the window with NEXT.

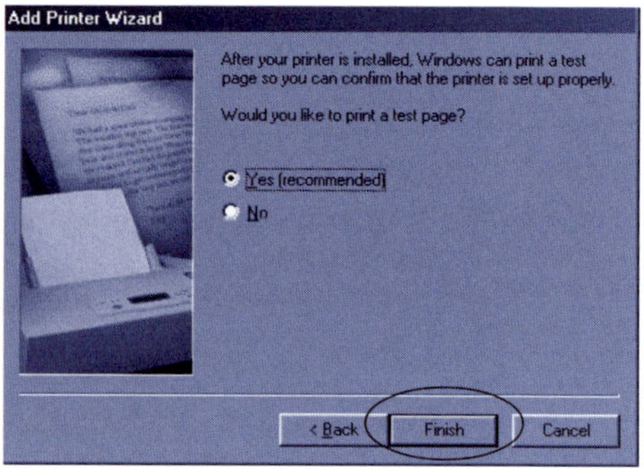

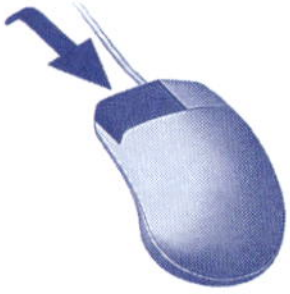

10 This windows asks you whether you wish to print a test page. If this the case, tick the *Yes (recommended)* radio button, switch on your printer and insert paper. Click on FINISH. Your printer should start printing a test page after a few seconds.

What do I do if the driver is not compatible?

If you buy a second-hand printer, you may find that the installation disks are no longer available or they may be set up for a different operating system.

Moreover, because modern operating systems such as Windows 98 no longer list old printers, you will not be able to use any default driver.

In this case, you could try to use the following **compatible drivers**; in this way, you will be able to use all the main functions of your printer. If your printer is not matched in the following list, try all of the listed printer drivers. Do not be afraid, nothing bad will happen!

Your printer is ...	Try the driver ...
Dot-matrix printer	Epson FX-80
Ink-jet printer	HP Deskjet
Laser printer	HP Laserjet

Printing documents

After printing a first test page, which is what we did in the previous exercise, you should now be sure that your printer has been correctly installed and is working properly.

You can now create, format and print your first test text. Start the program in which you wish to create your document, or open an existing document, and print it.

If you need some help, you will find it in the following step-by-step guide. Create a short text in Windows WordPad and, when you are happy with it, send it to print.

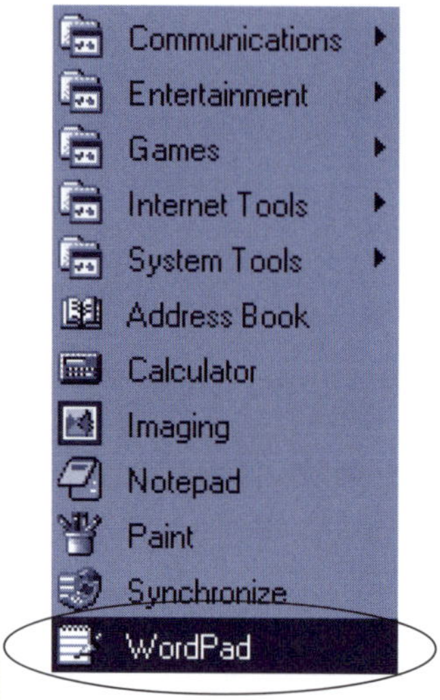

1 Click on the START menu button and then choose PROGRAMS/ACCESSORIES/WORD PAD.

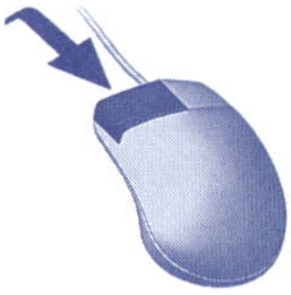

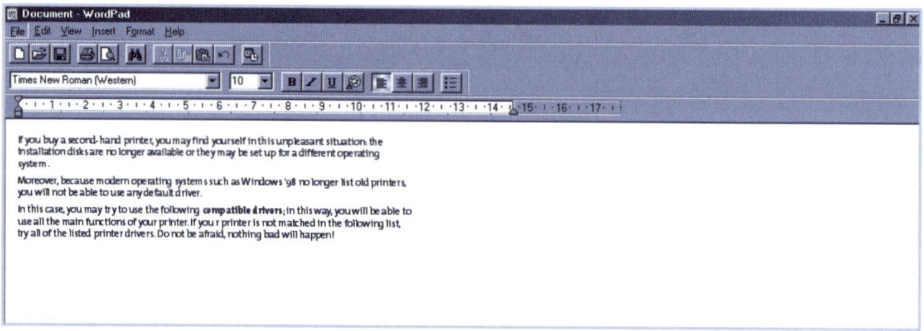

2 Enter several lines of text. For example, you can type a few sentences taken from this book.

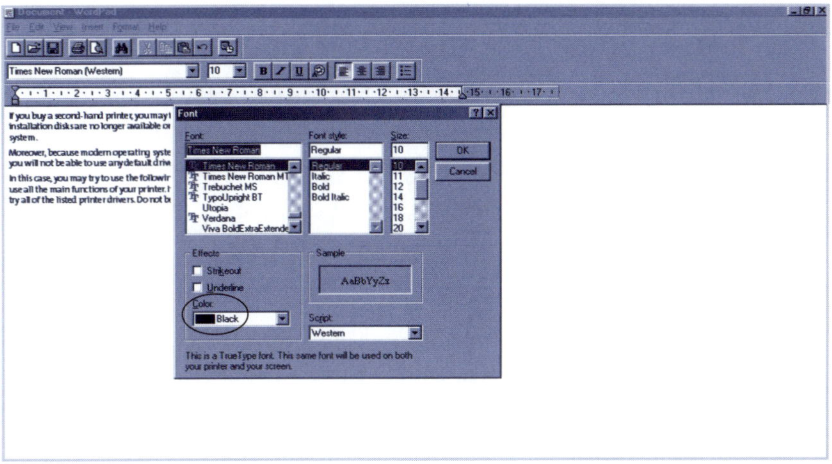

3 If you are using a colour printer, select the text you wish to print and click on FORMAT/FONT. Go into the *Color* field. The highlighted text changes to the selected colour, if a colour other than black is chosen.

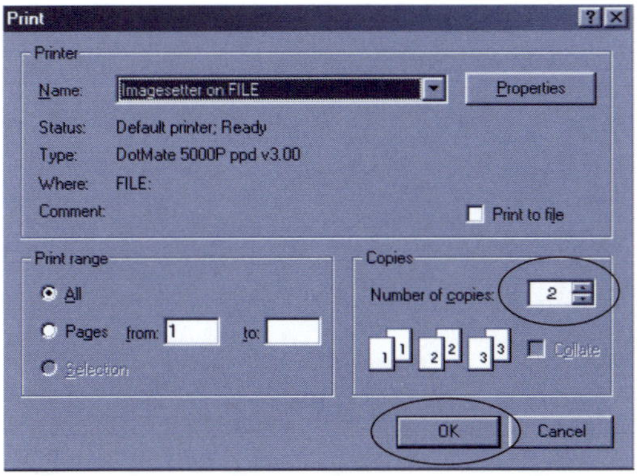

4 Click on FILE/PRINT. The default printer you have installed is displayed in the *Printer* field. Increase the number of copies to be printed to 2 and click on OK. The printout now starts; as a result, you should get two printouts of the same text.

Managing your print process

All current operating systems offer the **batch printing** option. You can send several documents from various applications to the printer at the same time. The printer works through the Batch command.

A printer buffer, called the "spooler", accepts all print jobs, even when your printer is busy, when it stores them and releases them to the printer one after the other, in a queue.

WHAT'S THIS?

By using the **Batch Printing** function, different applications can send print jobs at the same time. Print jobs are received by the **spooler** and passed on to the printer in a queue.

You can always check the current spooler and printer status. In Windows, there is a utility called Print Manager, which manages and coordinates all printer resources within the system.

The following step-by-step guide will show you how to view and modify a print job which you have already sent, in Windows 98.

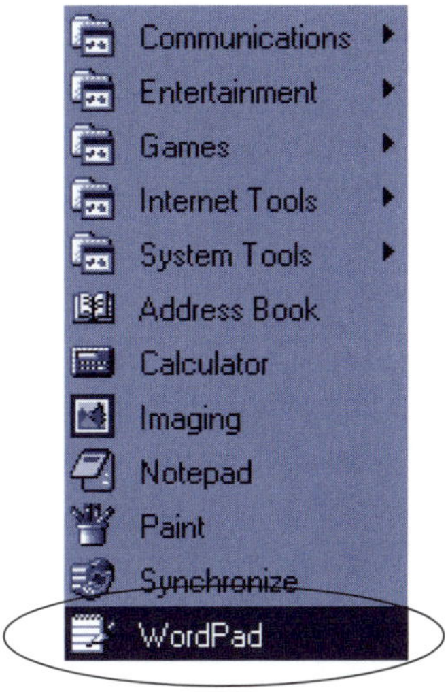

1 Open Wordpad by clicking on START/PROGRAMS/ACCESSORIES/WORDPAD.

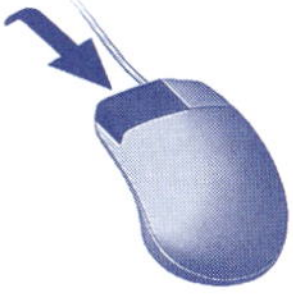

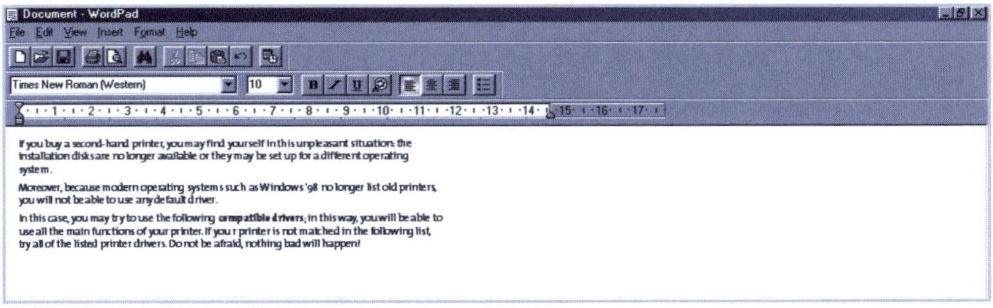

2 Enter a few lines of text, for example, a few lines from this book or use the text from the previous exercise.

3 Turn your printer off and choose FILE/PRINT. Confirm the print job with a click on OK. Windows 98 displays an error message, informing you that it is not possible to print the document.

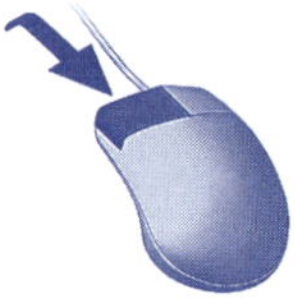

4 Click on MY COMPUTER, then on *Printers* and then double-click on the icon of your printer.

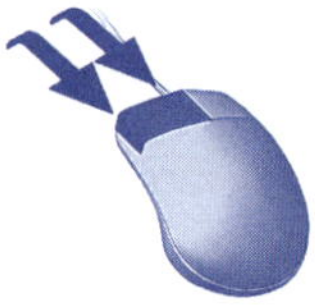

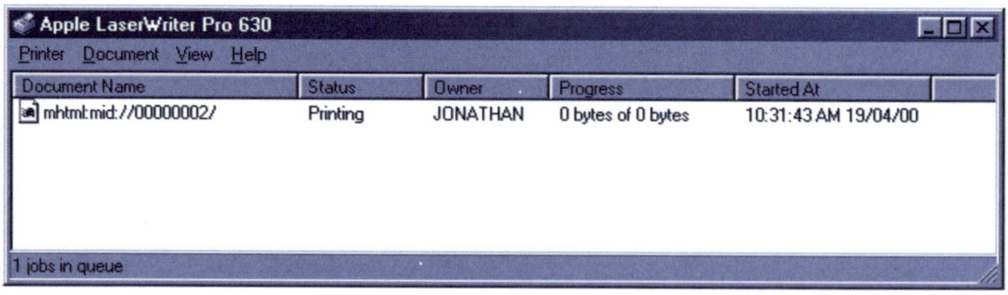

5 The window that opens represents the spooler. This window will display the position of your document in the queue as well as information concerning the current print job.

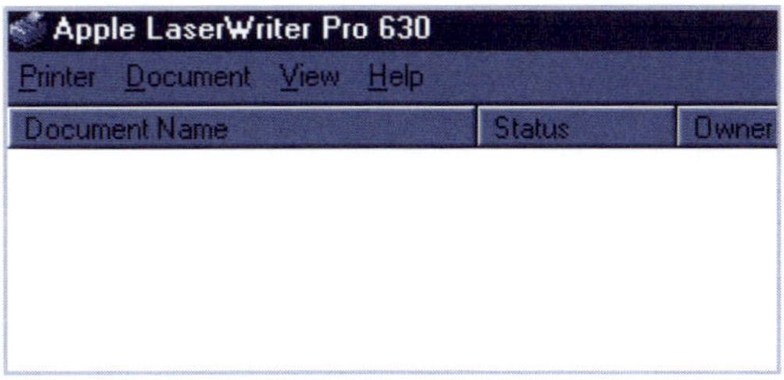

6 Click on Document in the window menu. You can delete the current print job by pressing the Del key.

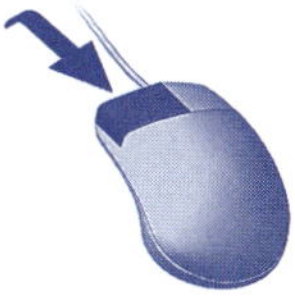

8 As fast as television

What's in this chapter:

This chapter explains the difference between a computer monitor and a television screen.
You will then learn about the function of a graphics card, the definition of "resolution", and how large your monitor should be.
We are also going to discuss the requirements a graphics system needs in order to function properly.
Finally, we will introduce you to some of the current graphics processors.

You already know about:

You are going to learn about:

From TV screen to computer monitor

You have already been working with your computer screen throughout the previous chapters, and are therefore familiar with its shape: this chapter will discuss the **monitor**, the most complex interlinked graphics system.

The monitor can be considered as a very close relation of the television screen, if the tasks performed by the two items were not so different. While the TV viewer is expected to sit at a distance of a couple of metres from the television screen, the computer monitor is used as a close-up visual display unit, where users enter and check data.

PCs could certainly work without a monitor, if there is no direct user; but this is not the case if a direct user is involved, because he would not be able to interact with the computer without a monitor. Monitors are unnecessary if no human action is required: network servers, for example, are usually installed without a monitor for cost reasons, and the monitor is then only temporarily connected for routine maintenance purposes or for checking breakdowns.

Although monitors and television screens have a different function, as we have just seen, their technical relationship is obvious. It could be said that computer monitors developed and evolved in line with video technology, but with a number of modifications aimed at the specific requirements of the computer market.

The graphics card

How do computer data reach your monitor? A graphics card, which is on the motherboard, translates the image you have produced so that the user can view it and manipulate it; it is therefore the interface between processor and monitor.

WHAT'S THIS?

A **graphics card** is the unit which produces images. It is the immediate interface between computer and monitor.

Early graphics cards were not graphics cards at all: text could be represented only in one colour. Later graphics cards introduced the concept of pixel management for monitors to be able to handle graphics.

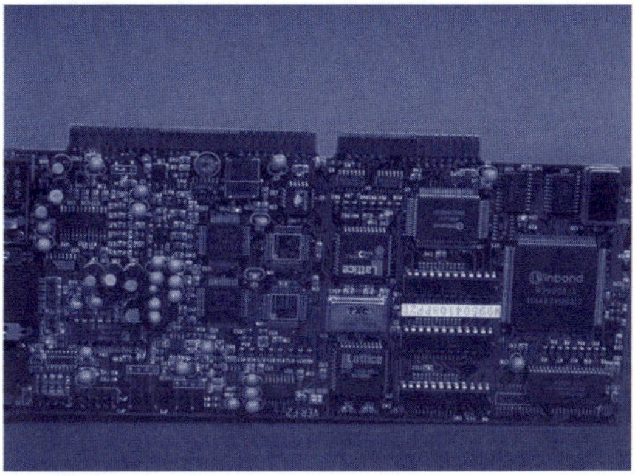

Does this development reminds you of what happened with printers? For example, the fact that early daisy-wheel printers could only handle text, while later models, such as dot-matrix printers, were able to print graphics.

WHAT'S THIS?

VGA is the abbreviation for Video Graphics Array. It is the sole graphics standard currently used.

Current graphics cards follow a common standard, called **VGA**. Most current manuals and publicity material no longer refer to VGA, simply because all PC-based graphics cards follow the same standard and everybody in the industry is aware of this.

Resolution

WHAT'S THAT?

The **resolution** indicates the maximum number of representable pixels, both horizontal and vertical.

Graphics card and monitor resolution is indicated in pixels, translated into dots for printing purposes.

The more pixels can be represented, the more detailed the image is. Unlike printers, monitor resolution is not indicated in dpi, but in horizontal and vertical pixels.

For example, a resolution of 800 x 600 means that the monitor can represent 800 pixels on the horizontal orientation and 600 dots on the vertical orientation.

Because a larger screen area can handle a larger number of pixels, larger monitors always have a higher resolution than smaller ones.

You can check the resolution of your monitor in the Control Panel of the operating system. The following step-by-step guide shows you how to set up the resolution of your monitor in Windows 98.

1 Click on the START menu button and choose *Settings*. Choose CONTROL PANEL and double click on DISPLAY.

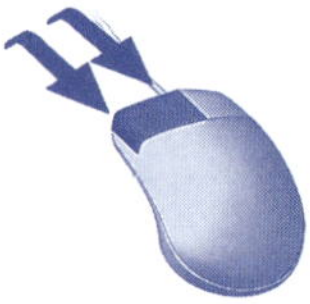

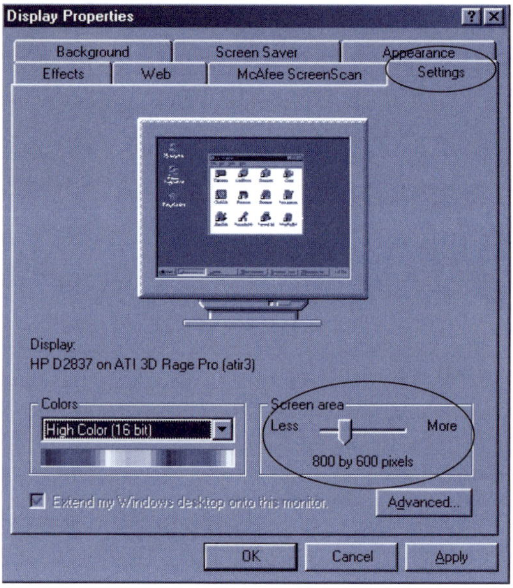

2 The *Display Properties* dialog box opens. Click on the SETTINGS tab in the top right-hand corner.

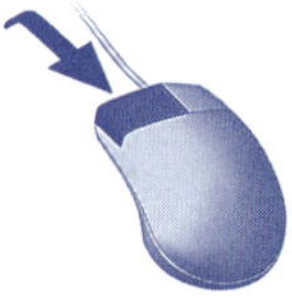

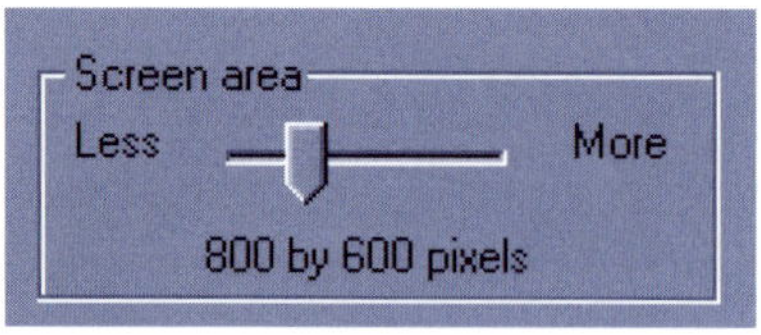

3 The *Screen area* field displays the current screen resolution, expressed in horizontal x vertical pixels.

Screen size

"Screen size" describes the size of the tube in a monitor and is measured in inches diagonally across the screen. Therefore this measure is very important, because the screen diagonal is not necessarily the same as the visible screen. You will be familiar with the the way the picture is shown on a television screen; the picture is enclosed within a black frame.

While earlier VGA monitors had screen diagonals of 14" or 15", today there are 17" and 20" or even 21" monitors. Even 19" monitors are reasonably common; some manufacturers have become reluctant to produce larger monitors because of the increased costs involved.

The monitor size you choose depends primarily on your needs, requirements and the size of your budget. But you also need to consider the type of applications you will be running. A 14" or 15" monitor is not recommended for long hours of work with a word processing package, for health reasons and ergonomic considerations. If you are working with a graphically oriented operating system such as Windows, and graphic user interfaces such as KDE on Linux, you would be well advised to buy at least a 17" monitor, so that the graphics, icons and documents do not appear too jagged.

For work where detail is important, you should use a 20" or 21" monitor. In computer-aided design (CAD), for example, it is important that the screen should be able to display a whole A4 page, something that smaller screens are unable to do.

Generally speaking, a larger monitor also allows a higher resolution, because the size of the cathode ray tube is larger. The following table details standard resolutions for various screen sizes.

Screen diagonal	Recommended resolution (pixels)
14" up to 15"	640 x 480 up to 800 x 600
17" up to 20"	800 x 600 up to 1024 x 768
20" and 21"	1024 x 768 up to 1600 x 1200

Screen refresh rates

If you watch television from a distance of about 30 cm, you will notice that the picture is constanly flickering. This is because the screen replaces the visible picture approximately 30 to 40 times every second; so we can say that a TV screen has a refresh rate of 30 to 40 Hertz.

If you were to work on a computer with this quality over a long period of time, the least you can expect is a headache.

WHAT'S THIS?

The **refresh rate** (in Hertz) measures the frequency of the complete picture in a second.

Obviously, the **ergonomic** standards regulating the **quality** of a computer monitor are stricter. This explains the high price of a monitor and answers the question asked by many beginners: "Why can't I use my television screen to work with my computer?"

While a TV screen works with a refresh rate of 30 to 40 Hz, high-end equipment such as computer monitors build the displayed picture with up to 200 Hertz, which means their refresh rate is up to five times higher.

When pictures **refresh frequency** is below 60 Hz, the human eye will perceive a flickering image; therefore, working with a 50 Hz system over a long period of time causes tiredness and eye irritation. These effects start to decrease from a frequency of 70 Hz. This is why current computer monitors work at a frequency of 80 and 100 Hz; this allows users to work for a longer period of time without experiencing any negative symptoms.

The table below shows refresh rates and their effects.

Refresh rates	**Working conditions**
Below 60 Hz	Clearly perceptible flicker
From 60 to 70 Hz	Perceptible flicker
From 70 to 80 Hz	Barely perceptible flicker
Above 80 Hz	Satisfactory ergonomic working range

Most operating systems allow you to find out the refresh rate of your monitor. The following step-by-step guide will show you how to identify and modify the refresh rate of your monitor in Windows 98.

1 Click on the START menu button and choose SETTINGS and CONTROL PANEL. Double-click on the DISPLAY icon.

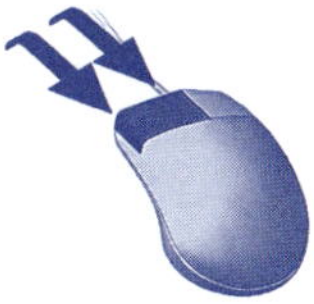

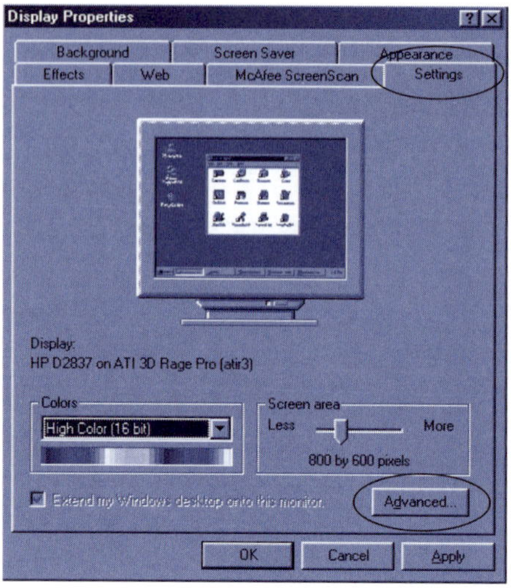

2 A window named *Display Properties* opens. Choose the SETTINGS tab and click on the ADVANCED... button.

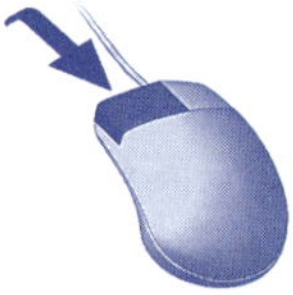

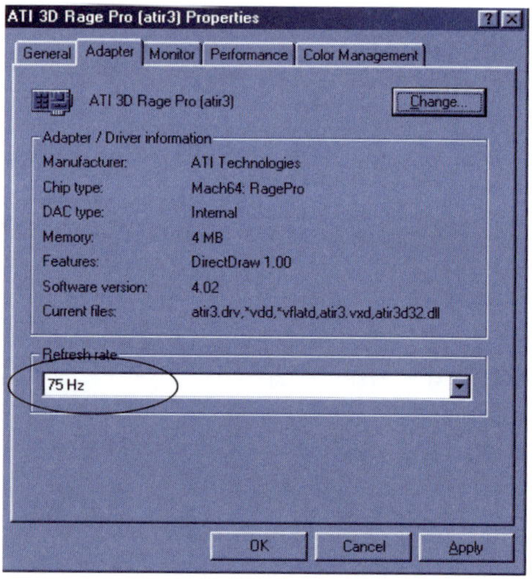

3 Click on the ADAPTER tab. The current Hertz frequency reported in the *Refresh Rate* field tells you the refresh rate frequency.

4 Click on the arrow button on the right-hand side of the Hertz number. You will notice that the drop-down box contains additional refresh rates which your monitor is capable of representing. It should select 80 or more for ergonomically sound working conditions. The settings available to you depend on your adapter.

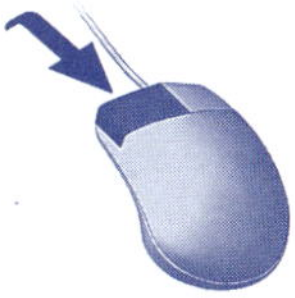

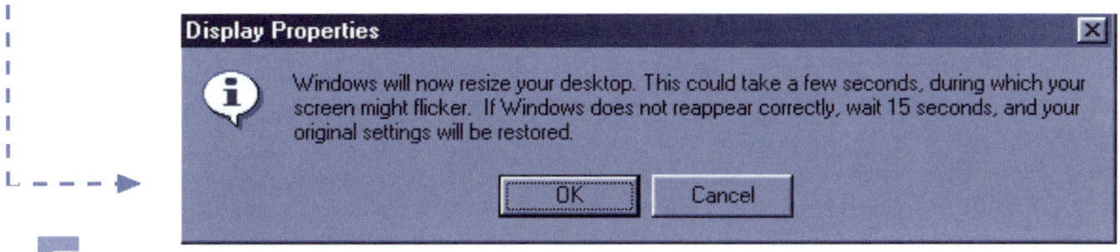

5 After modifying the refresh rate, click on the APPLY button. This menu looks different depending on your adapter. Windows 98 generates a testcard which is clear and should not flicker.

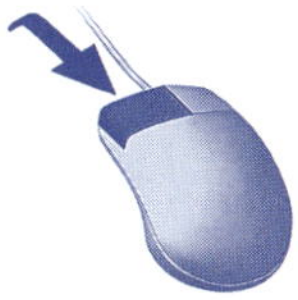

Driver software

Early VGA standards allowed a refresh rate of only 60 Hz, therefore it was not possible to achieve satisfactory ergonomic conditions.

You will need a driver to be able to use the utilities offered by graphics card and monitors in current operating systems. If you work with Windows 95 or 98, their integrated automatic recognition will have already connected a suitable driver.

Such drivers work in exactly the same way as mouse and printer drivers, with which you are familiar: they constitute the interface between operating system and hardware, and this applies to graphics cards as well.

The following step-by-step guide shows you how to connect a graphics driver in Windows 98. If you encounter some differences, do not worry and do not get confused.

1 Click on the START menu button and choose SETTINGS. Choose CONTROL PANEL and double-click on the DISPLAY icon.

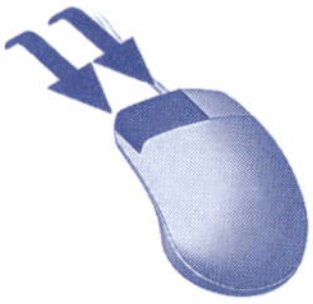

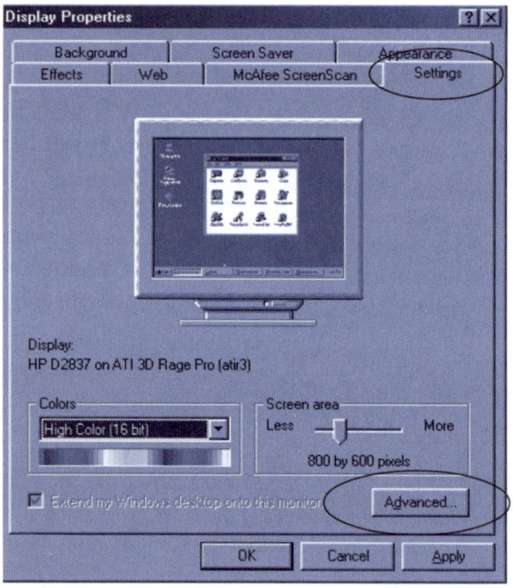

2 A window called *Display Properties* opens. Click on the SETTINGS tab and click on the ADVANCED... button.

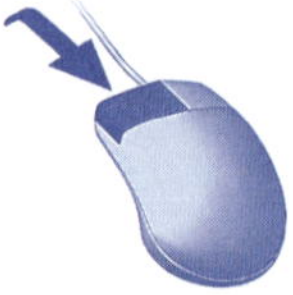

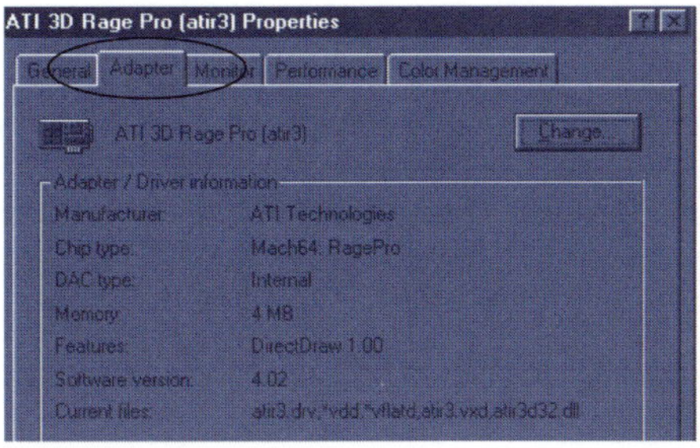

3 Activate the ADAPTER tab. This contains the list of currently used adapters and drivers.

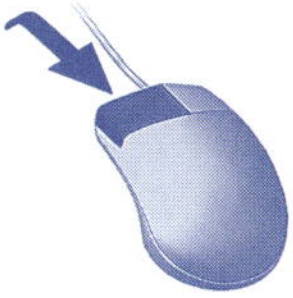

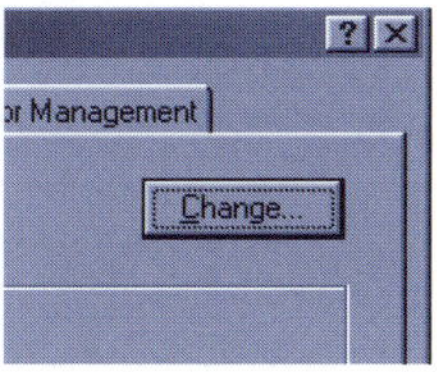

4 If you wish to connect a different driver, you must know the correct model name of your adapter. You will find these details in the adapter manual or on your PC system. Click on CHANGE.

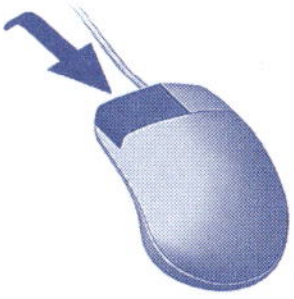

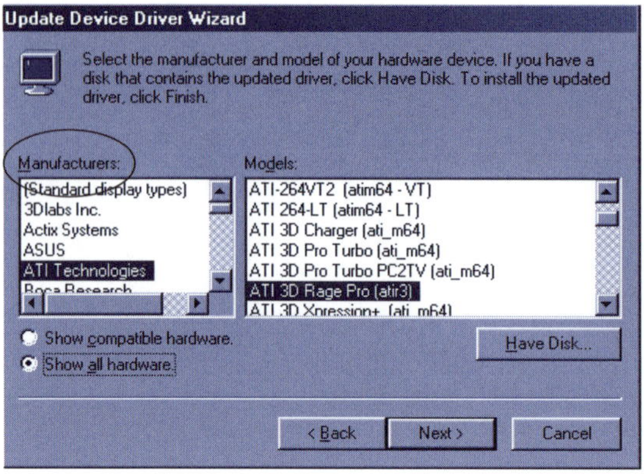

5 In the *Manufacturers* list, select the manufacturer of the adapter, for example ATI Technologies.

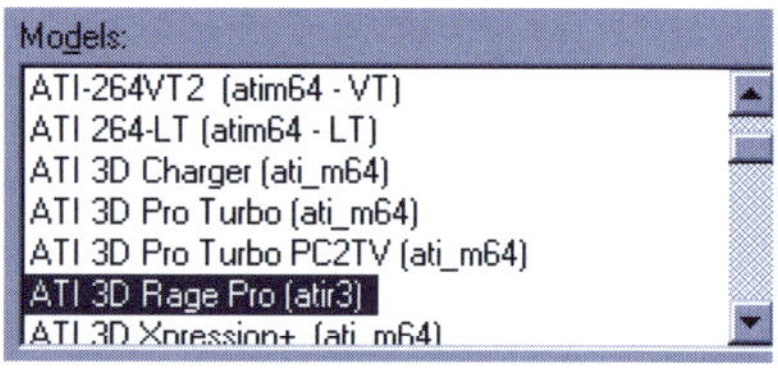

6 The models of the corresponding manufacturer are listed in the *Models* field. Click on the entry of your adapter and then choose OK.

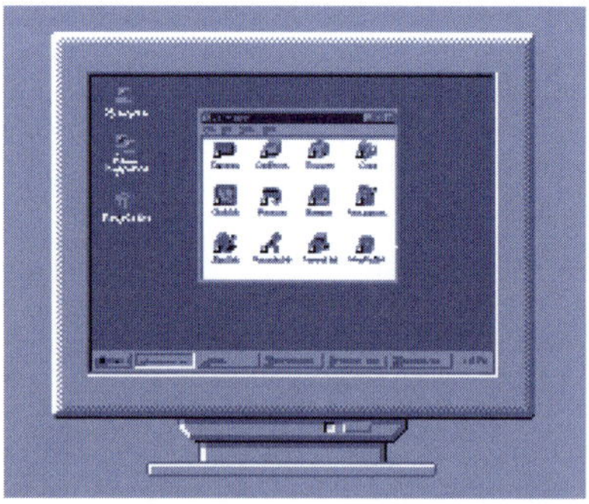

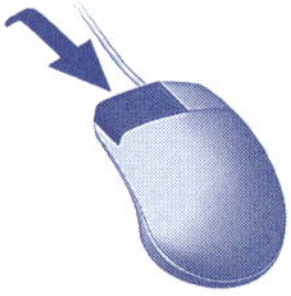

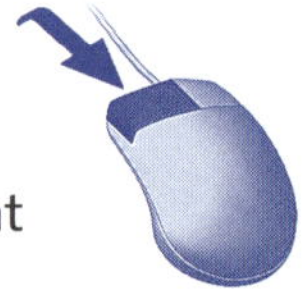

7 After copying some files, you should make sure that your driver functions as it should, by clicking on APPLY.

LCD monitors

The liquid crystal display monitors, or LCDs for short, are a new technology. The three main advantages that this technology offers over standard tube monitors are the fact that screens can be flat, easy to use, and they are energy-efficient. Notebook computers use LCD monitors by default.

Unfortunately, LCD monitors are still three to five times more expensive than a good comparable standard monitor, though prices are coming down fast.

Graphics processors

Today, many graphics cards are equipped with an internal **graphics processor** as a standard. This graphics processor is independent from the main processor and is used for representing graphics.

Because the graphics processor is highly specialised, but it can only execute commands specific to graphics processing, it works faster than the main processor.

Moreover, the graphics processor takes over from the main processor as well as from the Bus system: the main processor must specify the position and colour of every pixel of a graphical element in a system without an intelligent speed board, so the card works like a reception point for all graphics.

A typical example of a graphics processor is the 3DFX chip, which works with various graphics cards.

WHAT'S THIS?

Graphics processors are processors which perform their function on powerful graphics cards specialised in the representation of image information.

3D graphics cards

Current high-end games, such as *Tomb Raider*, which contain film and interactive scenarios, as well as many graphics programs, use 3D technology.

3D graphics cards work with specialised technology, for example Riva, Elsa, Diamond and so on, and represent tridimensional objects on a 2D monitor. The objects can rotate freely, so they can be viewed from all sides. This involves complex calculations, which are executed by 3D graphics cards. Modern PCs are usually equipped with 3D graphics cards as a standard.

Test your knowledge

Main theme: Printers and graphics systems

1. Which interface do you need to connect a printer to your PC? Explain the advantages and disadvantages of this.

2. Which units are used to measure printer resolution and graphics resolutions? Explain the meaning of the abbreviations.

3. List the advantages and disadvantages of a dot-matrix printer. Which printer can be used to print carbon copies or forms?

4. What is a refresh rate and how is it measured? Why should a graphics driver be installed at a rate higher than 60 Hz?

5. What is a graphics processor and which are the most common ones? The graphics processor takes over from two components of the motherboard: which are they?

6. You have printed a colour graphic, and you notice that the printout is different from the image colour represented on screen. Why is that?

7. Why is the image quality (and therefore the price) of a computer monitor higher than that of a TV screen? Which refresh rate is recommended for a good ergonomic performance?

8. What is a printer spooler and for what is it used?

9. What does VGA stand for?

10. Which sizes of VGA monitors are currently on the market? Why is a 17" or larger monitor recommended to work with graphics programs?

9

The Internet and going on-line

What's in this chapter:

This chapter introduces you to the new media, the Internet, and shows you what you need in order to access the Internet.
We will describe the difference between a modem and an ISDN line and between digital and analog communication. We will also explain what a protocol is and show you how protocols are used on the Internet.
You will also find a step-by-step guide, to accessing the Internet, and an explanation of the software you need.

You already know about:

You are going to learn about:

The seventh continent

Some time ago, computer experts realised that linking one computer to another would be an extremely useful improvement for computer functionality. How old is the personal computer? Let us take a "journey back into time", to the beginning of network technology.

On November 21st, 1969, Prof. Leonard Kleinrock sat at his computer in the Computer Science lab at the University of Los Angeles, and typed the sentence "Can you see this?". After a few seconds, he received the answer "yes" which was the birth of the age of **computer networks**.

Kleinrock had connected an early IBM with a computer 400 miles away, and had transmitted the text on a standard land line. Today, he is regarded as the "father of the Internet".

But what is the **Internet**? A popular quotation describes the Internet as "the seventh continent", almost like a virtual country. The American writer William Gibson has written, in his novel *Neuromancer*, of a continent where the citizens no longer exist bodily. He called this continent "Cyberspace".

The Internet is a worldwide computer link-up, where linked computers can communicate with each other. It consists of a variety of cables and a technically defined structure.

It is very important that the Internet should not belong to anyone, and should not be influenced politically or otherwise. Because the Internet is worldwide, you can send items of news and any file or document you want to any other computer connected to the Internet, anywhere in the world, for the price of just a local telephone call.

Because other computers can provide you with information, the Internet is also the largest information database in the world, with a speed, variety and immediate relevance no other medium can match.

Railway timetables, weather forecasts from the national meteorological office, on-line orders to various companies, banking, insurance, travel and customer services find the Internet the fastest and most direct media. On-line shopping and on-line banking are quickly becoming second nature. Moreover, customers can find the latest software or upgrades available as shareware. Communication with friends and business partners all over the world is easy and fast.

- What do you need to set up your computer for on-line communication?

A modem or an ISDN line and card, to process computer data via telephone. A modem is suitable for all analog telephone connections. You can use an ISDN card only with a digital ISDN connection.

- All current operating systems, such as Windows 95, 98, NT 4.0 or OS/2, include programs capable of enabling your computer to control data exchange between the local computer and the local server computer. For example, the upgrade to Windows 98 encloses a free version of Internet Explorer 5.
- A telephone connection to transfer data.

The modem: an analog bridge

There are two different technologies involved in sending data over the telephone network: the **digital** world of the computer and the **analog** world of the telephone, which has a much wider use. To establish a bridge between these two worlds, you need an appropriate connection: a modem.

A modem is the same as a transducer. The word modem is a combination of two words, modulator and demodulator. The modulator transforms the digital signals issued by the computer into analogous frequencies (tones), so that they can be transferred over the telephone network. The demodulator converts these sound sequences into bits, so they can be recognised by the computer.

A modem therefore creates an electrical connection to the telephone line.

WHAT'S THIS?

A **modem** is a transducer that connects the analog telephone network to your computer. The term is an abbreviation of the words "modulator" and "demodulator".

The term acoustic coupler, which a modem is, after all, clarifies the principle of data exchange over a telephone line. An acoustic coupler does not have any direct connection with the telephone network. It will therefore require a standard telephone socket. The coupler enters data translated into tones in to the speaker of the telephone mouthpiece and receives the distant terminal over an internal microphone. Acoustic couplers are no longer used.

WHAT'S THIS?

An **Internet service provider** gives users access to the Internet. Examples of ISPs are America Online, the Microsoft Network and CompuServe.

Mobile telephones are becoming more and more common today, and it is now possible to connect with on-line services from a mobile phone whenever one wants and almost from any place, using special hardware.

WHAT'S THIS?

bps is the abbreviation for Bits per Second, the speed of the modem transmission rate.

Choosing a modem is an important decision to make, because the modem is the communication interface between the user and the on-line service. A modem which cuts its connection to the internet every few seconds, because it uses an uncompatible product, will interfere with your communication needs. Traditionally, an external modem has ben perceived as being better, because the user can see that the connection is taking place, by checking the light indicator on the front of the modem box.

Today, modems with a data transfer rate of 28,800 bps (bits per second) are the absolute minimum requirement and cost less than £50. If you do not have a modem yet, and you need to buy one, then buy a 56,000 bps model.

Configuring your modem

Up to a few years ago, the user of a modem had to configure the modem by entering cryptic codes provided by the modem manual.

The complexity of installing and configuring such hardware drove even experienced Internet users mad. No wonder that users demanded, and got, more user-friendly alternatives.

With Windows 95, 98 and NT, the "Plug & Play" principle was brought into play, to satisfy the requirements of modem installation and configuration. You should not have any problems now in getting your modem to work.

The following step-by-step guide shows you how to set up a modem in Windows 98. The complete operation should only take a few minutes.

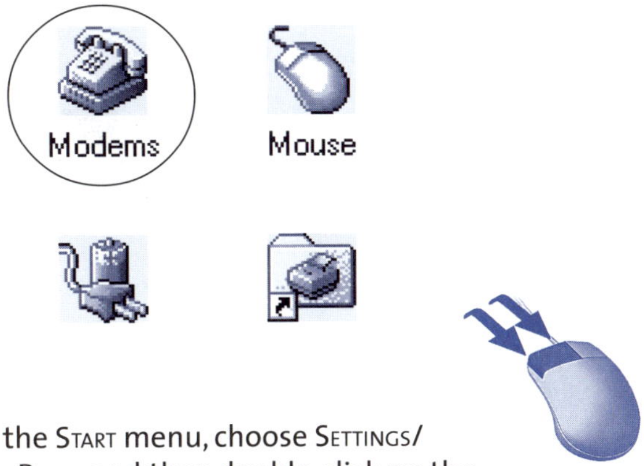

1 In the START menu, choose SETTINGS/ CONTROL PANEL and then double-click on the *Modems* icon.

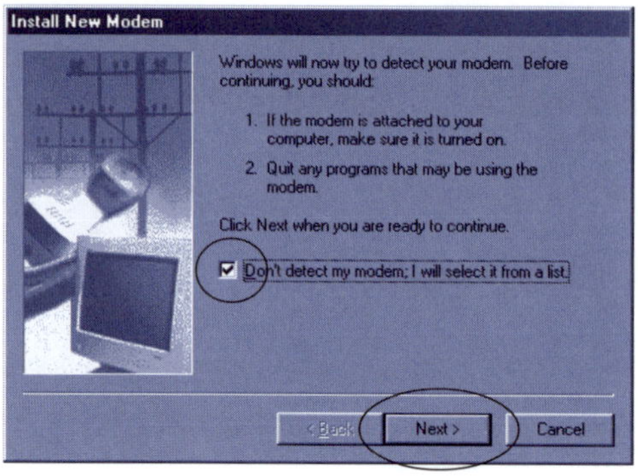

2 The Modem Installation Assistant welcomes you. Switch on your modem, if you have not yet done so. Tick the option *Don't detect my modem...* and then click on NEXT.

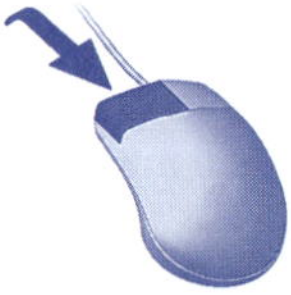

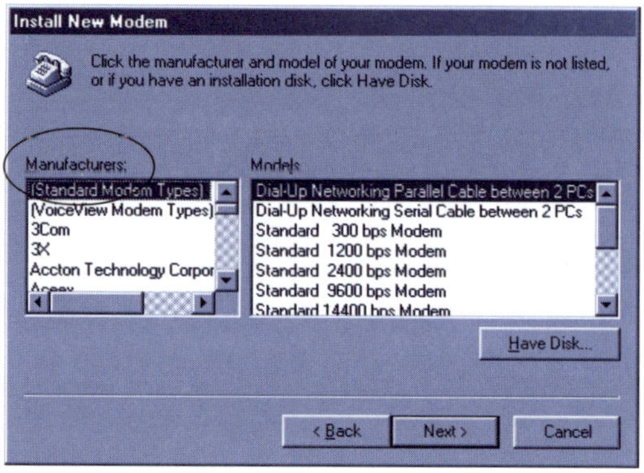

3 You must select the manufacturer and the model of the modem you wish to install. Click on the entry in the *Manufacturers list* corresponding to your modem. Then select the model on the right-hand side of this window. If your modem is not listed, go to step 4, otherwise go straight to step 5.

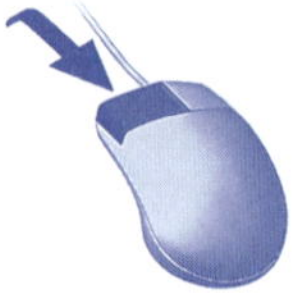

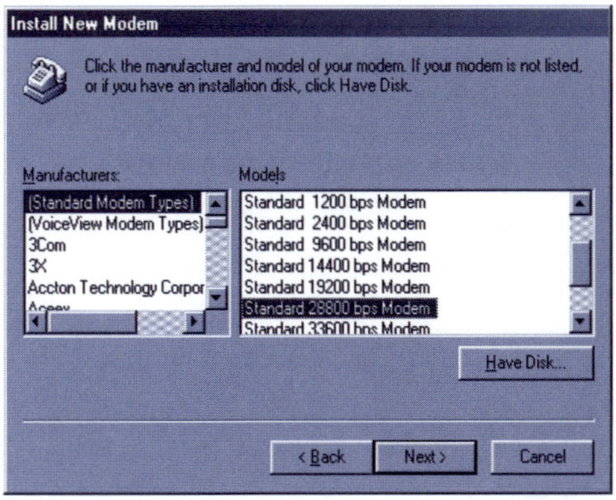

4 Several modem drivers are available, just as with printer drivers. If your modem is not listed under Manufacturers, select *Standard modem types* and, under *Models*, select the entry with the suitable transmission rate, for example *Standard 28800 bps Modem*. If you are not sure, select this category anyway.

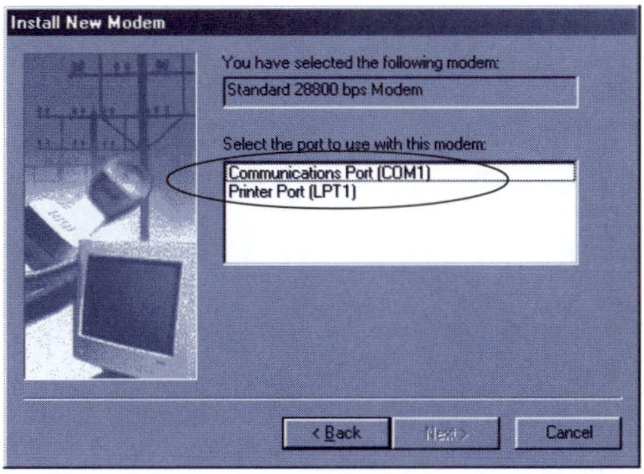

5 Select the port to which your modem will be connected. This is usually COM1.

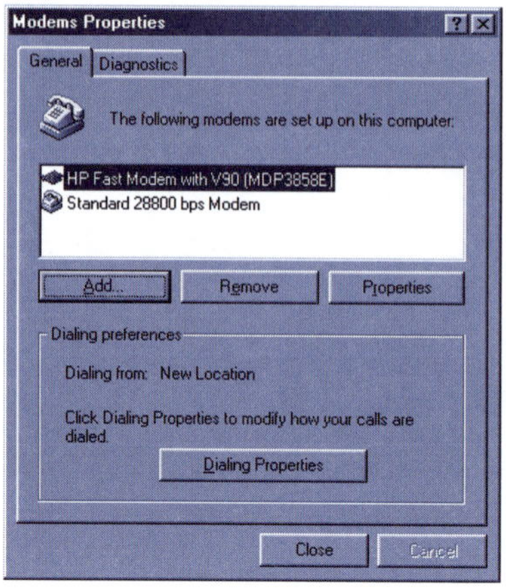

6 After installing your modem, this will be listed in the *Modem Properties* window.

ISDN technology

Data can be transmitted as modulated, but can also be transferred digitally using the ISDN **digital telephone** network. For this, you need an ISDN card instead of a modem.

WHAT'S THIS?

An **ISDN adapter** replaces the modem in digital data traffic. It works as the interface between the digital ISDN network and your PC.

The ISDN card is a direct interface between your computer and the telephone network. The ISDN card is just like a modem. All you need for this card to be able to function is a British Telecom ISDN connection.

ISDN transmission rate is 64,000 bps; therefore, an ISDN card reaches **twice** the speed of an average modem. With a large amount of data to be exchanged, an ISDN connection is therefore more economical than an analog connection, because the charging basis for all transmission is the time spent on-line, either via a modem or via ISDN. The ISDN reduces the time you spend on-line, therefore reduces your costs.

Since some software is not compatible with ISDN adapters, the ISDN adapter requires a modem simulator called CFOS, which makes your system believe that it is in fact working with a standard modem.

WHAT'S THIS?

A **CFOS driver** simulates the operating system, so that an ISDN adapter can be used as with normal modems.

Be careful that your ISDN adapter is authorised. You will know that it is recognised by BT if it carries the BT kitemark on its casing, with a serial number.

ADSL: the latest Internet technology

The latest on-line telecommunication technology is based on analog technology, like a modem. ADSL (short for Asymmetric Digital Subscriber Line), is catching on quickly worldwide in the analog communication field. British Telecom has planned some pilot projects, which will test ADSL in some large cities in the UK.

Because of the need to be able to transmit graphically advanced multimedia information faster, therefore requiring a larger frequency range, the ISDN frequency range works on a multiple channel package. Video conferencing is already possible, via ISDN, though only a small screen size can be transmitted at a low frequency.

Generally speaking, up to 8 Mbits can be sent on a twisted-pair copper telephone line; the frequency required is close to the one used for small local networks (about 10 Mbits). The 64 Kbits of the ISDN network frequency is ten times lower than the ADSL frequency.

Apart from these considerations, the ADSL system uses the latest data transfer technology to achieve the maximum possible data transfer rate. This technology involves special terminals for both sender and receiver. However, if the distance between sender and final user is short, the achievable transfer rate is considerably reduced.

Internet protocol

At the beginning of this chapter, we explained that the Internet is simply a collection of transmission cables. To be able to transmit data through this cable system, you will need to use a defined transfer structure. Therefore, a "Transfer Protocol" is the basis for systematic data exchange. This protocol provides both sender and receiver with details of the transmission and, in addition, checks the integrity of the transferred data.

WHAT'S THIS?

TCP/IP is an abbreviation for Transfer Control Protocol/ Internet Protocol. It is the transfer protocol of the Internet and forms the basis for a structured data exchange.

A structured data transmission is only possible if all participants work with the same protocol. The protocol used in the Internet is TCP/IP and is provided by every operating system, such as Windows 95, 98, NT 4.0, OS/2, and all UNIX systems.

It can be said that the TCP/IP protocol is resident on the telephone line, when you surf on the Internet. Before starting to surf, you must install TCP/IP. Windows 95, 98 and NT 4.0 provide a special Dial-up Networking function which connects automatically to a provider and must be set up before your first connection is possible.

The following step-by-step guide will show you how to set up Dial-Up Networking to connect to your ISP. The installation and configuration of the TCP/IP protocol varies according to different operating systems; always consult on-line help or the operating system manual.

Before starting the exercise, take the data sheet issued by your ISP. You will have been given this at registration. The data sheet includes all necessary technical data.

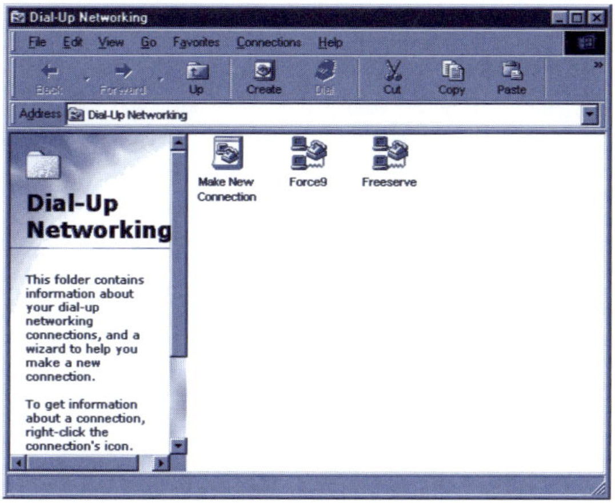

1 Double-click on My Computer and then choose *Dial-Up Networking.*

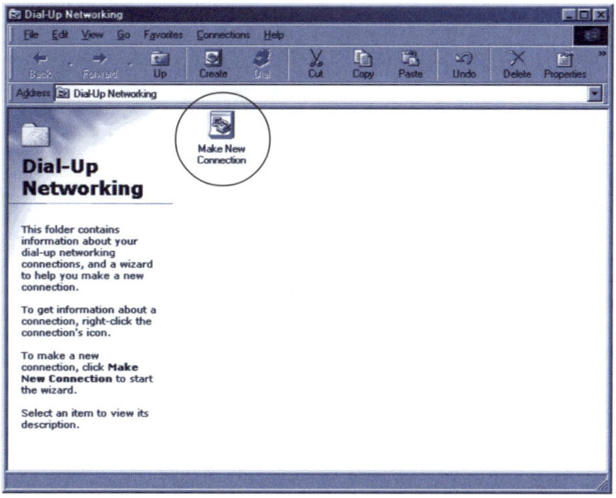

2 You will find a list of the connections which are already set up. To make a new connection, click on the *Make New Connection* icon.

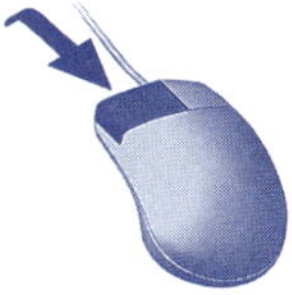

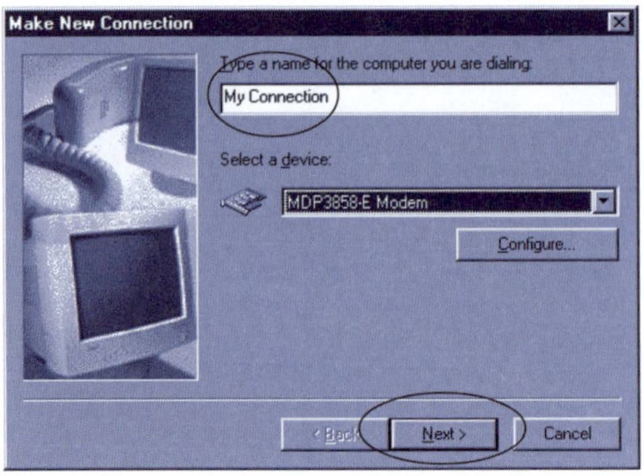

3 In this window, enter the connection name, for example "Force9", if you are connected with the provider "Force9". In the *Select a device* field, choose your modem or your ISDN card. Confirm your details with Next.

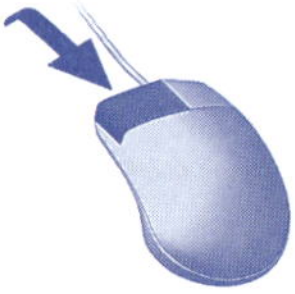

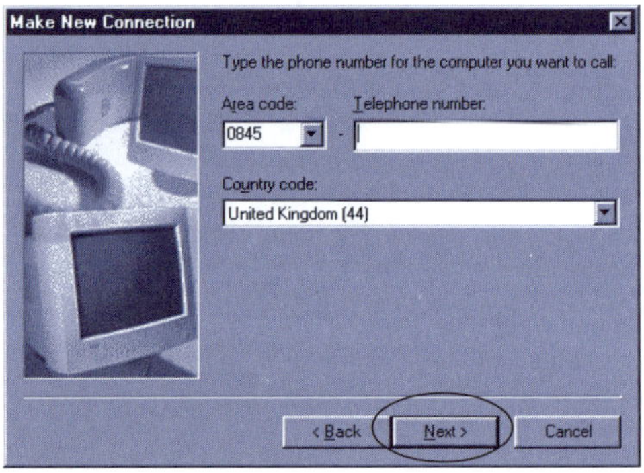

4 Enter the phone number with which you can connect to your ISP. You will find this number on the data sheet the ISP gave you at registration stage. Confirm with Next and then click on Finish in the following dialog box.

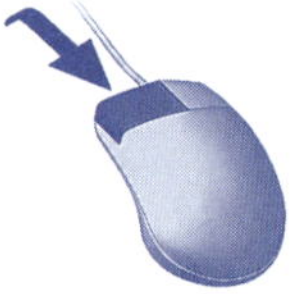

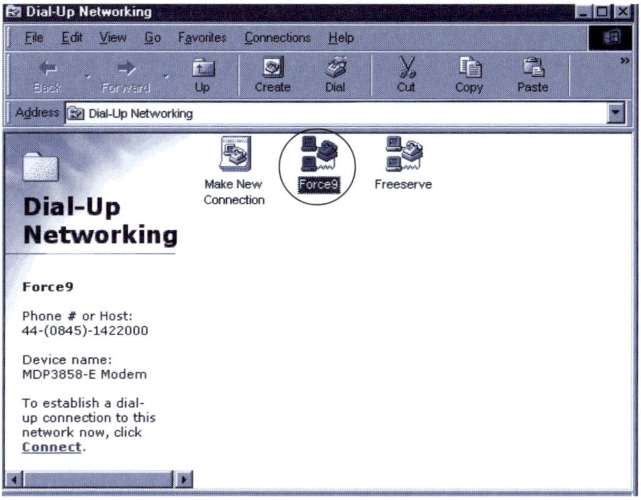

5 The new connection is now defined in *Dial-Up Networking*. Click with the right mouse button on the icon to enter additional data and select the PROPERTIES entry in the drop-down menu.

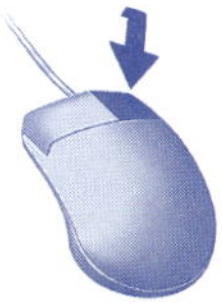

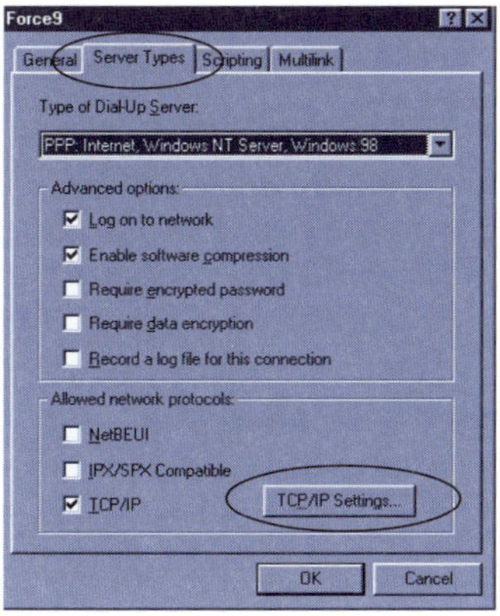

6 The SERVER TYPES tab contains TCP/IP settings. Click on *TCP/IP Settings...*

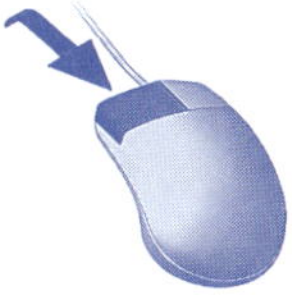

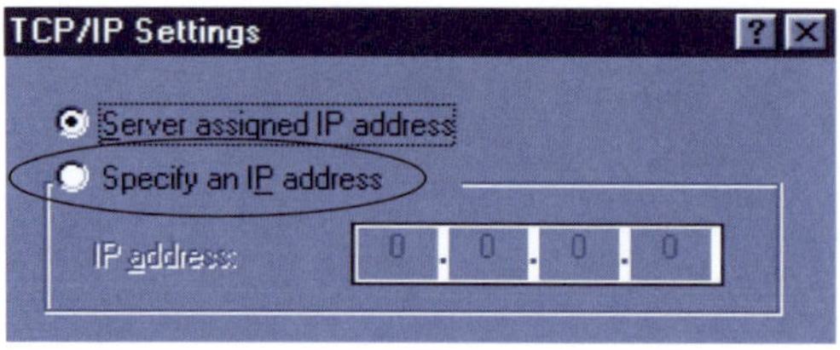

7 If the IP address is not server assigned (see data sheet), it must be entered in the *Specify an IP address* field. Otherwise, keep the address assigned by the server.

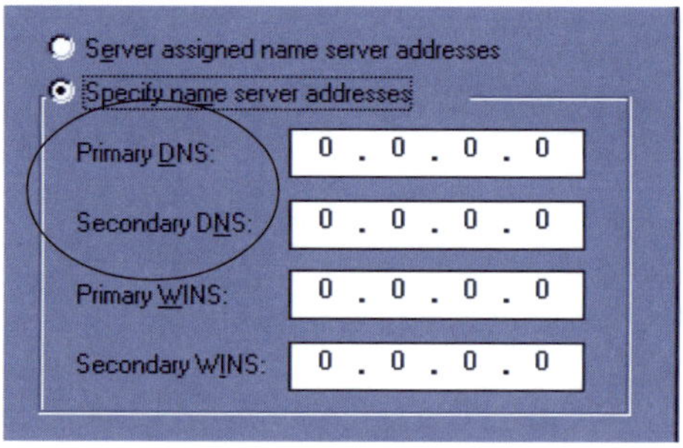

8 If your Provider has a 2-DNS server or "name server" (see data sheet), a further entry is required. Enter the corresponding details in the *Primary DNS* and *Secondary DNS* fields. Otherwise keep the server address assigned by the server. Confirm these entries with OK and close the window.

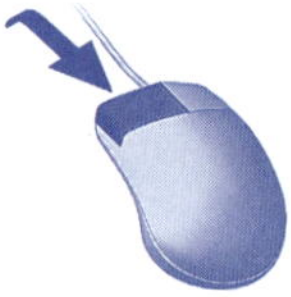

Connecting to the Internet

When your modem or your ISDN adapter is connected and set up, you are ready for your first "surfing trip" on the Internet.

With Dial-Up Networking, you can now set up your **first Internet connection** and confirm that your settings are correct.

The following step-by-step guide shows you how to establish an Internet connection to your ISP. You must always follow these steps when navigating on the Internet.

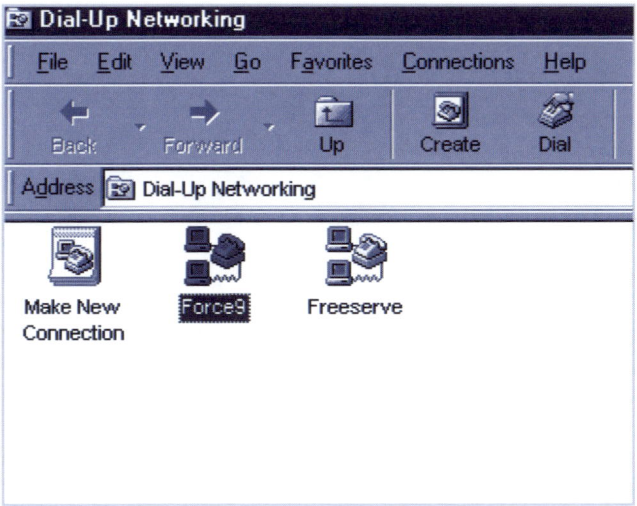

1 Double-click on MY COMPUTER and the *Dial-Up Networking* window will appear. The connection established in the previous exercise is displayed as an icon.

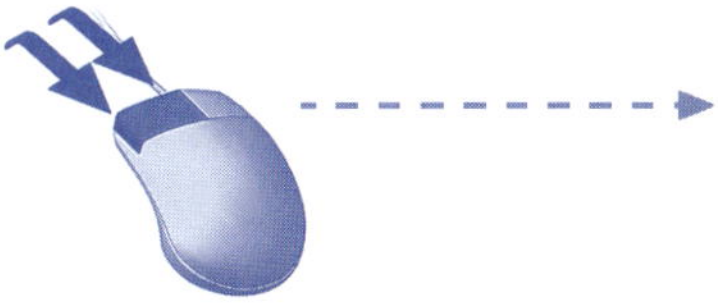

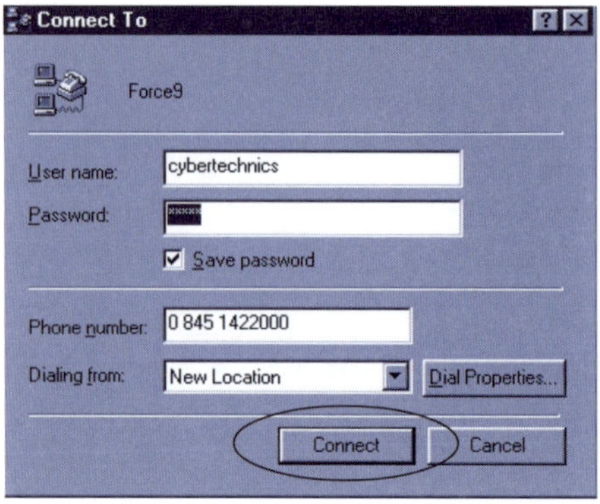

2 Double-click on this icon. A window opens which contains all your ISP's details, including the telephone number you will use to connect to the Internet. In the *User name* field, type the name registration (see data sheet from your provider). Your password must be entered in the *Password* field. In both cases, pay attention to the use of lower and upper case characters! Click on CONNECT to establish the connection.

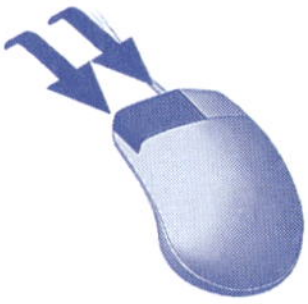

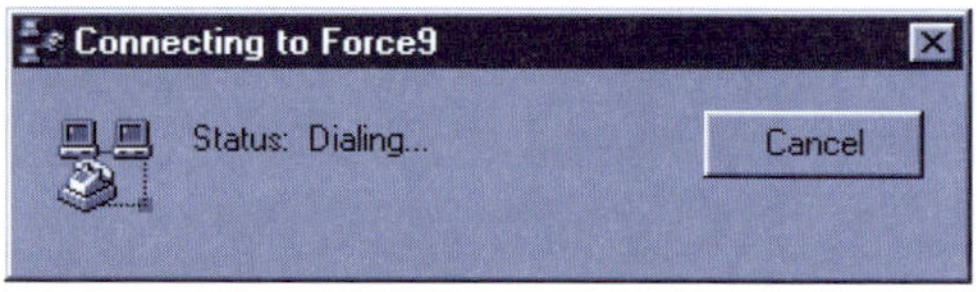

3 A few seconds later, your modem will start to dial the connection. Your computer gives a message "Verifying the user name and password" and "Registering to the network". The next report, which comes soon after, tells you that you are connected and gives the speed of your connection.

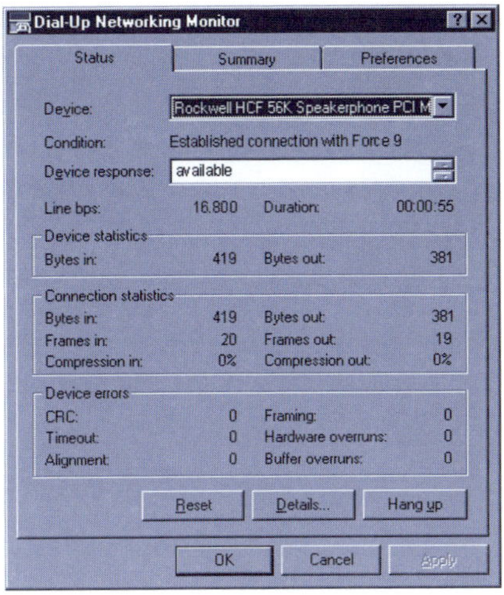

4 To check the connection, you can click in the bottom right corner of the Windows screen on the Modem icon. A program named *Dial-Up Networking Monitor* appears.

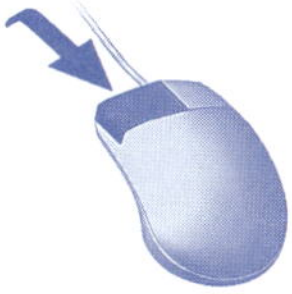

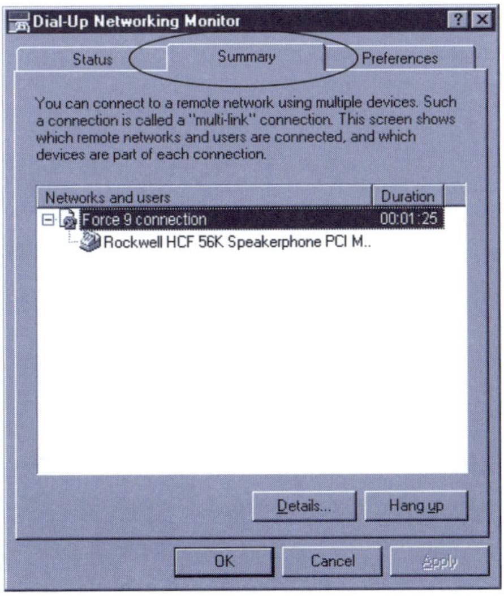

5 Click on the SUMMARY tab. If the connection is established correctly, your ISP will be listed here.

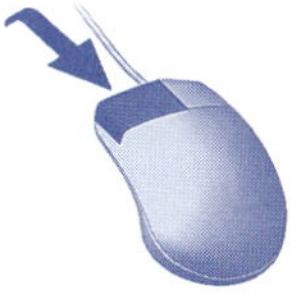

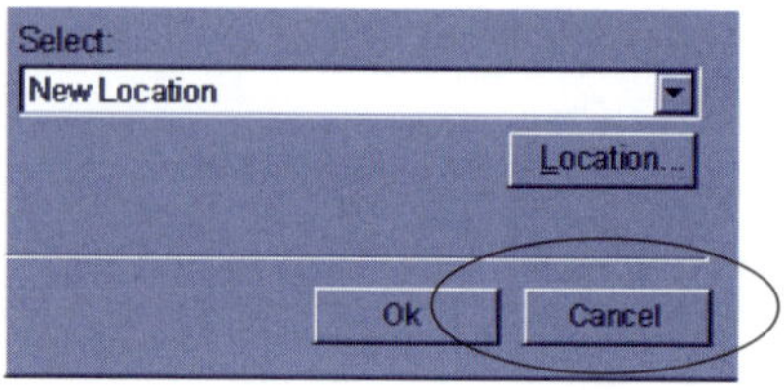

6 Click on CANCEL if you want to interrupt the telephone connection to your ISP. Windows does not end the connection automatically, so you need to interrupt the connection with your ISP manually each time.

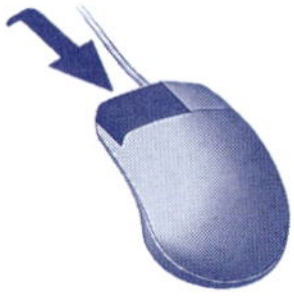

Surfing the Internet

Just as you need word processing software to be able to insert, edit, save and print text, the Internet needs software too.

The basic Internet software is called a **Browser**, because it allows you to 'browse' through the network. With a browser, you can navigate on the Internet, retrieve information, search databases, send files to your local hard disk and carry out many other activities.

> **WHAT'S THIS?**
>
> A **Browser** is the basic software to navigate on the Internet and to retrieve information from it. We can say that it is like a "decoder" for the Internet.

While there is a variety of word processing packages, there are only two programs in the browser market: **Netscape Communicator** (now in version 4.7, used to be called "Netscape Navigator") and **Microsoft Internet Explorer** (currently in version 5.1).

The decision of which browser software to choose is up to you. The second version of Windows 98 includes Internet Explorer 5 free , and Explorer is completely integrated in the system. The differences between the two programs are marginal for non-expert users. The software supports different hardware and operating system platforms for all Windows derivates, for UNIX, OS/2 and for Apple Macintosh.

Browser software is generally available for free. If you work with Windows 95, 98 or NT 4.0, Microsoft Internet Explorer is already installed on your PC or at least is on the installation CD.

You can find browser software, for example, through:

- Professional journals and magazines: many professional journals and magazines include a free CD-ROM where you can often find current browser programs.
- Internet Service Providers: large ISPs will send you a free CD-ROM with special access software after you have registered with them. This CD will often contain more than one browser.
- The Internet: if you have access to the Internet from other places (friends, a company, or at university), you can download browser software directly.

Internet security

A topic which attracts a lot of media attention is security on the Internet. We believe it would be useful to discuss this to conclude this chapter. The subjects of this discussion are **hackers**, who are simply data thieves, and tend to carry out their mischievous (and usually illegal) work by breaking into official organisations' computers, such as the Pentagon; their aim is to copy data and files from hard disks and even raid bank accounts.

Although these activities are usually carried out by isolated individuals, they tend to gain wide media coverage and therefore spread panic: many users are frightened of trusting Internet technology. It is true that only a computer that is not connected to the Internet is safe from intruders. However, it is also true that intrusion is very rare, and there is an increasing variety of security mechanisms and technology to stop hackers from stealing data.

If you are on the Internet and you stay on-line with your browser, you should use the same precautions that you take in real life. For example, you would not broadcast your credit card number in real life, so do not do it on the Internet either.

Test your knowledge

Main theme: The Internet and going on-line

1. What are the three prerequisites for setting up an on-line connection?

2. What is a modem and why is it called a modem? To which PC interface is a modem connected by default?

3. What is an ISDN card and how is it different from a modem? Which kind of transmission is possible with an ISDN card?

4. What does a CFOS driver do?

5. What is an Internet service provider? List some ISPs you know.

6. What does a transmission protocol do?

7. What does TCP/IP mean and how does it work?

8. What is a browser and why is it called a browser?

9. There are two main browsers available on the market. What are their names and in which current versions are they available?

10. What security measures should you adopt when navigating on the Internet?

10

The "personal computer"

What's in this chapter:

In this chapter, we will explain why your computer is called a PC. We will introduce you to the concept of upgrades. We will show you how you can extend the functionality of your PC with special add-ons. You are also going to learn what a soundcard is, how you can insert photos and text in your PC, and what an A/D convertor is.

You already know about:

You are going to learn about:

Expansion cards

Experts seem to agree on the fact that technical superiority is not the explanation for the success of the personal computer.

The concept of **extendibility** was unique and was soon copied by several computer manufacturers. All users should be able to organise the hardware and software of their computer as they require and to replace components, which have become too slow, with new and more powerful ones.

The computer's ability to adapt to users' needs gave it the name of **personal** computer.

Early PCs could only display black and white text. If users needed colour graphics, they could buy the appropriate accessories. Data carriers, for example hard disks, which are no longer large enough, can be easily replaced with higher capacity media.

Colour graphics cards and hard disks are standard equipment today, but you can still install other functions in your computer's expansion slots, if your PC does not have these functions already.

WHAT'S THIS?

With an **expansion card** (expansion adapter) you can expand the functions of your computer.

The expansion card consists of an electronic platinum board which is assembled with several components. On its back you will find the connections to link it to the back of the computer case.

The expansion card is inserted into the appropriate slot in the motherboard and connected directly with the bus system.

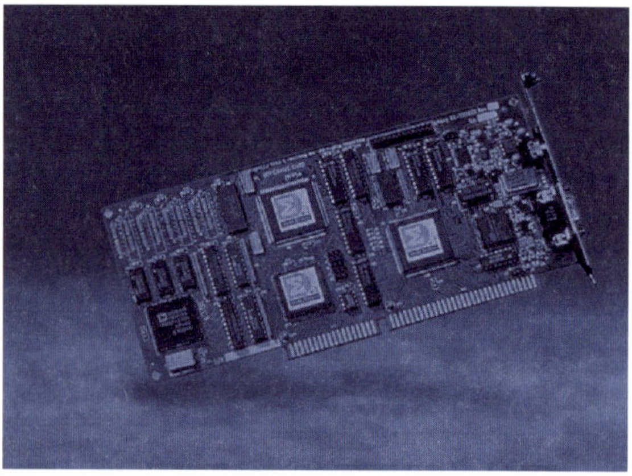

What are the available functions for expanding your computer? In this chapter, we will introduce you to the most important of these cards. In this list, you will probably find a number of expansion cards which in the future you may need to install on your PC.

WHAT'S THIS?

The expansion card is **inserted** into a slot in the motherboard. This is how the card gets connected with the PC bus system.

Technical parameters

Inserting the expansion card in the slot of the motherboard is not the end of the installation process.

Imagine you work with three expansion cards in your PC: the first one is for playing music for computer games, the second one connects your PC to a local network and the third one allows you to indulge your hobby of recording weather data.

For these different expansion cards to work together without clashing in your PC, every card must have **three technical parameters**. These parameters are independent from the type and specific function of the card, but they allow smooth internal communication between the PC and the card.

Base address

The base address (I/O port) of the card is comparable with your postal address. A base address is assigned either before installation by using switches on the board, or after installation by the software.

When the processor accesses the expansion card, it will use this base address. Each card should be assigned a unique base address, to avoid conflicts.

Base addresses are usually reported in hexadecimal format, for example "330h" or"220h"where the small "h" represents the hexadecimal value.

Interruption request

Imagine, for example, that you are recording current weather data with your system. The music expansion card is not used during this procedure.

The processor never accesses all the installed expansion cards at the same time, and so saves computing time. What it does is absorb data from cards when required. The expansion card "requests access" to the processor, checking whether it is ready to process data: it sends a request for interruption ("Interrupt Request" or "IRQ", for short), which induces the processor to process the available data from the expansion card.

It is unusual for the Interrupt procedure to be used by more than one card at the same time; usually, expansion cards will take it in turn to send an Interrupt message.

Direct memory access

In some cases, it is important that expansion boards should be able to load data directly into the main memory, without intervention by the processor.

For example, scanners send photographs directly to the memory, and, because of this, their operating speed is considerably increased.

The third parameter is therefore "direct memory access" (DMA, for short) which indicates the channel used by the expansion card to send data directly into the memory.

Plug & Play

In the past, and in some cases even now, base address, interrupt request and direct memory access had to be set up manually by the user. To change the parameters, the user needed what in computer jargon is called a "jumper".

This procedure was different for each case and required the user to have considerable technical knowledge. This configuration set-up has now been replaced by what Microsoft calls Plug & Play.

Plug & Play expansion cards configure themselves. They assign their own parameters to themselves during installation, and this procedure avoids possible conflicts which may be caused when the user creates the set-up.

The following step-by-step guide shows you how to select parameters for the interrupt request and the base address, as well as the direct memory access, under Windows 95 or 98.

1 Click on the START menu button and choose SETTINGS/CONTROL PANEL/SYSTEM.

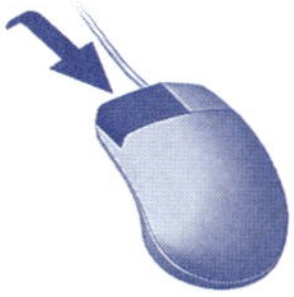

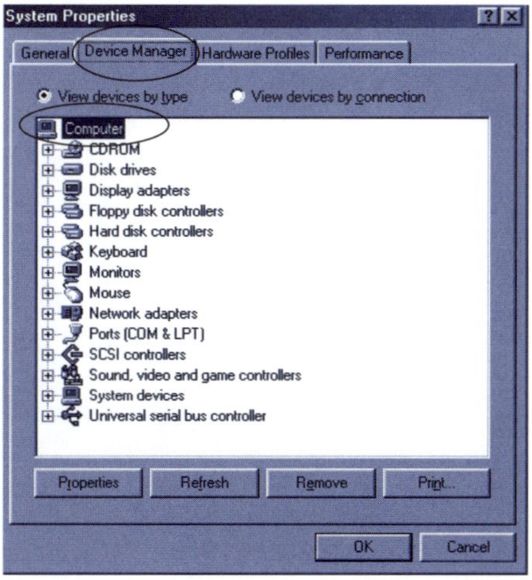

2 The *System Properties* window is now open. Click on the DEVICE MANAGER tab, where there is a list of the expansion cards installed on your computer, sorted by category. Double-click on the first heading, COMPUTER.

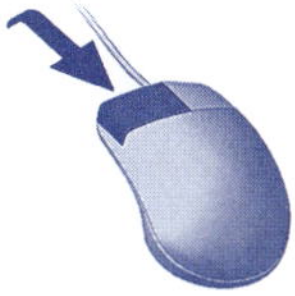

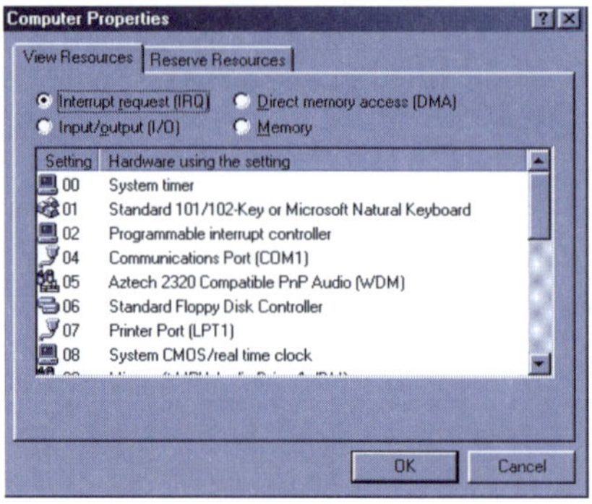

3 A window which reports the current Interrupt request now opens. The list in the *Setting* column contains the IRQ number, the list *Hardware using the setting* tells you the corresponding expansion card.

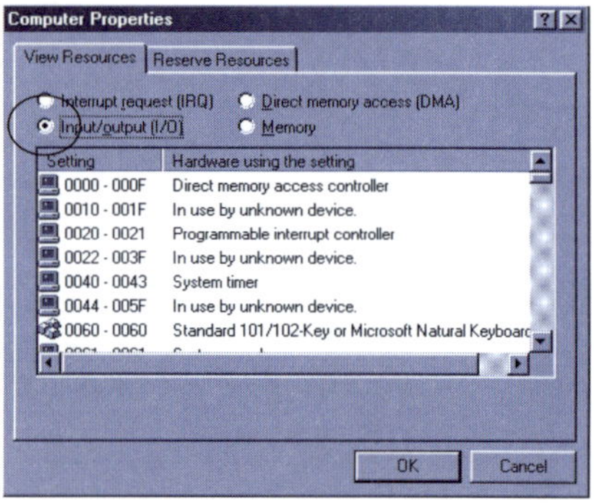

4 Click on the INPUT/OUTPUT radio button. Now the window contains the current base addresses which have already been assigned on your PC system.

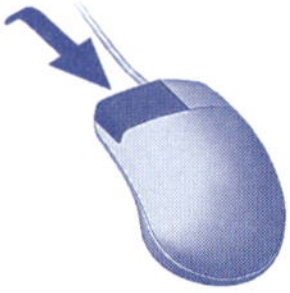

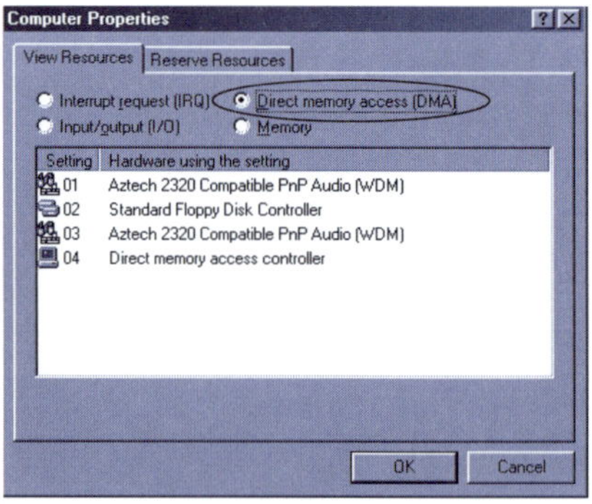

5 Click on the DMA radio button. This will display a list of the channels occupied by the direct memory access.

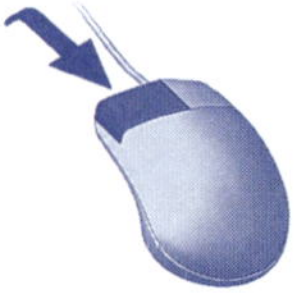

Driver cards

Just like the mouse, printer and graphics card, every expansion card needs a special **card driver**. This driver communicates with the card; it must therefore know the number assigned for IRQ, DMA and base address.

Plug & Play systems accept a variety of drivers for additional expansion cards and connect them directly after installation, when switching on your PC. Windows 95 and 98 connect suitable drivers even after the hardware recognition process, which you are already familiar with.

TIP

An expansion card does not work without a suitable driver, even if the DMA, IRQ and base address numbers are set correctly!

In the following step-by-step guide, we will show you how to identify the hardware parameters and drivers with which an expansion card will work under Windows 95 and 98.

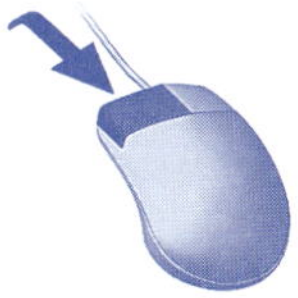

1 Click on the Start menu button and choose Settings/Control Panel/System.

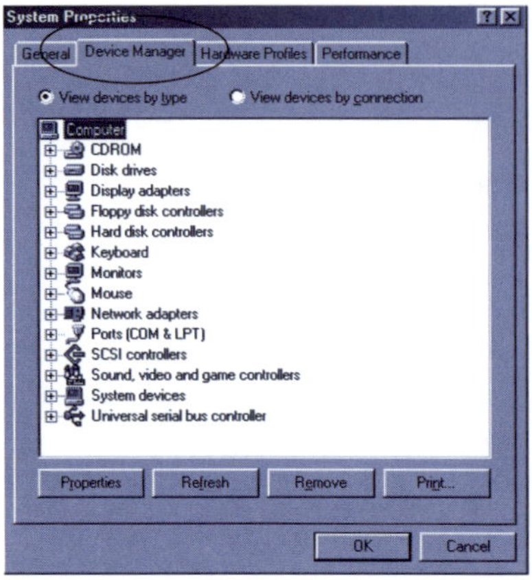

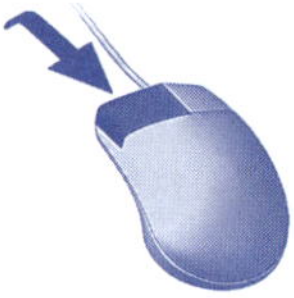

2 The *System Properties* window is now open. Click on the DEVICE MANAGER tab, which has a list of the expansion cards installed on your computer, sorted by category.

3 Now, choose the appropriate category for the desired expansion card. If you want to check your soundcard, for example, double click on *Sound, video and game controller*.

4 All devices in this category are now listed. Double-click on the desired expansion card, for example the *soundcard*.

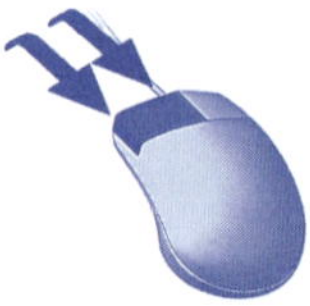

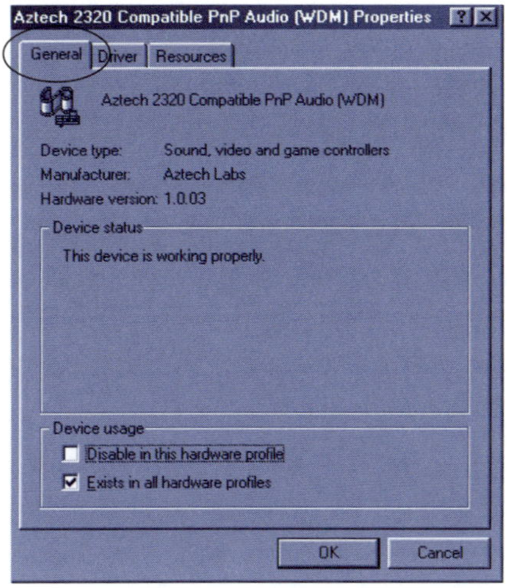

5 The General tab contains some general details and status information on the card, for example the information *This device is working properly*. It will also display error details if the expansion card does not work.

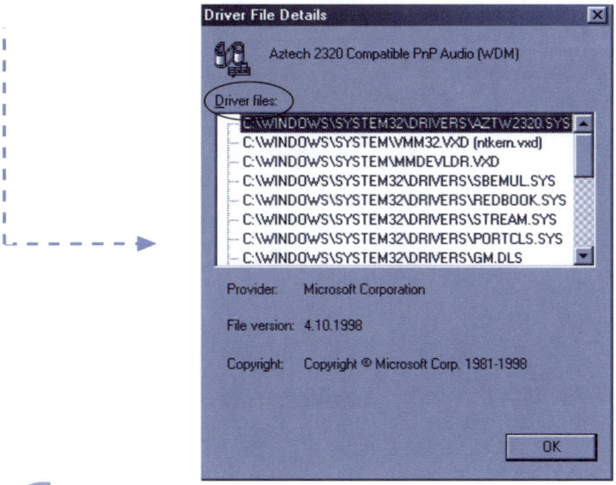

6 Click on Driver. You will find a list of the installed drivers, and the *Driver files* box tells you the version number of the driver.

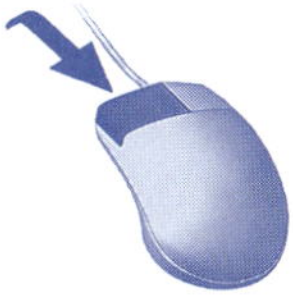

Soundcards

In the past, a PC generated sound via an internal speaker which frequently caused errors.

The trend towards **multimedia applications** and operating systems capable of handling multimedia has required not only a processor which is powerful enough for memory-hungry graphics, but is also capable of handling sound. By sound we mean anything to do with audible signals, such as music, speech, background noise and so on.

Traditional PC speakers are not able to provide the required sound quality, because users' expectations have become more sophisticated. In order to be able to meet these expectations you will need a **soundcard**, and therefore an expansion adapter. A soundcard is usually the first expansion card bought by many users.

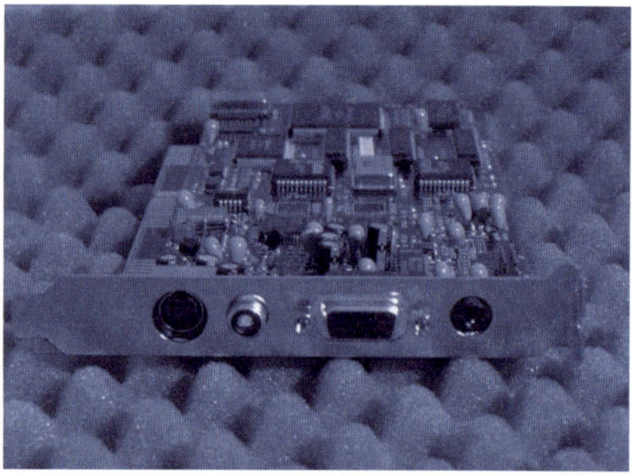

Each computer game supports a number of different soundcards; this is because you may need a different soundcard according to the technology used to produce the game soundtrack. The sound quality in current games is often very high: **realistic effects**, provided by music of CD quality with Dolby Surround Sound, are relatively easy to create and are therefore becoming widespread. The Interactive Movie environment is also very sophisticated.

However, there are substantial differences in the technical capabilities of sound equipment, which affect price. While for PC games you only need a simple and cheap soundcard, multimedia applications or semi-professional sound processing require more expensive and sophisticated equipment.

Scanners

A **scanner** is used to produce digital copies of printed images. A very sensitive and precise optical recognition system – such as the one used by photocopiers – reads the image, for example, from a book or a magazine, and sends the received picture information to the PC.

The image transmitted to the PC is viewed on the screen, and can be printed or saved to the hard disk, using the appropriate software. Powerful graphic applications, such as CorelDraw or Photoshop, enable users to manipulate and retouch the scanned image very easily; effects such as distortion and mirroring are as easy to achieve as enlarging and reducing, or cutting out (cropping) part of an image.

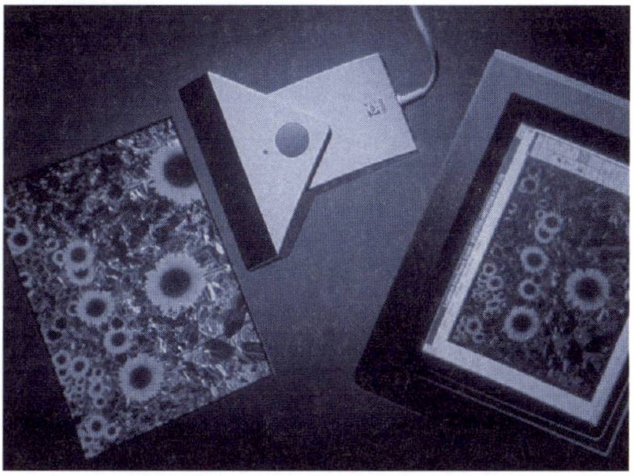

A second application field for a scanner is computer-controlled **optical character recognition** (OCR).

Entire text pages, such as pages from a book or a newspaper, can be scanned just like an image. Special programs with a specific cache algorithm **recognise the characters** and translate them into a text document which you can then edit in Word, for example, or any word processing package.

The copy of the text to be scanned in OCR must be clean and clear, and easily readable, because the presence of spurious marks, such as spots, on the page may create recognition problems. So far, only typed documents are capable of being scanned using this process; computers are currently unable to recognise handwriting.

Network cards

If you use your PC in your office, you may want to connect to an existing local network. A "network map" connects your PC to the network.

On your PC, there is a port to which a network cable is connected and which establishes the connection to the network.

You can set up a **small network** in Windows 98 in about an hour, but, since it may cause some problems to the way you work, it may be better for you to become more familiar with this subject matter by reading a book on the subject. If you are on a network, you would be able to carry on working while you are printing, and in Windows 98, you can even surf on the Internet with a modem or an ISDN connection while you are carrying out other activities on your computer.

A/D convertor cards

As a conclusion to this chapter, we would like to introduce a universal card which is not linked to a specific function. In science and technology, **Analogous Digital convertor expansion cards** are frequently used.

You know about this technology, because at the beginning we introduced the difference between analog and digital signals, and explained that analog signals can be saved as bits. The A/D connector is also used in different areas, which may not be immediately obvious to most users.

A **modem** is an example of this, since it converts from analog to digital signals using an A/D convertor.

The application field of an A/D convertor card is fairly wide. The list below gives its most common uses.

- Measuring tension and current. An A/D convertor can be used to determine tension and power.
- Determining chemical conducting ability. A wider application area for the A/D convertor is the determination of the chemical conducting ability of a substance which, for example, could provide information on the load of industrial waste in water.
- Measuring revolutions per minute. Strobe lights are used to determine the rotational speed per second of an engine in motor engineering.
- Reading weather data. An A/D convertor is used to translate analog signals to assess wind speed, rain and temperature and translate the information into digital data, so that it can be used for weather analysis.

11 Software

What's in this chapter:

We end our journey through the PC world with a chapter on software. We will introduce different types of programs and explain the differences between programs. You will learn why some software is so popular, and why some software may be very expensive. We will introduce some widely used standard applications, for example programs that handle text or graphics.

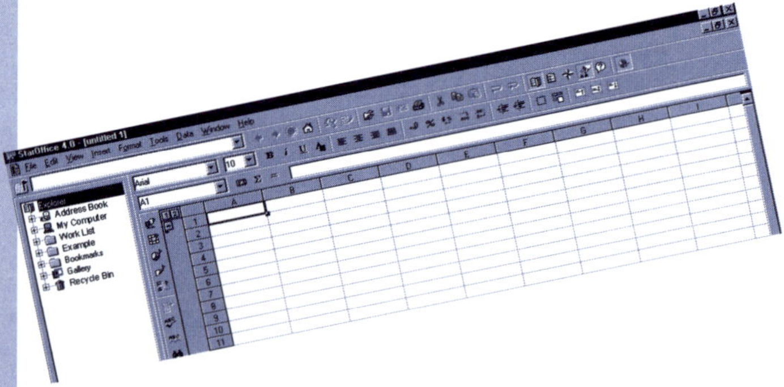

You already know about:

You are going to learn about:

Nothing works without software!

The most efficient and most modern PC cannot help you with your daily work if it is not equipped with the appropriate software.

You have already been introduced to some software packages in previous chapters: Windows 98, WordPad, Microsoft Word and Internet Explorer.

Software applications are software packages that support you in your work. In this chapter, we will introduce you to the most important types of software, and give you an overview of current packages.

Standard software

Programs which you can buy in computer shops off the shelf, standard software. These are relatively cheap, but are general, that is, not specifically adapted to your personal requirements.

Standard packages are used for basic functions, required by most users. **Word processing**, **graphics programs**, **spreadsheets** and **database programs** are standard software.

Horizontal software

Standard software, limited to specific tasks and application, is called "horizontal software". **Accounting packages and statistical packages** are typical of this type of software.

Vertical software

Software which offers extensive functions in a specific field, is usually programmed for a restricted number of specific operations. "Vertical software" is always expensive and can be **adapted** to the user's needs.

Typical PC users of vertical software are doctors, lawyers or insurance brokers.

Customised software

If the type of standard software mentioned so far is not suitable for your needs, then you require software which has been designed by a programmer according to your precise specifications.

Customised software will match all your requirements and can be modified to suit your changing needs. Of course, customised software is very expensive; a single program can cost tens of thousand of pounds, or even hundreds of thousands.

Software packages

Software suites contain a number of single applications which have complementary functions. The most popular and common example is Microsoft Office, which contains a word processor package, a database program, a spreadsheet analysis and a presentation software. With the new edition Office 2000, you can connect directly to the Internet. Other software producers have copied this system, for example, Star Division (which is part of Sun Microsytems) has produced a comparable program called StarOffice.

Importing data between individual packages within a suite is often standardised, so that you can easily take addresses from your database and use them for word processing functions, such as MailMerge.

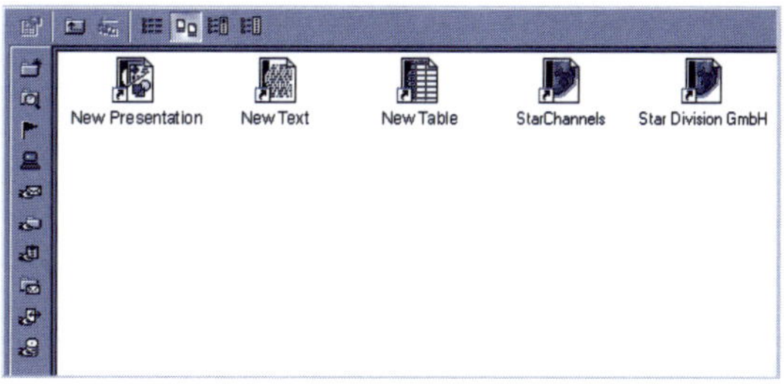

If you add up the price of individual packages in a suite, you can see that buying the suite saves you money. Office-based packages are often a basic requirement, because most PC users require word processing, database handling and spreadsheet analysis for their office work.

Light editions

Light editions are software packages which have a reduced **performance range**. If you only work with spreadsheets and only require basic functions to calculate a table, you can purchase a Light version of a software package. Light software is obviously cheaper and, if you want to buy the standard edition (the "full product") at a later stage, you will only need to pay the price difference.

Bundle software

If you buy hardware or a new computer system, there is usually a **bundle software** offer in the package. The manufacturer of the hardware provides these programs in addition to the components or the PC system; this is because the hardware manufacture has usually made a special deal with the software manufacturer.

Shareware, Public Domain and Freeware

Shareware, Freeware and Public Domain are all examples of software which is **completely free**. You can download these programs from the Internet, for example, or get them from friends, from stores or from CD-ROMs which come included with PC magazines.

Shareware often has a reduced performance, compared to the full version that can be purchased, or has an expiry date for trial purposes, and can therefore only be used for, say, 30 days. If you like the program, you can have the registered edition after a trial period. If you do not like it, after the trial period, you must remove it from your hard disk, for copyright reasons.

Word processors

The most common type of software installed in most computers, is the word processor. A word processing package will allow you to insert, manipulate, format, save and print text.

Modern word processing software offers very powerful functions. You can create a whole book (for example this one) using a word processor. You can **insert page numbers**, or **headers and footers**, create **standard letters**, **indexes and contents** and you can execute **automatic spelling** and **grammar checks**.

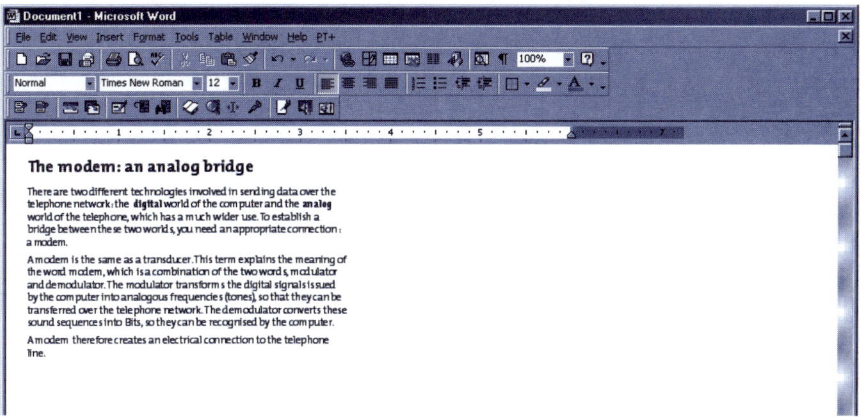

Most operating systems, such as Windows and OS/2, include a word processor in their basic functions. However, you should not expect advanced functions from them.

The most widely used word processing software are Microsoft Word 2000, Starwriter by Star Division and Lotus WordPro by Lotus.

Spreadsheets

When you use a spreadsheet, the screen is divided into rows and columns. You can type in numbers and link the cells to each other so that you can **calculate** the contents of these cells.

In this way, you can calculate **bills**, create **financial plans**, calculate **interest** and represent figures in attractive diagrams.

Microsoft Excel 2000, Lotus 1-2-3, StarCalc by Star Division and Corel Quattro Pro are some of the most widely used spreadsheet programs.

Database software

A database manages **addresses**, **appointments**, **customer details**, **delivery dates** and other such information like **stock levels** for a company warehouse, but also stamp collections or any other scalable data. A powerful **search mechanism**, called query, will then allow you to search for specific data in the database, or produce a list organised according to your search criteria.

You can create "masks", where you define a form into which the requested information is entered. You can even set up calculations in specific fields on the mask. For example, you can calculate minimum order or a minimum stock, and request information to your database whenever you need it.

Microsoft Access 2000 and Oracle are the most widely used database programs.

Graphics programs

You can draw **colour graphics** and combine them with other elements, such as text, using a graphics software program. Virtual tools such as brushes, erasers and pencil, and functions such as airbrush and filling are available.

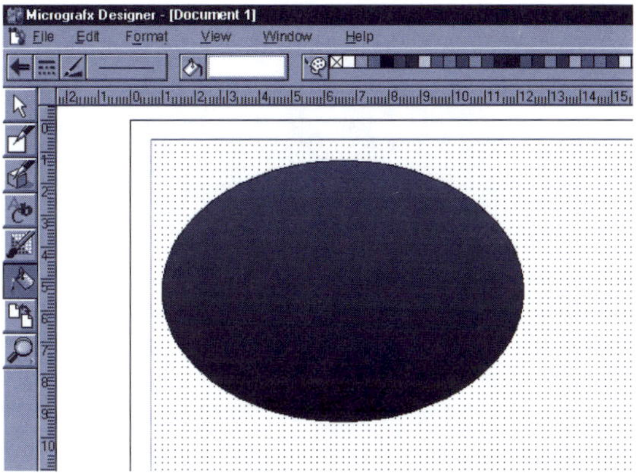

Many graphics programs contain a clipboard library with thousands of pictures and graphics ready and available for use. In this way, you can easily design invitations or letterheads.

Graphics software also allows you to retouch scanned photographs. You can alter contrast and brightness, change colours, remove parts or manipulate pictures by creating a number of different effects.

CorelDraw 9, Paint ShopPro and Adobe Photoshop are some of the most widely used graphics packages.

Test your knowledge

Main theme: Software

1. List at least two programs which are supplied with Windows 98 and which we mentioned in the previous chapter.

2. Why is standard software relatively inexpensive?

3. What is bundled software?

4. What is customised software and what are its main features?

5. What is the difference between Public Domain and Shareware? Within this context, what is "registration"?

6. What are light editions of software and what is a full product edition?

7. List two of the most widely used word processing programs.

8. Give three main areas where database software is useful.

9. You would like to do a presentation to the board concerning your quarterly sales statistics and you want to use diagrams and pictures. Which software is suitable to do this?

10. What is an office package? List two of the main products in this field.

Glossary

What's in this chapter:

In this glossary, you will be able to find all the essential technical terms used in the world of computers.

You will find the solutions to the Test your knowledge questions on page 343, followed by some useful tables containing relevant data that you are likely to encounter frequently when working with computers, on page 348.

Glossary

Computer jargon has a number of abbreviations and technical terms that you need to understand and become familiar with, whether you want to read through computer brochures, professional journals or advanced technical literature, or just be able to understand your system's on-line help facility.

This glossary explains the most frequently used terms and abbreviations.

Accelerated Graphics Port (AGP)

This is a special port that started to appear on motherboards in the second half of 1997. The port bypasses the PCI bus and allows much higher throughput from the graphics card to the processor for speedier 3D graphics. You will need special graphics cards to fit into this slot. It is not compatible with current PCI cards.

Advanced Configuration and Power Interface (ACPI)

This power management interface takes the power management out of the BIOS and gives control to the OS. Typically, a system's BIOS is only able to turn a device off after a certain period of inactivity. With ACPI, the user can instruct the OS to slow down the processor or enter sleep mode. This basically gives the OS, and thus the user, more control over power management.

Aliasing

When pictures are processed at a too low resolution, they become pixelated, which means the edges of the image will appear rough.

Analog

Analog refers to a representation of a quantity that varies over any continuous range of values. Analog signals are pure and unprocessed. Hence, the debate over whether record albums (analog representations of sound) sound better than CDs (digital representations of sound). Think of analog as the natural mode.

ANSI code

Abbreviation for *American National Standards Institutes.* This organisation represents the United States in the ISO (International Organisation for Standardisation). They work to develop coding and signalling standards.

Anti-aliasing

This is a method to better define higher resolution objects using a lower resolution.

API

Abbreviation for *Application Programming Interface.* APIs allow you to program to a preconstructed interface (the API) instead of directly programming a device or piece of software.

ASCII- code

Abbreviation for *American Standard Code for Information Interchange.* Pronounced "ass-kee". This is a means of representing characters as standardised. The first 32 characters are control codes which can be used for text formatting or actions, such as making the computer beep. After the 32 control codes, the next 96 standardised characters represent numbers, letters (both upper case and lower case) and punctuation marks. The last 128 characters represent different things on different platforms.

ASPI

Abbreviation for *Advanced SCSI Programming Interface.* This was developed by Adaptec so that different devices could be controlled by different SCSI cards so that various SCSI cards could be used. Basically, if the correct ASPI driver is being used, you can send the same command to any Adaptec SCSI card to make something happen to a device. Most commonly, ASPI is associated with CD-ROM drives.

Asynchronous

This method of transferring data does so without a specific timing mechanism between the two communicating parties. The party receiving data does not expect data at a set interval (synchronous).

ATAPI standard

Abbreviation for *Advanced Technology Attachment Packs Interface*. The ATAPI describes a standard hard disk controller, E-IDE. It can also operate with other equipment, such as CD-ROM drives and streamer disk drives.

AT BUS

Abbreviation for *Advanced Technology Bus*. Another name for this is the IDE-bus system.

Autopark function

When the computer is switched off, current hard disks "park" the read/write heads, automatically, at the edge of the disk, so that no data lanes can be damaged if a crash takes place. Earlier hard disks needed to be moved into a park position manually.

AV-Optimise

Abbreviation for *Audio Video optimised* hard disks. It plays audio and video sequences with the computer as a conventional hard disk. AV-optimised hard disks are equipped so that they can deliver a continuous data stream without interruption.

Bad clusters

Physically faulty sectors on a hard disk are put into a list of bad clusters so that these parts cannot be used by the operating system any more.

Bank

A bank of memory chips. The term applies to the expansion of the memory. In the past, these were usually a minimum of 4 Mbytes; their size has increased, in steps, to 16, 32, 64, 128 or 256 Mbytes, with current sizes becoming larger all the time.

Bank switching

The memory is divided up into banks which are managed by a simple form controlled by the BIOS.

Basic Input/Output System

This is a program stored on your motherboard that controls all the interaction between your components and your chipset. Standard access to video and the keyboard are included in the BIOS.

Baud rate

Baud is the measure of how frequently sound changes on a telephone line. This used to be the measure of the speed of modems because they actually made a sound for each bit of information. Now, modems work on a more sophisticated level. The baud rate should not be mistaken for the data transfer rate. A modem with a speed of 28,800 bits per second works to 3,400 bauds, but can transmit 28.8 Kbps.

Beep code

When you turn on your PC, and all is well, you typically hear a single beep from your computer speaker to signal that all is OK. If there is an error, and the computer BIOS discovers the error, a series of beeps will be emitted. This is the beep code. Based on the number of beeps, you can look up the meaning in your motherboard documentation and often diagnose the problem. Obvious things to check are whether your video card, processor and/or memory are plugged in.

Benchmarking

This is a process of measuring the performance of hardware or software in a specifically defined and strictly controlled environment. The test results are usually represented by a time or a number rating that corresponds to how quickly certain tasks can be completed. The benchmark must be reproducible, of course, to have any meaning.

Beta version

The different stages of development of a software package are often marked by Greek characters. A beta version is the first operational version before the alpha version is released. It is still full of faults and is usually released to a restricted number of users to let them test it under normal business conditions, to provide the manufacturers with useful feedback on bugs and features.

Binary code

Binary consists of a string of bits, i.e. 0101011100000000001.

BIOS

See *Basic Input/Output System.*

Bit

This is the smallest unit of measure in a computer. It is represented by a 0 (off) or 1 (on). Think of a bit as a switch. If it is in the on position, it's a 1, and if the switch is off, it's a 0. All levels of your computer communicate in bits.

BNC connector

This is a connector type for 10Base2 or Thin-Net networks. Shaped like the letter T, it connects coaxial cables. The 'T' has two male connectors and one female connector. The female connector can connect to the male connection of an Ethernet card that supports BNC connections, or remain empty. The male connectors link to a coaxial cable or a terminator. The BNC part stands for either British Naval Connector, British Nut Connector, or Bayonett Neill-Concelman. Neill and Concelman are the names of the inventors of the BNC connector.

Boot sector

This is the first sector of a bootable partition. It contains the information needed to start loading the operating system.

bps

Abbreviation for *bits per second* or *bytes per second*. This is generally a measure of how fast some devices communicate, usually in thousands of bits per second (Kbps) or millions of bits per second (Mbps). If you are using a capital B (KBps and MBps), then you are talking about bytes, which are equal to eight bits.

Buffer

This is a temporary location to store or group information in hardware or software. Buffers are used whenever data is received in sizes that may be different from the ideal size for the hardware or software that uses the buffer. For example, a 64-bit processor on a 16-bit bus may have a buffer to hold 16-bit requests until they equal 64 bits. Another use of buffers is to keep hardware from becoming overwhelmed with information. You use a large buffer to hold data until a device or program is ready to receive it, instead of just pushing it on to a device that might not be ready. Buffers must be optimised in size to work efficiently for the purpose they are designed.

Bug

This is a design or programming error in a hardware device or piece of software. The effects of a bug may be as harmless as an extra graphic on screen, or as harmful as a system crash or loss of data.

Burn-in

A burn-in test is an endurance test for a computer. Since error probability increases with the increased temperature of a component, faults may arise at a raised temperature level. Testing time is usually 24 or 48 hours.

Bus

A bus is simply a data path between devices. The computer's system bus is what peripherals use to send and receive data to and from the processor and main memory.

Bus mouse

A mouse that uses the smaller 6-pin connector instead of your computer's serial port. Also referred to as a PS/2 mouse because of its early adoption by the IBM PS/2 series of computers.

Bus speed

This is a measurement, usally in Mhz, of how many times data can be transferred over the bus per second.

Byte

Simply put, it is eight bits. Think of it as a string of 1s and 0s that represents a number from 0 to 255. For example "01100101" is one byte of information.

Cache

Generally a small chunk of fast memory that sits between either a smaller, faster chunk of memory and a bigger, slower chunk of memory, or a processor and a bigger, slower chunk of memory. This is to provide a bridge from something that is comparatively fast to something that is comparatively slow. Most computers have cache memory that holds some of the information from their main memory. When the processor needs the information, it takes it from the speedy cache instead of the slower main memory. Cache memory greatly increases the speed of a computer by storing the data that is most often accessed.

CAD

Stands for *Computer Aided Design*. This refers to the use of computers to design things. There are specific CAD programs such as AutoCAD that are generally resource-intensive, requiring fast processors, lots of memory, and a big, clear monitor for best results. CAD has enabled people to easily model, create, walk through or view designs of 3D objects or floor plans from different angles on a computer without taking the time to make a physical mock-up. This is a huge time-saver and has revolutionised design in general.

Caddy

Caddies are protective covers for CD-ROMs. They protect the sensitive disks from scratches and dust. CDs are inserted with the caddy in special CD drives.

Calibration

Fluctuation in temperature may cause small changes in the size of the highly sensitive magnetic parts in a hard drive. This could cause data pathways to be altered, because their physical position may have shifted. For this reason, current hard disks have a recalibration function. Write and read heads on drives have a tightly defined position and are capable of making the necessary adjustments to maintain this position relative to the interface. Calibration lasts approx 0.5 to 2 seconds, after which work can be resumed.

CAPI

Abbreviation for *Common API*. The CAPI is a software interface required for internal ISDN modems. The communication program uses the CAPI functions of the driver to check the use of the ISDN modem. There is a difference between the earlier CAPI 1.1 version, which is responsible for the national ISDN, and the current CAPI 2.0 version, which supports the European standard ISDN.

Cardbus

This refers to the 32-bit PCMCIA card slot and cards that can work in this slot. Standard PCMCIA, or PC card, slots were originally 16-bit slots. This caused problems when 100 Mbit network cards and fast SCSI cards were used and throughput would not go high enough because the 16-bit slots were too slow.

Cathode Ray Tube (CRT)

This is one of the main components of monitors and TVs. A beam of electrons is shot towards the CRT and, as they collide with phosphors on the inside surface, they produce light. Today, other technologies perform better than the heavy and bulky tube monitors. LCD panels and projection units are both in contention, but they still cannot come close to the low cost of a CRT monitor or TV.

CD-A

Abbreviation for *Compact Disk – Audio*. CD-A is the standard form for music CDs.

CD-I

Abbreviation for *Compact Disk – Interactive*. The CD-I standard was developed together by Philips and Sony especially to cater for interactive video applications in CD-ROM format.

CD-R

Abbreviation for *Compact Disk – Recordable*. CD-R drives record up to 650 Mb of data onto specialised CD-R media. The medium is more expensive than the mass-produced CDs that software is generally distributed on, but cheap for the amount of data you can store on it. CD-R media is a WORM technology. You can Write to it Once and Read Many times, but you can't erase anything you have written.

CD-ROM

Abbreviation for *Compact Disk – Read Only Media*. CD-ROMs hold 650 Mb of data. It is the current standard and easiest way to distribute software. CD-ROM drives can also read music CDs even though they are a different format from CD-ROM media.

CD-ROM-XA

This standard is an expansion of the standard CD-ROM for the combination of various data on a track (audio, video and computer data).

CD-RW

Shortened form for *Compact Disk – Rewritable*. These special CD-ROMs can be written to (burned) and deleted up to 1000 times. You will need a special CD-RW disk drive for reading and burning a CD-RW.

CE norm

Since the beginning of 1996, all electronic equipment or components must conform to the rules of the Conformité Européen, according to *European Union* legislation.

Centronics interface

The printer interface (or the parallel interface) was standardised by the company Centronics. Current printer interfaces allow a much higher data transfer rate.

CGA

Stands for *Computer Graphics Adapter*. This is a video standard that allowed a resolution of 320 x 200 with four colours. It was replaced by EGA. You can get 16 colours on CGA if you go down to 160 x 100 resolution. This is the first real graphics standard for IBM-compatible computers.

Character

This refers to a single letter, number or symbol. This term applies to data typed into a computer, shown on a computer screen, or printed on paper.

Chassis

Pronounced "chassy". The frame which holds your computer components.

Chip

Short for microchip.

Chipset

These are the chips that control the functions and features on a motherboard. The chipset determines how much memory you can put into a motherboard and which processors you can use with it. Of course, there are physical connectors on your motherboard that limit these things as well, but motherboard manufacturers use the chipset as a basis for what type of connectors they can put on a motherboard.

chkdsk (check disk)

This is a Microsoft program that checks your drive for logical errors, as opposed to physical defects. This program is supported in DOS and all versions of Windows. Windows NT still uses it as its main disk-checking program. DOS and Windows replaced this program with the friendlier Scandisk, but chkdsk.exe is still available.

CISC

Stands for *Complex Instruction Set Computer*. Intel x86 chips are CISC chips because of the complexity of the instruction set. On the other side of the coin, you have RISC chips that use a reduced instruction set. RISC chips split big operations into lots of simple, tiny instructions that are processed very quickly. Some people argue that RISC chips are better. Several Intel competitors use RISC chips with CISC converters to compete against Intel's chips.

Clip art

Non-copyrighted generic art distributed for use in word processors and desktop publishing. Graphic designers often use clip art as a shortcut for producing images.

Clock cycle

Think of a clock cycle as one tick of the second hand (but generally at a much higher speed). Computer clocks run voltage through a tiny crystal that oscillates at a set speed to give a meaningful timing method to the computer. One clock cycle does not necessarily mean that the processor does one operation. Today's high end processors often complete more than one operation per clock cycle, and sometimes, in the worst case, it will take several clock cycles to complete one operation.

Cluster

A cluster is defined by the MS-DOS operating system as the smallest indivisible unity for data storage on the hard disk. Depending on the size of the hard disk, clusters form eight or more sectors.

Clustering

Clustering is a new technology using two or more computers that function together as a single entity for fault tolerance and load balancing. This increases reliability and up-time in a client/server environment. One computer will sense when another computer is failing or becoming overloaded and will take over its tasks.

CMOS-RAM

Abbreviation for *Complementary Metal-Oxide Semiconductor.* CMOS describes a technique of circuits integrated into the production. This is the common reference for the BIOS preferences in your computer. Actually, it is a low power version of a chip. The low power comes into play because it is what commonly holds your BIOS preferences through power off, with the aid of a battery. The basic information about the hardware configuration is stored in the CMOS-RAM of the PC. Data saved in the CMOS is evaluated and processed by the BIOS.

Coaxial cable

This is the original ethernet cable. It consists of a single, insulated copper wire, surrounded by a copper braid or foil. The wire is then coated in plastic. Coaxial cable is used in bus systems.

Code

A series of instructions that make up a program.

Code generator

A code generator is part of a compiler. It takes intermediate code and translates it into final workable code in the target computer language.

Combination controller

Another name for a multi I/O card.

Command prompt

This is any blinking cursor waiting, or prompting, for user input. In DOS, the C: prompt greets you on most systems. This is a type of command prompt. As well, if you use any version of Windows, you can get to a DOS-looking window that allows you to type in commands. For novice users, a command prompt can be confusing, but for experts, a command prompt is a necessity.

Compiler

A compiler translates a computer program from one language into another, catching any errors in syntax along the way. Most commonly, high level language, such as C++, is translated into optimised machine language. This form of compilation puts your programs into a form that computers can understand without any translation, thus speeding them up.

Compression

This takes something large and makes it smaller. Compression generally comes in two forms, lossy and lossless. Lossy compression is best used on graphics files and sound files. It crunches down the data at a much higher ratio, at the expense of quality, thus ending up with an image or a sound that isn't quite the same as before it was compressed. In the best scenario, the data takes up less space, but the person viewing the graphic or listening to the sound file will not be able to tell. Lossless compression squezees data down so that at some later stage it can be uncompressed and returned to its exact structure with no loss of quality. Lossless compression is best used on data files and programs.

Convergence

The ability of the three electron beams (red, green and blue) in a CRT monitor to meet at a single point and produce one dot. Convergence in a monitor describes the correct relationship of these three primary colours. If this relationship is not correct, and the monitor is mis-converging, you will notice shadows of blue or red around any white images and the picture may appear as blurred. Often, this will only occur in some parts of the screen. Some monitors have convergence controls, but most do not.

Cookie

Web sites send these to your browser so that the site is customised, based on your previous actions on that site. For example, a site you are visiting may send a cookie to your browser to find out whether you are a new visitor or if you have been there before. The site would then check the cookie next time you visit the site and may well show you some different information, if you are a repeat visitor. If you want to view your cookies, look for a folder called Cookies on your hard drive.

CPU

Abbreviation for *Central Processing Unit*. Think of this as the brain of the computer. When most people think of processors, they think of Intel, Motorola or IBM. The Pentium II, III and K6 are popular CPUs. The CPU's first instruction is to check the system BIOS and do what the BIOS tells it. The CPU is designed to run a group of instructions or instruction set. CPU instructions can consist of adding together numbers, subtracting, fetching information from memory and numerous other simple functions. The computer's operating system feeds the CPU instructions after the BIOS locates it and puts it into memory.

Cracker

This is the common term used to describe a malicious hacker. Crackers get into all kinds of mischief, including breaking or "cracking" copy protection on software programs, breaking into systems and causing harm, changing data or stealing information, commonly credit card or bank account details. Hackers regard crackers as a less educated group of individuals who cannot create their own work, and simply steal other people's work to cause mischief, or for personal gain.

Cross-linked files

Files may be cross-linked by the file administration (FAT) because of a system crash. Often, it only concerns data, and most cross-linked files are deleted by a special program (such as Scandisk) before they create serious problems.

Cross-platform

Cross-platform is a term given to software that can be used on multiple hardware platforms, such as Digital's Alpha, SGI's Indigo or Intel's Pentium. One such piece of software is Java.

Cushion distortion

This affects monitors. The edge of the picture is curved outwards or inwards. The curve is more noticeable closer to the edge.

Custom

The American measurement unit custom (or inch) is frequently used for the length of the diagonal screen of a monitor. A custom corresponds to exact 25.4 mm (e.g., 15" = 38.1 cm / 17" = 43.18 cm).

Cyberspace

This term was coined to refer to the vast expanses of the Internet. Just as space is infinite, the Internet is, well, pretty big. "Cyberspace" just sounded cooler than "Internet" to the news media.

D/A Converter

Abbreviation for *Digital/Analog Converter*. This will change digital information into analog signals (the reverse of the analog/digital converter). So, for example, the digital information of the CD is translated into analog acoustic signals in the CD player.

DAT

Abbreviation for *Digital Audio Tape*. This type of magnetic tape at one point threatened to supplant the normal audio cassette with a better quality alternative. Unfortunately, it never really took off due to licensing issues that kept its price high. However, the small tapes were widely used in the computer industry for back-up copies. You can get DAT drives today that hold up to 8 Gb of data. Audio DAT tapes are not compatible with data drives.

Data

Information. Any series of bits, characters or objects that has meaning. Data is stored and transmitted by computers.

Data entry

This describes a job function where the employee is expected to enter data into a computer. Typically, the only technical skill you need for such jobs is typing. Some people use data entry positions to springboard into low-end technical support and head towards more technical jobs.

Data type

This refers to the type of data that is being used in a computer program. Different types of data take up different amounts of space. Some common data types are integer, float (for floating point numbers) or strings (for a text string). If a procedure is expecting one data type and it gets another, you usually get an error message or a crash.

Database

An ordered set of data.

Daughter board

This is a circuit board that plugs into a larger circuit board or motherboard. Often, processors are contained on daughter boards, along with cache memory. For example, Intel Pentium II processor ships on a daughter board that plugs into slot 1 on the motherboard.

Daylight saving

New BIOS versions can change the time on the computer clock automatically. The computer knows the difference between summer time and winter time. Although the date of the changeover is different in the USA and in the UK, this function will still work.

DCI

Intel and Microsoft have developed the uniform *Display Control Interface* for accelerating video applications and games under Windows 3.1 x. (DirectDraw).

DDC

Abbreviation for *Display Data Channel*. Information is replaced by these standardised "channels" between monitor and graphics card. This Plug & Play function allows energy-saving measures, as well as offering support.

Default

Ths is the fallback value. If no other setting is specified, the default value will be used. If you install a program, it generally installs with the default settings, and you can customise it afterwards with your preferences.

Defrag

This is slang for the act of defragmenting a hard drive. See defragment.

Defragment

When you defragment a hard drive, you use a software utility to arrange the order of your files so that each file is represented in a physically continuous segment. Defragmentation can improve your hard drive performance, because it can read any particular file in a continuous stream, instead of jumping here and there around a hard drive to locate each fragment.

Degaussing

Latest monitors often have a *Degauss* key. This key can demagnetise the cathode ray tube. If it is too magnetised, you may occasionally experience colour shifts.

Device driver

This is synonymous with the term "driver". It is a piece of software that tells an operating system how to communicate with a device.

Dhrystone

A special benchmark test that checks the performance of the processor. This test shows how many times the CPU can execute small programs (Dhrystones) within one second.

Digital

Digital implies a value represented by a group of discrete steps. Some claim that digital representations of images and sound are more accurate; others that the translation of analog sounds and pictures into digital representations cause a loss in realism. The bonus to digital reproduction is that, if done well enough and designed to correct errors, digital reproduction can sound good over a long period of time. Records and tapes are analog, CDs are digital. Play a CD a million times, and it should sound the same. Play a record a million times, and it will degrade due to the weight of the stylus and the inherent friction involved in analog systems.

DIP

Abbreviation for *Dual Inline Package*. A DIP system unit describes two row chip construction, which means the pins are on two rows. SIP (Single Inline Package) stands for one row pins.

DIP switch

This is one or more switches that are housed in a rectangular box on a circuit board. The switches are binary in nature, either on or off for each switch. Dip switches were more common on ISA cards, and are often used in place of groups of jumpers. You can adjust the switch, for example on your printer or on the motherboard, usually by inserting a pointed object.

DirectDraw

Microsoft has developed the DirectDraw standard primarily to accelerate games and graphics applications under Windows 95/98. To be able to use this, the appropriate driver must be installed for the graphics card.

DMA

Abbreviation for *Direct Memory Access*. At the start of the DMA process, data streams are initiated by the processor, then continued by the DMA controller, between the peripherals and the working memory. The DMA provides relief to the processor and also allows a much faster data transmission. PCs have DMA channels that allow certain devices to directly access memory in order to speed up processes.

Domain

This term describes the Internet's addressing scheme, and also a security construct in Windows NT. For the Internet, domains are represented by domain names such as Geek.com or UGeek.org. These domains are mapped to TCP/IP addresses by DNS servers so that browsers can find Web sites.

Domain Name Service (DNS)

This service maps TCP/IP numbers such as 123.12.4.245 to a more easily remembered name, such as www.ugeek.co.uk. In this way, when you type www.ugeek.co.uk into your browser, it goes out to the DNS server you specified when you installed dial-up networking (or TCP/IP services) and asks for a matching TCP/IP address. If it finds a DNS entry for the name you typed in, you will see the site you have requested. If not, it lets you know. Every domain name on the Web has a corresponding TCP/IP address that maps to the Web site. When you set up a site, your ISP adds a DNS entry to their DNS servers. This entry is replicated across the Internet in a matter of hours, and, once fully replicated, you can reach your Web site from any Internet connection in the world.

Dongle

This is the slang term an for external hardware device with some memory inside it, which attaches to your computer and dangles off it (hence the name dongle). It is a copy-safe device. It is mostly used on the parallel port and instructs the computer to select that interface. A dongle usually contains an individual code. This code is questioned by the corresponding program. If no dongle is available, the program may refuse to run, or run with limited features. When a software program is dongle-protected, it is not possible to copy it. Often, companies that sell expensive software packages use dongles as proof that a computer actually has a licence to use the software.

DOS

Abbreviation for *Disk Operating System.* This OS is what got it all started for PCs. It was produced by Microsoft (MS-DOS) and was a 16-bit operating system, designed to run on 16-bit chips and then on 32-bit chips. The DOS describes the operating system responsible for cooperation between the single hardware components and the software. Today, you can find a similar command line interface in all Windows products for quick and easy mouseless file manipulation.

Double-speed disk drive

A CD-ROM drive with double speed works with a data transfer rate of approximately 300 kbytes/s. (see also Quadspeed).

DPI

Abbreviation for *dots per inch.* Most often, this term is used to describe printer resolution. If a printer is said to print at 300 dpi, it will be capable of printing 300 dots horizontally and 300 dots vertically over a square inch. Therefore, if you have a printer with a higher dpi value, you should have a cleaner image. Besides printers, dpi is often discussed when referring to flat panel displays. As flat panel technology increases, you get a higher dpi value, and therefore can display a larger image in a smaller space, without losing any detail. The goal, in both printers and displays, is to keep dpi values high enough so that the user gets a high-quality image and cannot see the individual dots (or pixels) that make up the image.

DPMI

Abbreviation for *DOS Protected Mode Interface.* This software interface standardised by Microsoft moves programs from safe mode, by switching over the processor to 4 Mbyte memories.

DPMS monitor

Abbreviation for *Display Power Management Signalling.* The graphics card is aware of and supports the corresponding energy consumption of a DPMS monitor and can make any necessary adjustments to save energy.

DRAM

Dynamic RAM memory. This is the most common form of computer memory. It needs to be continually refreshed in order to properly hold data, thus it is called "dynamic". DRAM chips situated in the PC must usually be refreshed every 15 microseconds.

Driver

A driver is software that works to communicate between an operating system and a peripheral. Think of it as a translator. If you use a poor driver, your OS won't understand your video card and may become unstable and crash. Hardware manufacturers constantly update drivers to make them faster and more stable.

DSL

Stands for *Digital Subscriber Line.* This is a form of high-speed Internet access currently competing with cable modems. DSL works over standard phone lines.

DSP

Abbreviation for *Digital Signal Processor.* A DSP is a microprocessor designed to work with analog signals such as video or audio, that have been digitally encoded. The DSP then takes these digital representations and performs operations on them. DPS are used in video, sound and modem technology. Intel's MMX instruction set is an attempt to make the Pentium processor line capable of DSDP operations.

Dual ported

Dual ported memory chips have two separate bus versions. They can be described and selected simultaneously. This technology finds its application primarily in memory for high-quality graphics cards. See also VRAM, WRAM.

Duplex

This is a telecommunications term that describes part of the communications between a local modem and a remote computer. In full duplex mode, the remote computer is set up to return the characters that are sent to it, so that they can be displayed on your screen. In half duplex mode, the remote computer does not return the characters sent to it.

DVD

Abbreviation for *Digital Video Disk*. Much like a CD-ROM, except that it stores up to 12 times as much data and is rewriteable. Although not everybody in the industry seems to be convinced by DVDs, the fact is that this is the successor to CD-ROM technology. It is the same size as a CD, but holds between 4.7 and 18 Gb of data. The first wave of DVD drives are read-only devices, but future versions will work with rewriteable media. In the consumer market, these drives are expected to replace VCRs and Laserdisc players.

Dynamic Link Library (DLL)

This is a library of procedures that programs can call with input. The DLL produces output related to that input.

ECC

Abbreviation for *Error Checking and Correcting*. Generally refers to memory chips, or motherboards, that support this type of behaviour in full-parity memory chips. ECC memory uses some extra memory on the memory chips for parity information and checks to see whether a memory error has occurred. If a minor error occurs, the ECC logic will handle it. With full-parity memory (one step below ECC), you will be alerted of a memory error and your system will stop. With non-parity memory, you will experience random results, usually crashing and possible data corruption. Because ECC is expensive, it is only used in safety-critical areas.

EEPROM

Stands for *Electronically Erasable PROM*. Not as fast as RAM, but maintains data through power loss. Very similar to flash memory, except EEPROM is written in one byte at a time and flash memory is used in blocks. See PROM.

EIDE

The *Enhanced IDE* interface is an expansion of the normal IDE standard, as it allows for two IDE channels that can each support two devices, so it would support up to four hard disks, instead of two. Unlike the capacity of the IDE system which is limited to 504 Mb, the enhanced standard can handle up to 7.8 Gb. The E-IDE standard is fully compatible with IDE equipment.

EISA

Abbreviation for *Extended ISA*. 16-bit ISA was extended to 32-bits and was renamed EISA. It is generally used only in server machines, and it never caught on because of VL-Bus and PCI. It is better than PCI because you can have a large number of EISA slots in one machine without any complex wiring. VL-Bus and PCI generally support fewer than four slots, and that can be a problem if you want to install seven network adapters and five RAID cards. EISA makes this possible.

Email

This stands for electronic mail. It is a service provided over the Internet that allows you to send information to another person or list of people.

EMM

Abbreviation for *Expanded Memory Manager*. MS-DOS contained a program managed in accordance with EMS specifications and this makes it possible to use an extended main memory.

Emoticons

These are groups of text characters that, when viewed sideways, look like facial expressions. For example, the most common one is the happy face :-) which is a colon, a hyphen and a close parenthesis. There are many more, such as ;-) to represent a wink or :-p that looks like you are sticking your tongue out. The purpose of emoticons is to convey a feeling in a text-based message that may or may not be obvious to the reader. They are typically used in informal communications.

Emulator

This is usually a program that performs the same operation as another program, or a piece of hardware. For example, there are programs that allow a PC to act like a Commodore 64, a Nintendo or even a MacIntosh. These emulators are often developed by talented programmers just to prove that something can be done.

Environment

Normally, this is your surroundings. In your computer, think of it as your computer's surroundings.

EPP

Abbreviation for *Enhanced Parallel Port*. It is an enhanced version of the parallel port specification for PCs. It makes data transmission twenty times faster. The great advantage of EPP technology is that it is fully compatible with earlier equipment, therefore can work with old printers as well. Nowadays, most parallel ports support EPP mode, and EPP mode should be used for maximum performance when frequent bidirectional communications are necessary through the parallel port.

EPROM

Stands for *Erasable Programmable Read Only Memory*, read only memory that retains its information until it is exposed to ultraviolet lght. You can often tell a chip is an EPROM by the little window on it.

Ethernet

This is a network topology that is able to send data at 10 Mbits/second. Workstations can exist on the same cable, but only one can communicate at a time. To get by these limitations, switched ethernet and fast ethernet were invented, and can also be combined.

Expansion slot

Refers to any type of slot in a computer where you can plug an expansion card. Generally, it is limited to ISA, EISA, PCI and PCMCIA, but thre are other types and there will be more in future.

Export

When you export data, you take that data from a program, database, or file and save it in another format that is generally easier to manipulate or import into a different program. An example would be selecting data from a database, such as Access or SQL or Oracle, and saving it as text, so that you can use it in a mail-merge. Thus, the exporting frees the mail-merge program from having to understand the complex database format, because it just uses the exported files.

External cache

The second level cache is a back-up for the cache memory on the motherboard.

Extranet

An extranet is an Intranet that extends onto the Internet. Confusing? Yes. Extranets are external extensions of a company's intranet that allow certain people to interact from the Internet. Not all intranets are extranets.

Facsimile (Fax)

Almost always referred to as fax, this is the term for the electronic transmission of printed documents over a telephone line. Usually, transmission occurs between fax machines, but you can also use a computer with a fax modem, or a dedicated fax card. A fax machine will be able to scan documents and transmit them over a phone line to another fax machine. A fax machine can also receive faxes from other machines and print them out.

Fan

This is a device designed to move air by sucking air into one side and pushing it out the other. Fans are a necessary part of most computing devices because microprocessors heat up when run at high frequencies. Fans move the hot air away and allow the microprocessors to be cooled off. Fans are used in power suppplies to keep them cool.

FAQ

Frequently Asked Questions. This is a document that lists the most common questions and answers on a topic, for example a software package.

Fast-ATA

Together with the EIDE bus, Seagate has developed the ATA standard. VL Bus or fast ATA PCI systems transfer data up to 13 Mb/s and need no further hardware. This standard is fully downward compatible with the IDE bus.

Fast-ATA2

This fully downward compatible system is a further development of the ATA standard and can increase data transmission up to 16 Mb/s.

Fast page mode

This increases speed for software administration. This technology, also called FPM, for short, is used in normal DRAMs as main memory.

FAT

Abbreviation for *File Allocation Table*. The FAT manages the way MS-DOS operating system (and now Windows as well) handles files on floppy disks and hard disks. The file allocation table is like a table of contents. It contains an exact entry for every cluster on the hard drive, relating to tits contents. In addition, single clusters in the list have been interlinked with each other. So, if a file extends over several clusters, then the FAT refers to the next cluster. Of course, the file system tries to cover cluster which are next to each other when saving a file. If this is not possible, because of lack of space, then a file may be scattered over the whole disk. This is called "fragmenting". Damage to the FAT can lead to total loss of data, in a worst case scenario. For this reason, DOS always defines a second copy of the FAT.

FAT-32

This is the newest file system creation from Microsoft. It expands on their aging FAT-16 fle system and allows for much larger partitions. FAT-32 was created as a quick fix to the problem of computers shipping with hard drives over 2 Gb. Prior to FAT-32, computer manufacturers had to messily split hard drives into multiple partitions under 2 Gb in size. FAT-32 is faster and works more efficiently, and is used by Windows 95/98.

Fat client

Today's fast PCs are fat clients. They've got lots of memory and big hard drives. They store information and run programs locally off their hard drives. Fat clients usually work in client/server environments, where they leave the servers free to serve. As a rule, fat clients are much more customisable than thin clients.

FCC

Abbreviation for *Federal Communications Commission*. This American authority checks electronic equipment for unwanted emission. The restrictions apply to computers and any digital equipment of class B in accordance with part 15 of the FCC guidelines. Equipment should not cause any damaging interference and must be able to cope with interference without being affected.

Feature connector

This is a connectivity to be found on most higher order graphics cards. It provides additional processing power for additional cards, which must be able to cooperate directly with the graphics card. The first in line is the video card. Unfortunately, these interfaces are not always uniform, so only some cards will work together.

FIFO buffer

Abbreviation for *First In/First Out Buffer*. An area of memory that holds information in the order in which it was received until the computer has time to use it, for example for print output.

File extension

DOS, Windows, and to a lesser extent UNIX and Linux use the last three characters of a filename, after a full stop, to signify what type a file is – such as text, movie, sound and so on. The MacOS has a file system that contains an identifier for file types that is invisible when looking at the filename, and allows you to call files whatever you want without an extension. Examples are .exe (executable file), .bat (batch file), .wav (wave sound file) and .txt (text file).

File format

Applications save files in a certain way. They organise the data in a way that makes sense for the information they are saving. There are many standard file formats, such as GIF and JPG. These are graphical formats and are in common use.

File server

This is any computer that allows other computers to access files stored on its hard drive or other storage media. The file server also controls who can and cannot access these files. Most other types of servers, including database and Web servers, are just glorified file servers. Web servers serve up Web pages, but Web pages are files. Database servers serve up data, but the data is contained in files. However, the distinction is that file servers typically allow access to the files in raw format, such as through a file management program or command, while Web and database servers may not allow that form of access.

File sharing

This describes the access to a file by several programs at the same time. This function is only required in multitasking operating systems, or in a network. Sufficient protection must be ensured to prevent loss of data or files crashing. For example, MS-DOS has the SHARE command.

File Transfer Protocol (FTP)

This is the method of moving files from system to system using TCP/IP.

Firewall

This is a form of Internet security that stands between a private network and the Internet. It is like a wall in that it can prevent unwanted traffic from passing either way. Some firewalls have proxy functions built in. In fact, the distinction between a firewall and a proxy is often blurry. Add in the differences and similarities between a firewall and packet-filtering router, and you've got a very confusing situation. True firewalls support packet-filtering, proprietary application filtering and some proxy functions.

Firewire

A new serial technology that promises to speed data at 200 – 400 Mbps. This standard may eventually replace your serial ports, parallel ports, game ports, USB and maybe even SCSI.

Firmware

This refers to the software that is embedded on to a piece of hardware to control that hardware. Generally, firmware can be upgraded and is placed on an EEPROM. Sometimes, if a new driver for a piece of hardware is released, new firmware will also be released to provide the full functionality or performance of the driver. In other cases, firmware will have some bugs or undesired features, and can be upgraded to work out the problems. Of course, the rest of the hardware cannot be upgraded without replacing pieces of it, so manufacturers try to store as many critical function controls as they can in the firmware, in case they need to change them. For them, it is the difference between recalling a product and simply telling their customers to upgrade the firmware.

First level cache

The *first level cache* on the CPU is usually meant for holding instructions as they are executed.

Flag

A flag is a variable which can be used to represent specific conditions. One can insert, delete or select a flag and also create the specific conditions.

Flash BIOS

The BIOS uses the EEPROM or Flash PROM for storage. This BIOS contains a flash ROM chip that can be updated under certain conditions, but is otherwise static.

Flash PROM

Another name for EEPROM.

Flash ROM

A rewritable ROM that does not lose its information when the power is turned off.

Flat screen

A CRT that is made more flat than a standard tube by using more than one electron gun. It is most useful to professionals who rely on the precision of their monitors. It is also better for the standard user, because a straight line across the monitor looks straight.

Floating point

This refers to a three-part representation of a number that contains a decimal point. The number is represented first by the sign, then the number itself, then the decimal position. Some examples of floating point numbers are 4.23423412, 1234.1234234 and 4.00. Floating point numbers offer a specific amount of precision, often 8-bit, 16-bit, 32-bit or 64-bit. This precision controls how accurately floating point results are represented and calculated during arithmetic operations between floating point numbers. For a simple example, you have a low level of precision and, when you divide 1 by 3, you will get 0.33. With a higher level of precision, you would see that the answer is 0.33333333333, and so forth. Thus, your calculation is inaccurate by 0.003333333333 (which is 0.333333333333 - 0.33). A small inaccuracy such as that may not matter if you are pumping out frame rates on a 3D game, but if you are building an aeroplane's engine, you might want to make sure that your design program handles a proper amount of precision for the job you are doing. When writing software, larger floating point precision takes more space to store, and may be slower depending on which hardware you are running it.

Floptical

Abbreviation for *Floppy Optical*, a flexible visual storage unit. Data is saved magnetically as on a floppy disk. This in addition has a write-reading head which is kept in place by a laser beam. Because of this, the number of possible paths is much higher. Standard floptical disks can save up to 20.8 Mb.

Floppy disk

This is any type of disk medium which is not rigid. Often, it is contained in hard cases, which may lead to confusion in identification. Commonly, the term is used to describe 1.44Mb 3.5" diskettes, but it applies to any medium, such as Zip disks, which are floppy in nature if removed from their casing.

Floppy disk drive

This commonly refers to a 3.5" disk drive that uses 1.44Mb 3.5" diskettes, but the term can also be applied to any drive that uses floppy disk media.

FM

Abbreviation for *Frequency Modulation*. Method for artificially producing real life sounds.

Folder

This is a term used by Microsoft to be synonymous with "directory". Currently, folders tend to be a more graphical interface for managing files than directories used to be.

Font

In current computer language, a font is a specific style of displaying characters (a typeface), such as Arial often scalable to a variety of sizes. This differs from the traditional definition of font, where each style and size was its own font (such as 9 point Arial). A groups of fonts, which includes all the varieties of that specific font, is called a "family".

FPU

Abbreviation for Floating Point Unit. FPU is the name of the mathematical coprocessor designed to handle floating point calculations. It is integral to current processors (later than 486 DX) for a faster execution of such operations. Often, the efficiency of this part of the processor will decide whether a processor is successful or not. Some chips have a weak floating point unit compared to Intel Pentium III processors.

Fragmentation

Fragmentation is a typical problem for FAT file systems. This occurs when a hard drive writes a file in multiple segments (fragments) instead of in a physically contiguous area. A low level of fragmentation means that most files are in one piece and that, if files are fragmented, there are only a few fragments. If the level of fragmentation is high, the disk will have difficulties in retrieving them and will therefore take longer to do so. In the worst cases, parts of a file lie scattered in single clusters around the hard disk. Such incoherent storage can be resolved with tools present in the operating system (in MS-DOS). Defragmentation should be carried out at regular intervals, but especially when you notice that your computer performs at a slower pace than usual.

Frame

This concept is often used in the computer world to describe a section from a large amount of data. "Frame" can also mean an individual picture in a video sequence.

Freeware

This is software that is free for use and does not require a fee to be paid to access its full functionality. See also shareware and open source.

Frequency range

The frequency of data transmission indicates the speed (of the telephone line). A high frequency range makes the simultaneous processing of several signals possible. Fiber optic cables are currently the most efficient transmission medium, with a frequency of approximately 600 Mbit/s.

Front end

This refers to the part of a program or process which the user interfaces with and controls.

Fuzzy logic

This is logic without an absolute true or false. Instead, you have gradients of true and false. This is necessary for solving some problems, especially those involving artificial intelligence.

Game card

The game card or the game port is a 15-pin analog port on a PC, used specifically for game controllers such as a joystick. It also doubles as a MIDI connector. Usually, you will find one on the back of your soundcard.

Gateway

The computer or device which you PC needs to go access your network. A TCP/IP route uses many hops to get from point to point.

GB

Short for Gigabyte, approximately 1 billion bytes.

Gbps

it stands for *Gigabits per second*. This is a rate of data transfer of 1 gigabit of data per second.

GDI

Abbreviation of *Graphics Device Interface*. The GDI is a printer interface provided by Microsoft for the production of graphic output by Windows. Its advantage is that GDI printers are smaller and cheaper. Its disadvantage is that the equipment only works under Windows. The functions are device independent, but you can use them on any graphics card only as long as Windows is installed.

Glitch

This often refers to a bug in a program. Its effects are different from those of a freeze or a crash, and usually cause erroneous or garbage results to be displayed.

GLSI

Abbreviation for *Giant Large Scale Integration*. GLSI describes the integration degree of a chip. Over 1,000,000,000 transistor functions can be put in a chip at this level.

GND

Abbreviation for *Ground*. It means the earthing of a power cable.

Green function

Another name for the environmentally friendly mode.

GS seal

Abbreviation for *checked safety*. A seal with this imprint is on most technical equipment. It means that the equipment was checked for safety by an independent examining institute.

GUI

Abbreviation for *Graphical User Interface*. Unlike systems where users control events by input, a GUI simplifies access to functions. The most essential functions can be accessed intuitively using a mouse. Examples of GUIs are Windows or OS/2.

Hacker

This is someone who seeks to understand computer, phone or other systems strictly for the satisfaction of having that knowledge. Hackers will sometimes do legally questionable things, such as breaking into systems, but they generally will not cause harm once they break in. See also cracker.

Half duplex

The half duplex represents a method of data transmission. Originally, this was a modem communication term, but now refers mainly to network communications which transmit in one direction at a time.

Hard disk

This is the common slang term for a hard drive. It refers to rewriteable media that is not flexible, as opposed to a floppy disk. The hard disk contains multiple hard disk platters.

Hard drive

A device that physically stores data in your computer. much like a floppy disk, but the system is closed and the disks are hard (usually metal, although some glass versions have been developed). The closed system gives the possibility of more precision, so the drive is much faster and can hold much more data.

Hardware

This refers to any physical piece of a computer. For example, the computer itself, a monitor, printer, memory and a video card are all hardware. See also software.

Hayes standard

The company Hayes created the AT standard for modems to be distributed, which ensures high performance quality. All common modems are still defined as Hayes compatible.

Head crash

The head of a hard disk usually moves freely over the magnetic plate. If the head touches the plate even for a short time, it destroys a large part of the data on the magnetic pathway, which is caused by the disturbance. However, a head crash can also be triggered by a single dust particle, since the disk is very close to the head.

Hertz

Frequency is measured in Hertz (Hz) (vibrations per second), named after the German physicist Rudolf Hertz. The speed of a computer processor is measured in megahertzs (MHz). One Hertz means one time per second, so one megahertz means one million times per second.

Hexadecimal

This number system on base 16 is used for a more simple representation of binary numbers. These can be represented as an 8-digit dual number, with a 2-digit hexadecimal number. Such a number is often used for the name of a memory address in computers.

HFS

Abbreviation for *Hierarchical File System*. It compares to the file management system FAT, for example Apple MacIntosh computers work with the HFS method.

Hidden files

Most operating systems create invisible files. These files, which are provided with a specific attribute, are present in the system and therefore can be retrieved, but are not displayed in the file overview. This option offers low-level protection against curious unauthorised users, though it can easily be overun.

High colour

Colour representation is only carried out with a colour depth of 15 to 16 bits true colour. The colour palette contains 32,768 or 65,536 colours. This depth is suffcient for a reasonably faithful representation, thanks to a higher processing speed.

High resolution (HiRes)

This is used to describe a screen resolution which is higher than 800 x 600 pixels.

High Sierra standard

The first definition of a CD-ROM standard. This was then followed by the ISO 9660 standard.

Hit

When a user requests an HTML document on the World Wide Web, the server records that request as a "hit". The problem with measuring "hits" is that some Web servers also count each graphic on the page as a hit. For example, if you look at a page with five images on it, some servers count that as five hits. For this reason, "hits" are a questionable measurement of how popular a Web site actually is.

Home page

A home page is a page on the World Wide Web (WWW) that is the first page of a Web site. Usually, it is called index.html or index.htm. When you go to a Web address, this is the first page your browser looks for.

Host adapter

A SCSI controller is also called a host adapter.

HPFS

Abbreviation for *High Performance File System*. HPFS is the method with which the OS/2 operating system manages its files. It makes storage possible for FAT, which is not possible with standard administration, without any fragmentation. Furthermore, it allows file names to have more than the usual eight characters.

HPGL

Abbreviation for *Hewlett-Packard Graphics Language*. HPGL was developed by Hewlett Packard as a graphics and printer's language. It is vector-oriented and is capable of working to a higher standard, such as for laser printers.

Hub

A central connection point. Standard terminology for a device that connects multiple computers in a network.

Hyperlink

A hyperlink, or link, is part of the HTML language. When you view an HTML document using a browser, it is common practice to display the hyperlink in blue with an underlined font. When you click on a hyperlink, you will jump or link to another area in that document, or a different document.

Hypertext

A text format that allows for links from keywords in a document to other sections of the document or to other documents.

HyperText Markup Language (HTML)

A standard language made for typesetting, currently at version 3.2. It is mainly used for creating documents on the World Wide Web. Included in the language are provisions for including pictures and links to other pages.

Hypertext Preprocessor (PHP)

Created in 1994, this is a versatile embedded scripting language that can be placed into HTML documents and, as long as the Web server supports it, it can be used to generate HTML pages by contacting and accessing a database. PHP code is executed on the server, and offers an alternative to CGI or SSI calls, or the use of Allaire's ColdFusion embedded server-side scripting language.

HyperText Transfer Protocol (HTTP)

The way the data in an HTML document is transferred. It tells the program looking at the data what to use it as. So, a document coming in HTTP is read as an HTML document.

iComp

Abbreviation for *Intel Compare*. Processor comparison test brought in by Intel and used in their own advertising. It provides an overview of products with a view to enhance Intel processors. Since reference values for processors of other manufacturers are not included, no meaningful comparison is actually possible.

Icon

This is a graphic, usually a small one, that represents something, usually a file on the hard drive. Icons can also represent directories, folders, or devices. In a GUI environment, icons represent just about everything.

IDE

Abbreviation for *Integrated Device Electronics*. The IDE standard, also known as AT bus, indicates a fixed disk standard, which is the standard hard drive interface for PCs. You can connect a maximum of two hard drives to an IDE connection or channel. IDE hard drives are cheaper than SCSI drivs, but IDE is generally slower than SCSI and does not support sector remapping.

Import

This refers to the process of pulling data into a program. Normally, it refers to taking a plain text file and pulling it into a database format so that you can work with it using a database program. For example you call a company you need some data from and ask them to send you some data to add to your database. They send the data as a text file and import it into your database. Now, you can run queries on the data in your database program.

Incremental back-up

This is a method of archiving data. Basically, during an incremental back-up, all data that has changed since the last full back-up will be archived. Data that has not changed will not be backed up.

Indeo

Abbreviation for *Intel Video*. A standard for compression of digital audio, introduced by Intel for video data (similar to MPEG II).

Independent Software Vendor (ISV)

This term refers to a software company that creates software to run on a platform or platforms that it doesn't create. For example, Microsoft is not an ISV because it owns its own OS. Often, the term refers to companies that write "valuable" software applications. OS makers will often give them special deals and help them distribute their software if they feel it benefits their OS.

Industry Standard Adapter (ISA)

The 8- and 16-bit original connectors used in PCs. They run at a bus speed of 8 MHz. You can plug ISA expansion cards into an ISA slot modems, and soundcards are ISA due to their low bandwidth requirements.

Information Services (IS)

This term refers to the field of computer technology but has been replaced by the newer and sexier term, IT.

Information Technology (IT)

This term refers to the field of computers and technology, and all related jobs.

Inkjet printer

The next generation of dot matrix printers. It uses a head that sprays tiny droplets of ink on to print material. There are three major benefits to this method: 1) it is quieter than standard dot matrix printers, 2) it is able to make smaller dots, to make print look better, and 3) since the ink is in liquid form, it mixes better when printing in colour.

On the downside, they print more slowly than standard dot matrix printers, and since they do not print by impact, they cannot print carbon copies.

Input

Anything entered into a computer or system. This includes keystrokes, mouse movement and talking into a microphone.

Input/Output (I/O)

This abbreviation refers to any operation in a computer where data is transfered in or out of the computer. I/O may seem like a vague concept, but it refers to the basic throughput power of a computer.

Integrated circuit (IC)

This refers to a combination of multiple circuits into a single integrated device. Today, the common microprocessor uses many millions of transistors, with each transistor counting as a single circuit.

Integrated Development Environment (IDE)

This term refers to a development environment that is integrated into an application. For example many office suite programs feature a macro language that can be expanded by using a common programming language. Specifically, Microsoft Office allows development in Visual Basic for Applications inside of its Office products. Thus, the development environment is integrated into the applications.

Interface

An interface is a hardware or software component which looks after the exchange of information between different components (API). To be able to attach a printer to the PC, data must be distributed in standardised form by the computer. This is the task of the appropriate interface.

Interlaced

Interlaced means that the graphic data is split (usually in two parts) and is displayed alternately one half and one half. So, for video output, if you have 480 pixels rows shown vertically, an interlaced image will show 240 pixels rows (every other pixel row) at once. It will alternate fast enough that the image looks whole and complete. This is a trick used to increase resolution. However, it makes text and small shapes shimmer in a disturbing way. Today's systems also have a non-interlaced mode.

Internet

The global network of computers constantly connected to each other using standardised communications protocols, specifically TCP/IP.

Internet Protocol (IP)

This is a connectionless comunications protocol that forms part of the basis for the TCP/IP protocol suite. It is a fast protocol, but it has no mechanism for sequencing or error conditions. Error packets are simply lost.

Internet Service Provider (ISP)

An ISP provides Internet access to people or corporations. ISPs generally have pools of modems awaiting dial-up connections. Smaller ISPs buy bandwidth from larger ISPs. There are two basic ways of connecting: one is to get a PPP or SLIP account; the other is to get a UNIX shell account.

Interrupt request (IRQ)

This is a gateway for devices to request time for the processor to do their job. For instance, every time you hit a key on your keyboard, an interrupt is generated on the keyboard IRQ. This is generally only a concern for PC users. A PC bus only has a restricted number of fifteen IRQ addresses.

Intranet

Local network of computers using TCP/IP as the standard communications protocol. Usualy an intranet features some sort of HTML content that you can use a browser to look at. Think of it as a mini, private Internet.

I/O map

Abbreviation for *Input/Output map*. This is responsible for the mapping of data functions.

IOS

Abbreviation for *Input Output System*. The IOS is part of the operating system which is responsible for functions. This takes care of the IO.SYS component for MS-DOS.

ISA bus

Abbreviation for *Industry Standard Architecture*. The ISA bus is a standardised PC bus, which was originally developed in 1987 by IBM. This 16-bit bus system has contributed to the success of the PC, for it has assured high hardware compatibility. The 32-bit bus has made further PCI development possible.

ISDN

Abbreviation for *Integrated Services Digital Network*. This is a digital line often used to connect to the Internet. The ISDN integrates digital transmission of data and language. It generally comes in two forms: one is the 56 Kbps version, which in practice only uses half of the ISDN line's bandwith; the other is the 128 Kbps version, which uses both the 56 Kbps channels on the line. However, it still only uses 112 Kbps, as the other 16 Kbps are an 8 Kbps back-channel of each line. Connection to the PC is carried out with a simple and inexpensive ISDN modem.

ISO

Abbreviation for *International Standards Organisation*. This committee is responsible for creating standards for everything, from cleanliness to file formats. Approximately 90 countries currently belong to this organisation.

ISO 9660

The ISO 9660 is an international standard which regulates file formats on CD-ROMs. This regulates data, lists and numbers, as well as file names.

Iterative

This is a programming term. It refers to a process that can be described by a fixed number of variables and the set of rules that describes what happens to those variables to achieve the next step of the process. If the process is interrupted, it can be continued if you state all the variables. Contrast this to a recursive process. An iteration is a single step.

Java

This is a platform-independent programing language designed by JavaSoft. Java is like C++, but includes some restrictions. Java mainly runs on Web browsers at the moment, but it can also run on operating systems or in a Java virtual machine.

Javascript

A simple scripting language designed by Netscape to be embedded into HTML documents. It is unrelated to Java.

JAZ drive

The JAZ drive is a development of the Zip drive. It is a type of removable disk drive. The single media offers a capacity of 1 Gb or even 2 Gb. The speed is also higher than that of a Zip drive.

JPEG

Abbreviation for *Joint Photographic Expert Group*. The JPEG standard is a method of storing digital images. It was specifically made for storing more than 256 colour images. The method achieves a very high compression rate (better than GIF, which is designed to store images of 256 colours or less). Quality loss is relatively low. You can also set the amount of compression you would like for the graphic; however, the higher the compression, the less quality the picture has. On the down side, even at 100% quality (or zero compression), the graphic is not perfect. It is not suitable for professional printing purposes, and you cannot bring the image back to its original condition. It should be used as a reduction method, rather than a compression method. JEPD files use the extension .jpg.

Jumper

A jumper fits on to metal connectors. It provides an electrical connection between two wires to enable a semi-permanent hardware configuration. The Plug & Play initiative was designed to eliminate jumpers, but so far this has not worked out very well. Most add-in cards, hard drives and motherboards still have many jumpers that they can utilise to make devices act in different ways.

Kernel

This is the guts of any operating system. The kernel is loaded into the main memory and stays there, while other pieces of the OS are loaded in and out of memory.

Keyboard

The main input device on PCs, it consists of all the letters in the alphabet and numbers 0 through to 9. Usually, especially on computer keyboards, there are extra keys such as cursor keys and function keys.

Keylock

The keyswitch on the PC system unit cover can separate the keyboard from the computer to prevent unauthorised access.

Keyword

This is a term used to describe content on a Web page so that search engines can properly index the page. It is possible to put up keywords that do not apply to a particular page to get more traffic, but that is discouraged by most search engines and could result in having all of your Web pages go unlisted.

Kilobit

1024 bits (2^10 bits)

Kilobits per second (Kbps)

A measure of data transfer. A 14.4 Kbps modem transfers data at about 1.8 Kilobytes per second or about 100 Kb per minute.

Kilobyte

A kilobyte corresponds to 1,024 bytes.

KVM switch (Keyboard Video Mouse switch)

This is a switch that connects two or more computers to the same keyboard, mouse and monitor. The KVM switch fools each computer into thinking that they are actively connected to a separate keyboard, mouse and monitor. There is some mechanism (a button and or keyboard command) on a KVM switch to switch between which computer accepts the input of the keyboard and mouse, and displays output to the monitor. Thus, when you move the mouse connected to the switch, your mouse movement is only echoed to the computer which is active at the time. Some KVM switches also accept audio input, so that more then one computer can use the same set of speakers – although not simultaneously.

Landscape

The landscape format is an output format where the output is printed sideways or horizontally on the page.

Laptop

A computer small enough to fit completely on your lap.

Laser printer

A printer that uses a laser to etch out what is to be printed. Toner goes on this etching and then the toner is heated to bond with the print material.

Latency

This is a measure of how long, on average, it takes to get a response from something. This term usually refers to network response speed, and also to storage devices (hard drives, CD-ROM drives etc.).

Leased line

A phone line that can be purchased from the telephone company that is yours only. With the assurance that you are the only one on the line you can work at faster speeds and stay connected 24 hours a day.

Legacy device

This is a type of device or peripheral that is not Plug & Play compatible.

Legacy system

This is any old computer system which continues to work and need support. Often, legacy systems are problematic to upgrade because the people or companies that put them together are not around any more. One example is the year 2000 problem, or millennium bug. Legacy systems are another problem because no one programs in COBOL anymore, and lots of legacy code is written in COBOL.

Library

A library is a file which store complete program functions, which can be used by different programs. It is not always necessary to develop standard routines, since they are already present in a library. Under Windows, such libraries are called "DLL".

Line frequency

The line frequency determines the picture repeating frequency. If the line frequency is aproximately 64 kHz, then the monitor will conform to satisfactory ergonomic standards.

Linux

This is an open source UNIX-like operating system originally developed by Linus Torvalds. Linux is freeware by default, but may be sold for the cost of packaging, bundling and technical support. Companies such as SuSe, Red Hat and Caldera sell Linux packages. However, they also allow you to download them for free. Linux was first developed for x86 computers, but now runs on a wide variety of platforms.

Liquid Crystal Display panel (LCD panel)

This is a slab of specially treated glass which is used to sandwich liquid crystal. You can then send electricity through the treated glass to change the phase of the liquid, which then changes colour. This is a low power way of displaying images.

Local Area Network (LAN)

A small isolated network at one office location. Most office computers are connected to a LAN, but may also be connected to the Internet, or a WAN.

Log

This is a record of events. It is also an abbreviation for logarithm, which is a mathematical operation.

Log file

This is a file that records events. Many programs produce log files. Often, tech support will ask you to look at a log file to determine what is happening when problems occur. Log files usually record more system events than are shown to the user, such as pieces of Windows 95 starting. You may not want to see each part of Windows 95 start, but it is good to have a log of it if something goes wrong. Often, log files will have the extension "log".

LOL

On-line speak for "Laughing Out Loud".

Long File Name (LFN)

Since DOS only allows eight letters then a full stop then three more letters, there is a separate distinction for it. Almost all other file systems allow for longer names. With Windows 95 now so prevalent, long file names have become commonplace. They can be 255 characters long, contain spaces or even periods. The only real restriction is no backslashes.

LPT

Abbreviation for *Line Printer*. The LPT interface describes the interface between the operating system for the printer and the parallel interface.

Macro

This usually refers to a means of executing a group of instructions within a program. Many programs offer the capability to put together macros so that you do not have to do the same group of repetitive instructions one by one. You can program the macro to do any number of instructions. Many programs allow you to extend the simple macro languages that they provide with other, more complex, programming languages.

Mainboard

Another name for motherboard.

Mainframe

Basically, a large and powerful computer designed to be very fault-tolerant. Historically, mainframes with lots of memory and disk space are hooked to dumb terminals that can be used to access data on the mainframe, but can do nothing without the mainframe.

Mapping

The assignment of logical sectors is defined by mapping to the physical sectors of software. Mapping is necessary for compatibility reasons.

MCI

Abbreviation for *Media Control Interface*. The MCI is a software interface defined by Microsoft for Windows, for the use of multimedia hardware components (such as a soundcard).

Megabit

This is roughly one million bits.

Megabits per second (Mbps)

This is a measure of throughput roughly in millions of bits per second. More exactly, that is 1,048,576 bits per second.

Megabyte (Mb)

A Megabyte is roughly one million bytes. This is exactly 1,048,576 bytes (that is 1024 x 1024). The size of hard disks is measured in Mb.

Memory

Chips in a computer that remember data. Also commonly referred to as RAM.

MF2

Abbreviation for *MultiFunction keyboard*. MF2 keyboards have 105 keys and three control lights for a common PC keyboard standard.

MFM

Abbreviation for *Modified Frequency Modulation*. This method is only used by data stored on floppy disks. It was also important on earlier fixed disks.

MIDI

Abbreviation for *Musical Instrument Digital Interface*. The MIDI standard connects electronic musical instruments and sound mixers to the computer. To connect them to your computer, you need a MIDI cable and a MIDI port. The MIDI port usually doubles as a game controller port on your soundcard. It can be applied to different instruments.

MIPS

Abbreviation for *Million of Instructions Per Second*. This measurement unit is used to describe the speed of the CPU.

Mirroring

This can refer to many things in the land of technology. Most often, it is used to describe a method of redundancy where data is mirrored across two devices, whether they are physically separate devices or not.

Modem

Abbreviation for *Modulator/Demodulator.* A modem changes data from analog into digital information over the telephone line (and vice versa). It is used to send data transmission. The speed of current modems reaches 56 kbps .

Moire

An interference pattern that is created when small dots are placed in a tight pattern.

Monitor

A device for viewing the output from a computer.

Motherboard

The mainboard, also called the motherboard, is the central area of a computer. It is the circuit board that your CPU, IO chips and all the peripheral cards plug into.

Mouse

A pointing device that uses a roller ball on the bottom to detect motion.

MP3 (MPEG-1 Audio Layer 3)

This is a compression standard for music. It enables you to fit over 100 full length songs on a single CD with almost no loss of quality. You can find MP3 players and MP3 files on the Web - you just have to look. The music industry is unhappy about MP3 files being distributed and has shut down some sites that distribute them.

MPC

Abbreviation for *Multimedia Personal Computer.* This standard fixed by the computer industry describes a minimum requirement for multimedia computers. For example, since 1993, MPC-Level 2 has required a graphics card processor for a 16-bit soundcard and 8 Mb of main memory and an appropriate CD-ROM drive.

MPEG

Abbreviation for *Motion Pictures Expert Group*. This group of experts has developed a very efficient standard for compression of images and sound. There are special expansion boards which can use the current MPEG 2 method and compression of videos for PCs.

MPR

This is a standard for levels of electromagnetic field emissions by computer monitors, published by the Swedish National Board for Measurement and Testing. Monitors must have electromagnetic field emissions below specified levels, to meet MPR standards.

MTBF

Abbreviation for *Mean Time Between Failure*. This is the time normally given in hours that predicts the failure of a device. The larger the number, the better. CD-ROM drives have a MTBF of 10,000 hours.

Multi I/O cards

IDE controller for hard disks and floppy drives as well as further I/O devices contain interfaces (serial and parallel) which can operate simultaneous connections.

Multifrequency monitor

Monitors which can adapt to different frequencies and screen resolutions, unlike automatic frequency monitors. Multifrequency monitors can handle multinational frequencies, as opposed to normal monitors that can only work with a specific frequency and resolution.

Multiscan monitor

Another name for *Multifrequency Monitor*.

Multisession CD-ROMs

If a writeable CD-ROM or photo CD is not full after the first writing event (session), it can be filled in further sessions. Every writing event is completed with a special feature. These multisessions CDs may only be read by special drives.

Multisync

"Multisync" is a trademark of NEC and it applies to multifrequency monitors. Since NEC is one of the first manufacturers of such monitors, this term is currently synonymous with multifrequency.

Multitasking

This is the ability of an operating system to run two or more tasks at once. With one processor, you will not have more than one task using the processor at a given moment in time, but the tasks will be scheduled so that they can all appear to be running at the same time and do not interfere with each other. A task can be a program (i.e. the Windows Calculator), or an instance of a program (such as opening the Windows Calculator multiple times).

Nanosecond

This is one billionth of a second. Used most often to measure the speed of memory.

Narrow SCSI

This is the original form of SCSI, using 50 pins, and transmitting data at 5MBps. See also Wide SCSI. Drives and adapters that support narrow SCSI usually have an "N" in the part number.

Natural keyboard

The ergonomic keyboard developed by Microsoft. It is easy to take apart and the two halves stand close to each other at an angle.

Netiquette (Internet etiquette)

There is an informal code of conduct that most people follow on the Internet. Usually, people who break the code then receive flame emails. Netiquette no-no's include not sending email in ALL CAPS or with too many !!!!!'s and not asking repetitive questions in forums which have FAQs posted. Sending spam is also a violation of netiquette. You are not obligated to follow proper netiquette, but you may have an easier time communicating with others over the Internet if you do.

Network

This refers to a group of interconnected computers. The computers must be capable of transferring data to form a true network.

Normalise

This is a verb used to describe what can be done to data to remove useless or extraneous entries. For example, if you set up a survey with choices A, B and No Response and then wanted to list the percentage of respondents who picked A or B, you could cut out the no responses and thus normalise the data. Another example would be changing the volume of an MP3 file by analysing the file for the loudest part, and then setting the loudness of the entire file to a percentage of that. That way, if you are putting together a file from many sources, you get a more uniform volume.

Notebook computer

A computer the size of a notebook. Usually smaller and lighter than a laptop.

NTFS

The file system of Windows NT, called "New Technology File System". It can work with FAT, but not with FAT 32. NTFS also has standard password protection and data encryption facilities.

Null modem cable

This is a cable that connects two computers together via the serial port and allows them to communicate. Some hardware manufacturers of network hardware, such as hubs and routers, include serial ports for programming their devices. You use a null modem cable to communicate with these devices. It is basically a modem cable with some reversed connections.

Object

Objects can refer to the objects in object-oriented programming or the objects in OLE (Object Linking and Embedding). In OLE, an object is a piece of a document, a graphic, or a multimedia file. In object-oriented programming, an object can be a spell checker or a piece of a graphics program used to draw squares or circles. See OLE.

OCR

Abbreviation for *Optical Character Recognition*. It can recognise letters and translate printed characters into a text file.

OEM version

Abbreviation for *Original Equipment Manufacturer.* Other manufacturers use software and hardware components taken from an OEM manufacturer to produce their own equipment. The problem is that software manufacturers do not offer support or updates to OEM versions. The OEM supplier often produces its own manuals. Of course, this software is substantially cheaper.

OLE

Abbreviation for *Object Linking and Embedding*. The OLE method was developed by Microsoft to allow exchange of data between different Windows applications. See Object.

On board

Components that are integrated directly on the motherboard are referred to as being on board. For example, the hard disks controller and the interfaces controller are often present on modern boards. This is an advantage because these components have been built in a way that matches the motherboard.

Open source

This is software that can be freely distributed, and must be distributed along with its source code. Thus, the source can be changed easily and the program can be altered to fix bugs or add features. Depending on the open source licence, you may be unable to redistribute altered code, or charge money for the distribution of the software. Some popular examples of open source software are Linux and Netscape Communicator version 5.

OPL

The OPL chip is produced by Yamaha and used on soundcards to reproduce sound. The OPL 3 version works on Sound Blaster cards. The OPL chip produced by Adlib was the first to be used on soundcards. The current OPL 4 chip is now capable of handling sounds from a library of digitised tones.

OS

Abbreviation for the *operating system* of a computer (such as MS-DOS, Windows or OS/2).

OS2

This is an operating system originally developed by Microsoft and IBM. Microsoft dropped out of the project to concentrate on their Windows operating systems. IBM continued to develop OS/2 and to this day there are still many OS/2 users out there. OS/2 is a full 32-bit operating system.

OSD

Abbreviation for *On Screen Display*. Provides the setting for picture options, usually with a menu displayed on current monitors.

Output

Anything that comes out of a computer or system.

Overdrive

The overdrive processors of Intel represent an upgraded technology which is simpler to use. The overdrive processor is either plugged into a ZIF socket or simply replaces the old processor on motherboards. It improves performance from between 40% and 200%. Overdrive technology was offered by Intel starting with the 486 generation.

Overflow

When there is more information than can be handled. Often used to describe the production of a number larger than a variable can handle. For instance, if you are expecting 10 digits but receive 11.

P54C

This is the official part number for the Pentium processor from Intel.

P55C

This is the official part number for the Pentium processor with MMX technology from Intel.

Packet

A collection of information, often used to refer to the chunks of information sent over computer networks.

Page technology

Paging is a method for organising a computer's memory. Memory is organised in pages, which are subdivided into lines and columns, in order to be dealt with more easily. For example, a database program may deal with 2Kb pages of memory. If it needs 2.1 Kb of space to store some data, it will use two pages, or 4 Kb of data, since you cannot split pages up into smaller groupings of memory.

Parallel interface

The parallel interface (or LPT port) is a connection for external pieces of equipment such as printers, scanners and storage. It is a 25-pin interface found on most PCs. The parallel port can transfer data at a maximum speed of 512 Kbps.

Parity

The horizontal sum of one byte which is called parity can be either zero or one. It is used to check faults in storage or data transmission.

Parity memory

This can be thought of a PC memory's summary. The parity does not exactly have a copy of the original memory, but rather enough information to verify the integrity of the original.

Partition

This is a section of a hard drive. You must create at least one partition to begin using a new hard drive. You can create multiple partitions and keep chunks of your data separate. It is also possible to install multiple OSs on these multiple partitions. Usually, there is just one OS per partition, but some OSs, like Windows 95 and Windows NT, are designed to run together in the same partition.

Partitioning

You can partition your hard drive by breaking it up into one or more pieces or "partitions."

Path

This refers to the group of directories that are searched every time a command is entered in a command line, if that command is not found in the current working directory. You can specify additional directories to be added to the path.

PC card (early PCMCIA)

Abbreviation for *Personal Computer Memory Card International Association*. The PCMCIA indicates a standard of cards in credit card format. More than 300 hardware and software companies use this PC card architecture for network adapters, modems, hard disks and RAM memory.

PCI bus

The PCI bus is a Local bus system developed by Intel. It is a more efficient alternative to the VESA-Local bus system and has become established very quickly with newer systems, because older VESA technology has limitations for modern Pentium systems. The PCI standard is currently at version 2.0 (version 2.1 is in preparation) and is mainly used for expansion boards such as hard disk controllers or video cards. PCI has provisions for a Plug & Play BIOS. The maximum data throughput rate is 132 Mbps with PCI.

PCL

Abbreviation for *Printer Control Language*. The PCL is a page description language developed by Hewlett-Packard. In the current version, PCL 5, this language includes the HPGL standard for vector graphics. Most current laser printers work with the PCL 5 standard. It is preferred to PostScript in the semiprofessional area, for cost reasons.

Performance

Performance describes the efficiency and speed of PC systems or of individual components.

Peripheral

Any device that is not part of the motherboard, aside from memory and the CPU. For example, video card, soundcard, modem.

PGA

Abbreviation for *Pin Grid Array*. The PGA is a form of chip with a group of pins in concentric rectangles, designed to fit into a PGA slot. Current Intel processors are equipped with it. x86 compatible chips that fit into socket 7, socket 370 and Super 7 are designed in this format.

Photo CD

The photo CD is a special method developed by Kodak to save photographs digitally. Normal negative films are digitised and burned for the customer on to a CD. Approximately 50 pictures fit on a CD in three various formats. It comes with special software that you can load on to your PC, so that the pictures can be viewed and edited. They can be also be read with any standard CD-ROM drive.

Picture repeating frequency

The *picture repeating frequency* gives the number of lines per second. At low resolution, the human eye reacts badly. Monitors with 72 Hz resolutions or over are ergonomically sound. Cheap standard monitors usually work with lower frequencies, around 60 Hz.

Pipelined burst cache

This is a form of second level cache which uses pipelining to speed data access by being able to feed data to the CPU at the same time as it pulls data from memory. The burst mode also allows the cache to fetch additional data from the main memory before the CPU requests it. Data can be transmitted faster, because the complete memory address does not need to be used in this mode. It only needs the initial address and the number of data items. Several burst accesses can be started simultaneously with the pipelined burst cache.

Pipelining

Pipelining is the technique of processing multiple parts of an instruction at the same time. It applies to processors, whereby the elements are available and can work simultaneously for processing purposes.

Pixel

Abbreviation for *Picture and Element.* A pixel is the smallest representable unit of a picture at a particular resolution (a microdot). Screen size is often referred to in pixels, for example 800 x 600. This means that the screen is 800 pixels across and 600 pixels high.

Platform

This is a means of generically grouping like computers. Macintosh computers are a platform; so are PCs running DOS. It is not very specific, and multiplatform support can mean many things. If someone says to you "this application supports multiple platforms," ask them which ones they are talking about.

Platinum

Platinum is a physical disk on which electronic-components are soldered. Single components are added to electricity-conducting platinum using a chemical etching process. The main platinum presence is in the motherboard, but all other cards also have platinum.

Plug & Play (PNP)

This is a standard that was supposed to make adding peripherals to your computer as easy as plugging them in and using them. Its biggest contribution, apart from headaches, is the removal of jumpers from many devices.

Point of Presence (POP)

This is a local telephone number through which you can access your ISP. The largest national ISPs have POPs all over the country so that you can connect to the Internet for the price of a local call and not have to dial a long-distance number.

Point to Point Protocol (PPTP)

The mode of transport used to connect a computer to the Internet via a dial-up adapter.

Pointer

Think of a pointer as an address. The address can point to just about anything, including another pointer. Ultimately, if you follow the trail of pointers, you'll probably find some data. Pointers are most often used to point to data. The purpose of pointers is so that when you are programming, you can pass around a small address that points to some data, instead of passing the actual data around. Pointers can also refer to the icon on the screen that you move around with a mouse or other pointing device. In a GUI environment, you need a pointer to point to things so that you can select them.

Portable computer

Technically, any computer that is self-contained to allow easy moving. Most often refers to a computer that can work away from an outlet.

Portable Document Format (PDF)

This is a format originally developed by Adobe. Adobe makes a freeware Adobe Acrobat Reader that is available for a variety of platforms. Thus, using a variety of operating systems, you can download and read a PDF document very easily. In addition, the PDF format strives for easy printing, viewing and compact storage. On PCs, .pdf is the file extension for this type of file.

POST

Abbreviation for *Power-On Self Test*. POST is the self-diagnostic test routine that the BIOS carries out after switching on. The signals (tone signals) are transmitted in POST codes.

PostScript

Postscript is a standard language developed for telling printers how to print text and graphics. PostScript printers are used primarily for a high quality output by professionals operating in the graphics industry. Most Macs use PostScript to print, while PCs normally default to PCL.

PQFP

Abbreviation for *Plastic Quad Flat Pack*. The PQFP is used by Intel for its processors. It is a synthetic material system unit cover and is provided with 196 pin contacts on the outside.

Practical Extraction and Report Language (PERL)

Created by system admin Larry Wall in the mid 1980s, this programming language was originally intended to fill a gap and help out with administration tasks. From those meagre beginnings, PERL has become a programming language often associated with the Web and UNIX. PERL is the most common programming language used to program CGI scripts. It is a very powerful language that can be used to easily modify large amounts of text files with hardly any programming required.

Print screen

This button prints whatever is on your screen. If you are using DOS, or in your BIOS, and have a printer set up, the Print Screen button should do just that. In Windows OSs, hitting the Print Screen button will copy your current desktop, so that you can paste it into a graphics program, or a program that will support graphics, such as many word processors today. Additionally, hitting Alt-Print Screen will copy just the active window.

Printer

This is any device that makes an impression on media, usually paper, and is connected to a computer. The invention of the computer with printer has made the typewriter obsolete. The simplest printers are located in cash registers printing out receipts, while more advanced printers are capable of magazine quality photo images. Printers come in several types, including daisy-wheel, dot matrix, inkjet and laser printers.

PRN

PRN (Printer) is the default printer interface in the MS-DOS operating system, and is usually described as LPT1.

Processor clone

Intel processors have gained worldwide recognition as a standard for computer CPUs and are copied by other companies.

Processor upgrade

Motherboards can exchange the CPU for a more efficient processor at a later stage. It is easy to do and increases performance.

PROM

Abbreviation for *Programmable Read Only Memory*. This is a memory device. Once data is written to a PROM it is there forever, unlike an EPROM.

Protected mode

The main memory can work in protected mode. Data from various programs in the memory are protected from mutual access. The 386 processor is 32 bits, which corresponds to a memory of 4 Gb.

Proxy

This is commonly a form of Internet security. You can use a proxy or proxy server to pass data between your internal network and the Internet. A machine on your network sends a request to the proxy. The proxy sends the request to a server on the Internet. Thus, it stands in for the computer on your network. The server on the Internet never knows that the request is coming from anywhere but the proxy. Thus 100 machines on your network could all access an Internet server and it would look like the proxy was making all of the requests. Some proxies have caching and site filtering built in.

PS/2 module

The PS/2 module was introduced in the 1990s with PS/2 computers produced by IBM.

PS/2 mouse

An alternative mouse connection is offered on many Pentium boards. This has the advantage that no valuable serial interface is used. However, it has the disadvantage that it is a special connection and users will need a special PS/2 mouse or a corresponding adapter.

Push technology

This technology was first popularised by Pointcast, a company offering a client that would allow data to be pushed into it from an external server. The client would then display parts of that data based on what the user was interested in looking at – such as news, weather reports, stock information and so on. Push technology has lost popularity due to bandwidth requirements and the general undesirability of having data pushed into corporate networks. Now, the same services are offered through Web pages.

PWL

This is a type of file, ending in the .pwl extension. Windows 3.x/95/98 use encrypted .pwl files to save the local users' system passwords. PWL translates into *PassWord List*, or Listing.

QIC streamer

Abbreviation for *Quarter Inch Cartridge*. The QIC standard describes the form of a magnetic tape cassette, in streamer drives, for saving data. The storage capacities of the cassettes reach from 40 Mb to 2 Gb.

Queue

This is a first-in, first-out (FIFO) data construct. Think of a check-out queue at a supermarket, or any type of queue formed by people in society. Queues are used throughout the architecture of computers and are necessary in programming languages to accomplish certain tasks.

QuadSpeed

Quad speed CD-ROM drives reach data transmission rates of about 600 Kbps, six speed drives about 900 Kbps and eight speed drives about 1,200 Kbps. Current CD drives can reach up to 48 speed.

Radial stepper motor

The radial stepper motor is an extremely accurate engine. It is put into hard disks, and the read and write heads move around it switching from lane to lane.

RAID

Abbreviation for *Redundant Array of Inexpensive Drives*. It is a manipulation of SCSI technology that allows you to combine several hard drives to use as one. The benefits can be either speed increase or failsafe, so that if one drive dies or crashes, you do not lose any data, or a combination of both. There are several levels of RAID: RAID 0, which combines two or more hard drives into a single logical drive; RAID 1, which can be in two forms, disk duplexing and disk mirroring; RAID 10, originally called RAID 1+0, which consists of RAID 1 drives linked together with RAID 0; RAID 2, which stripes data across two or more drives for protection; RAID 3, a form of RAID protection that uses at least 3 drives; RAID 4, similar to 3, in that an extra drive is used to store all parity information, but data is striped by drive sector, instead of bits and bytes, so the read operations are faster; RAID 5, where the configuration uses three or more hard drives and stripes data across them, much like RAID 0.

RAM

Abbreviation for *Random Access Memory*; the memory chip where programs reside when running. You can access any part of the memory, and it can be easily overwritten with new values. See also S-RAM and DRAM.

RAMDAC

Abbreviation for *Random Access Memory Digital/Analog Convertor*. This is the part of the graphics card that transfers digital colour signals into analog signals that a CRT monitor can understand. Faster RAMDACs are necessary if you want to use higher resolution displays at higher colour and refresh rates.

Read-only

Usually applied to a file or other kind of document. Means that the object cannot be written to, which means that you cannot save any modifications you make to it.

Read-only memory (ROM)

Memory containing a program, data or information about the device that has been programmed on to the chip at the factory.

Real mode

The real mode was the only way operating systems could address memory in first generation PC processors (Intel 8086 and 8088). In this mode, program code and data are in a memory area and cannot be protected from each other. Every program has access to the complete area. Software positions are mentioned with the physical address and memory requests are passed on untested over the address bus. The next generation of processors also has a protected mode.

Reboot

To restart a computer. It comes from "boot", which is a term that means to start the operating system on the computer. When you are using your computer and have problems, you will be asked to reboot your computer to see if this resolves the problem.

Redundancy

In a redundant system, if you lose part of the system, you can continue to operate. For example, if you have two power supplies and one takes over if the other one dies, then that is a form of redundancy.

Refresh rate

How often something is rewritten or updated. The refresh rate of your monitor and graphics card can cause your monitor to appear to flicker if set improperly.

Register

A CPU contains registers that it uses for temporary storage of data. You can think of a register as a kind of cache. If the processor has to add the values of two memory locations, it may first fetch each from memory and place them into its registers, and then do an operation that adds two registers.

Remote access

This is a means of contacting a remote network and becoming a node on that network. The problem with remote access is that the connection to the network is generally slow, such as over a modem, so copying or working with large files is very tedious. The advantage is that the minimum hardware requirement is one server or remote access piece of hardware that can control many remote access lines.

Reseller

Anyone who buys computer equipment or software and sells it. In most states in the US, you need a reseller licence to purchase goods without paying taxes, and then you are responsible for collecting and paying taxes on the goods you resell. Resellers usually buy goods from distributors and sell them to the public.

Resident

This describes memory-resident programs, which stay permanently in the background of the main memory, for example, hardware drivers.

Resolution

This describes the size of pixels on a monitor. The higher the resolution, the more pixels that can be squeezed onto a screen, thereby giving the appearance that the pictures on your screen are smaller without losing any detail. Because the pictures are smaller you now have room to place more on your screen.

RET

Abbreviation for *Resolution Enhancement Technology*. This method developed by Hewlett-Packard increases the quality of the printout on a laser printer. It is a special method for smoothing edges. For the observer, it results in a higher constant resolution. This technology is now offered by various manufacturers.

Rewriteable

This means that what was written can be erased so that it can be written to again, for example, floppy disks are rewriteable.

RISC processor

Abbreviation for *Reduced Instruction Set Computer*. RISC chips use a simpler instruction set than CISC chips to get their work done. This results in more instructions that need to be procesed by the processor, but they are easier to process, so the chips can process more instructions per clock cycle than a CISC chip.

Router

A device that bridges an internal network to another network. Take a ferry as an example: cars that need to go to the other side of a body of water (another network) need to use the ferry (the router). If they want to stay on their side, they do not travel on the ferry. Also a device used to bridge a computer to a long distance digital communications network, such as ISDN.

RS232 interface

The RS232 interface is the standard serial interface. Most computers are equipped with one of such 9 or 24-pin hardware connections. It is used for peripherals such as a mouse or modem.

RTC

Abbreviation for *Real Time Clock*. The real time clock which provides the correct time and date on every computer on the motherboard is called the RTC.

RTFM

On-line speak for "Read The F***ing Manual".

RTM

On-line speak for "Read The Manual".

Runtime

This refers to the time when a program or process is running. When it is running it may need runtime libraries and have runtime variables with runtime values. Also used to refer to runtime versions of software that include functionality of the software as the means to an end of running some other software, such as packaging a DOS program with a runtime version of DOS, so that you do not need DOS on your computer to run the program.

Safe mode

This is a Windows 95 mode that is automatically loaded if Windows 95 crashes during boot-up. You can access safe mode any time if you press F8 when the screen says it is loading Windows 95. This will bring you to a menu that allows you to boot into safe mode. Safe mode is a special mode of Windows 95 that loads with minimal driver support. The purpose of it is to help resolve boot problems. For example, if you install the wrong graphics driver, Windows 95 crashes when it is loading. When you restart Windows 95, it will boot into safe mode and use the standard VGA driver with 60 Hz refresh rate. This will allow you to go to the Display Properties function and switch the video driver back to something that works. There is no reason to go into safe mode unless you are crashing during boot-up or you are trying to diagnose a driver problem.

Sample

A small portion representative of something, usually meaning a small amount of sound from an instrument, enough to reproduce the sounds of that instrument.

Sampling

Sampling describes the digitalisation or scanning of pictures or sound presentations in digital data processing. Video data can be scanned with a video camera, audio data with a soundcard.

Save

This term describes the movement of data from a computer's volatile DRAM to the non-volatile hard disk or other media. Basically, when you save something, you are making sure that if your computer loses power, you will be able to get back to the information that you have saved. This information may be saved to a floppy disk, a hard drive or a CD-R. The information also can be saved to these devices connected to your local machine, or to a server on a network.

Scalability

Scalability is the ability to grow with your needs. A scalable software package means that you only buy the parts you need, and that it has the ability to grow by adding on as you do.

Scandisk

This is a Microsoft program that was first shipped with DOS version 6, replacing chkdsk.exe. Technically, the program is scandisk.exe. It is available in MS-DOS version 6.x, and non-NT versions of Windows. It carries out a surface scan for physical defects on drive media.

Scanner

A device used to copy an image from a physical source (e.g. a photograph) in to a computer.

Screensaver

These programs generate the monitor background or screen contents when there is no activity. It was not easy to move away from the fixed screen contents, usually branded, in earlier monitors. Now it is very easy to change the screen contents, unless it is password-protected. There are thousand of amusing screen savers around, or you can create your own.

Script

This refers to a group of commands usually stored in a file and run one at a time so that you do not have to type them all in one at a time. Script is the newer, sexier term for batch.

Scroll lock

The scroll lock key is for most a way to turn the Scroll Lock light on and off on your keyboard and nothing more. The scroll lock key was intended to function as a third status key, such as the Caps Lock and Num Lock keys. Some software makes use of it, but most does not.

SCSI

Abbreviation for *Small Computer System Interface*. It is pronounced "scuzzy". The SCSI standard allows up to seven peripherals. Peripherals are attached along a single cable, one after the other. The last peripheral is provided with a terminating resistor (terminator) and signals the end of the bus.

SCSI 2

The common SCSI 2 standard which has consistent data transmission; unlike the SCSI 1 standard, it allows transmission of up to 10 MBps. SCSI 1 can only transmit 3.3 MBps in standard asynchronous mode and up to 5 MBps in the faster synchronous mode. (The expansion option for SCSI 2 standard is wide SCSI).

SCSI 3

SCSI 3 offers a data transmission rate of up to 100 MBps. This is not wide SCSI. It is also not ultra SCSI. In fact, the SCSI 3 specification does not yet exist. When it is created, it will probably use some sort of fiber-channel interface. However, wide SCSI and ultra SCSI are sometimes referred to as SCSI-3.

S-DRAM

Abbreviation for *Synchronous Dynamic Random Access Memory*. Like DRAM, but arranged with a more efficient data pathway which allows for faster throughput.

Second level cache

The *second level cache* memory sits between the first level cache of the processor and the main memory.

Sectors

A hard disk consists of several magnetically coated disks one of top of the other. Every disk is divided into tracks which move around the average axis and are subdivided into sectors.

Semiconductor

A semicondutor is a substance that selectively conducts electricity. The selection usually occurs by running another current through a different axis. Microprocessors are made of semiconductive materials. Today, semiconductor technology memory chips are produced which stand out due to a low access time and smaller size.

Serial interface

The serial interface (or COM port) is a connection for external equipment such as a mouse or a modem. Serial data here is sent one after the other, in both directions. It comes in 9- and 25-pin varieties, which are the same.

Server

This refers to a machine whose sole purpose is to supply data, so that other machines can use it. This also describes any software process that runs on a server machine, and responds to client processes or programs locally, or across a network.

Shadow RAM

Most BIOS types offer a Shadow RAM function. This copies parts of the slower system ROM into the faster RAM memory. Since currently the BIOS in most operating systems communicates directly with the hardware, this function has become increasingly irrelevant.

Shareware

This is software that can be installed and distributed freely. Some shareware is free but requires a fee to be paid to the author before all features become available. Other shareware is full featured but encourages you to pay the fee with extra screens that must be bypassed each time you load the software. Most shareware requires you to pay for it within 30 days of installation, or you must uninstall it from your system. See also freeware.

Shell

This most commonly refers to the various text-based user interface programs available for UNIX. The shell is the part of UNIX that interacts with the user and accepts typed commands. Different shells have different functionality, so it is important to have the proper shell loaded, or you may find yourself lost as things are displayed differently and familiar commands are not supported.

SIMM

Abbreviation for *Single Inline Memory Module*, those little memory cards we put into a computer as memory. It used to be that you needed eight or nine single chips (with parity) to put in to the computer to make a whole memory unit. Now, a single card or two is all that is needed. The maximum size of SIMMs is 4 Mb. SDRAM modules are currently the norm.

SIMM shuttle

The SIMM shuttle called SIMM PS/2 adapter allows users to carry on using old SIMM chips, also in PS/2 boards. Four or eight SIMM chips go into an adapter. This 72-pin adapter can now be used as a PS/2 module. The substantial drop in price has meant that this PS/2 adapter is no longer necessary, though its use would also be determined by a variety of possible technical problems.

Single session

CD-ROM drives are now capable of multisessions, unlikely earlier drives that could only handle one session.

SIO

Abbreviation for *Serial Input Output*. This chip controls serial data transmission. An example is the UART circuit, usually found in PCs.

SIP

Abbreviation for *Single Inline Package*.

Slot

Slots describe the plug-in places on the motherboard which take expansion boards.

Slow-refresh

In a PC, the D-RAM chips normally get refreshed in about 15 microseconds. It is possible for this time to be prolonged to 60 microseconds in some BIOS settings.

SLSI

Abbreviation for *Super Large Scale Integration*. SLSI describes the integration degree of a chip. 100,000 transistors can be put in a chip on this level.

Software

The programs that run on computer hardware. This can include operating systems, office suites, games, and Web browsers. Software runs on hardware.

Soundcard

A peripheral device in the form of a card used for producing sound and music. Although PCs come with a speaker, they do not do a good job of playing music. As for reproducing sound, it takes most of the processor's power to produce only marginal sound, whereas a soundcard does it effortlessly and produces a much better reproduction.

Spam

Besides being a canned meat, spam has taken on a new meaning. Spam is the common term for unsolicited email. Some common types of spam include adverts for pornographic sites, pyramid schemes, and advertisements for products that allow you to send spam. Other types of spam are messages that claim that you will win a prize or help a dying child by sending messages to all of your friends. In addition to being a noun, spam is also a verb, as in "Don't spam me!". Often spammers will take the list of addresses that reply to them and compile new lists to spam.

SPOOL

Abbreviation for *Simultanous Peripheral Operation On-line*. The spooler is a special program which manages and stores print jobs in a queue. The printer driver sends the next task during printing operations.

Spreadsheet

This is a type of computer program that displays a group of cells (a 2D graph pattern) and allows for easy mathematical operations and relationships between the cells. The first major spreadsheet was Lotus 1-2-3. Today's most popular spreadsheet is Microsoft Excel.

S-RAM

Static RAM memory.

Swap file

A swap file is an evacuation file. If the RAM memory available is no longer sufficient, parts of the RAM are evacuated on to the hard disk.

This technology is used by Windows. The advantage is that large applications can run on small hardware platforms. The disadvantage is that the hard disk naturally works at a slower pace than RAM memory.

Switch

This refers to a hub that directs network packets to the port they are intended for, without broadcasting them to all connections. Switching is an alternative to moving to faster architectures. Switched 10Base-T can move data faster in some cases than a 100Base-T hub, because the 100Base-T hub takes up the hub's entire bandwidth with each packet sent.

Synchronous

This means that transmitter and receiver transmit data at the same time. It is used in electronics to signify something occurring at the set pace of the clock, much like a metronome.

Synchronous cache

Another name for burst cache.

System software

This term can refer to all of the software that comes with a computer system, or more specifically, the operating system.

T1

Two pairs of copper wire that carry data at a rate of 1.544 Mbps. T1 lines are used to carry 24 DS-0 signals. They can be used to carry 24 phone lines or an Internet connection capable of 1.544 Mbps data transfer.

T3

28 T1 lines together make up a T3, which can carry 672 separate voice channels or up to 44.736 Mbps data throughput. Many large Internet providers brag of about having T3 backbones.

T4

Six T3 lines make up a T4 which carries data at 274 Mbps.

Tag Image File Format (TIFF)

This is a bitmap graphics file format. It was developed by Aldus in 1986 to provide a common format for scanners, and is mainly used for that purpose and desktop publishing.

Tag RAM

This is a bank of SRAM that only holds addresses so that when the processor makes a call for memory, it first checks to see if the data is in the cache by looking for the memory addresses in the tag RAM. If it is there, it gets the data from the cache. If not, it gets the data from main memory. Tag RAM controls the amount of memory that can be cached. For example, the Tag RAM used with most Intel 430TX chipsets only allowed the first 64Mb of RAM to be cached. You could use more RAM in your machine, but it will not be cached, and thus performance will be affected when memory over 64Mb is accessed.

Taskbar

This refers to the the space that normally sits at the bottom of the Windows 95/98/NT4/2000 interface. It displays the list of running programs so that you can easily switch between programs even when you have a maximised window taking up the rest of the screen. It can be moved to either side or the top of the screen as well.

TCO

Abbreviation for *Total Cost of Ownership*. This phrase was coined by the creaters of the Network Computer (NC) to describe the benefits of using a system that is more mainframe and less client/server. Their logic states that NCs, although they may cost the same up front as cheap PCs, have a lower TCO than a network built on PCs.

Terabit (Tb)

This refers to approximately 1 trillion bits. More exactly, it is 1,099,511,627,776 bits.

Terabyte (Tb)

One trillion bytes, or one thousand gigabytes.

Terminators

The two physical ends of a SCSI bus must be completed by a terminator. This terminator is required because of the possible length of cables. Without terminators, disturbances would be reflected at the end of the cable and cause additional disturbances.

Third Level cache

This type of cache is becoming more prevalent as microprocessor manufacturers ship more processors with first and second level caches built into the processor. This cache is an extra cache that sits on the motherboard between the processor and main memory.

Tophat

Hard disks consisting of several magnetically coated disks, one on top of each other. Every single disk is divided up into tracks which move circularly around the average axis and are subdivided into sectors. The tracks of all disks are combined to form tophats.

Topless SIMM

These are SIMM chips which are directly wired on to the platinum layer. These chips also are called COB (Chip on Board) SIMMs.

Touch pad

This is a pad that is electrically sensitive to touch. The touch pad replaces the mouse or the tracker ball and is often used as the pointing device in laptops.

TPI

Abbreviation for *Tracks Per Inch*. With TPI the number of the lanes is indicated per inch on a hard disk. It is a factor at the amount of data to be saved.

Trackball

This performs the same function as a mouse. The ball responds easily to the fingers' movement. The advantage of this input device which replaces the mouse is that it needs less space and does not need a smooth mat.

Transmission Control Protocol/Internet Protocol (TCP/IP)

This is the part of the TCP/IP suite of protocols responsible for forming reliable data connections between nodes, as opposed to IP, which is connectionless and unreliable.

Troubleshooting

Troubleshooting is searching for causes and remedies for hardware or software faults.

True colour

A colour depth which corresponds approximately to the colour perception of the human eye is defined as true colour. One could therefore also represent real colour and translate the image with realistic colours. The true colour palette contains 16.7 million colours, this means a colour depth of 24 bits.

Turbo LED

This light-emitting diode shows whether a PC is in the turbo mode.

TWAIN

Abbreviation for *Toolkit Without An Interesting Name*. This is a standard set for scanners to allow them to have a standard interface to software. TWAIN compatible scanners can be used from any TWAIN compatible application. This allows the use of your favorite graphics package with your favourite scanner without worrying about whether one will support the other. In practice, there are problems because the standard does not necessarily have a uniform translation. Check out www.twain.org for more information.

Typematic rate

CMOS can usually adjust the *button repetition* rate. This option always occurs when a key is held depressed for some time.

UART

Abbreviation for *Universal Asynchronous Receiver/Transmitter*. The UART constituent is the essential element of a serial interface. Types like NS 8250 or 16450 have been used in PCs in the past. Type 16550 is now exclusively used. It increases FIFO memory in multitasking surroundings and has built-in transmission security.

ULSI

Abbreviation for *Ultra Large Scale Integration*, ULSI describes an integration degree of a chip. It has over 1,000,000 transistors. Most popular chips today fit this description.

Upgrade

Normally refers to a newer version of software, or a version with an enhanced feature set. If you already own a previous version of the software, you can purchase an upgrade version for a lower price than a new version. In terms of hardware, you can upgrade your system by adding more memory, or any component that makes your system better or faster. Some graphics cards let you upgrade them by plugging more memory on to the board.

Upload

The act of transferring data from your computer to a remote system. This is most commonly referred to when sending files to a remote BBS.

UPS

Abbreviation for *Uninterruptible Power Supply*. This is a device that contains a battery and some circuitry to supply your computer with power for a limited time (depending on the battery) if there is an interruption in power.

URL

Stands for *Universal Resource Locator*. This is what is used to give Web addresses for HTML, VRML, WAV and other files. It simply contains the Internet name of the machine containing the data and the path to the file. The address also includes the protocol to be used.

VESA

Abbreviation for *Video Electronics Standard Association*. This is a group that sets standards for certain peripheral devices and their connectors, such as VESA local bus and VESA standard monitor specification.

VESA local bus

Abbreviation for *Video Electronics Standard Association*. It is a 32-slot extension of a 16-bit ISA slot. The standard, also called VL-bus, describes an improved bus system which accelerates communication between the CPU and peripherals. The current system is version 2.0 and is primarily used for graphics cards and hard disk controllers. This architecture pre-dated PCI and allowed users to break the bottleneck that occurred when the ISA bus slowed down graphics speed. It allowed speeds of up to 40 MHz, compared to ISA's 8.3 MHz and a data capacity of 32 bits compared to ISA's 16 bits. VL-bus was big on 486-66 machines, when it first came out, but was quickly displaced by PCI. PCI cards have some modest speed advantages and are much smaller. All VL-bus cards were full-length cards.

V-FAT

Abbreviation for *Virtual File Allocation Table*. V-FAT is an expansion of the FAT system found in Windows for Workgroups 3.11 and in Windows 95. Besides the advantage of speed, 32-bit file access is now possible under Windows 95, and file names can have a length of up to 255 characters.

Video card

A device in computers that deals specifically with displaying to a monitor. Without one, you cannot see what is going on in your computer and may have to resort to the ancient method of using a printer as a monitor.

Video CD (VCD)

This technology was developed by Sony and Philips in 1993, and allows around 70 minutes of compressed MPEG-1 video/audio to be stored on a CD. Typically, VCD movies are shipped on two CDs. VCDs were very popular in Asia, and were available before DVD. However, VCDs will eventually succumb to the higher quality of DVD. VCD resolution is 352 x 240 (NTSC) or 352 x 288 (PAL), which is comparable to the VHS resolution of 300 x 360.

Video Graphics Array (VGA)

This is a video standard that allows for resolutions up to 640 x 480 with up to 16 colours at a time. It also allows for 320 x 200 resolution with 256 colours. Many older games were written to take advantage of the 320 x 200 resolution because of the comparatively high colour depth. SVGA and XGA replaced VGA, but VGA compatibility remains an important part of most graphics cards.

Virtual memory

This is a section of a hard drive used to augment a computer's RAM. Different operating systems have different ways of dealing with virtual memory. UNIX and Linux use a separate hard drive partition dedicated to virtual memory, while Windows can use part of any hard drive partition. Virtual memory is used when the operating system runs low on physical memory or RAM. Virtual memory is also used to swap out lesser used portions of physical memory, freeing it up for other operations.

Virtual reality

Virtual reality is a world created for you that only exists in a computer, often experienced by looking through 3D goggles that detect which way you are looking and then display what should be there. Another form is a world created in your imagination by stories or interactive games on the computer.

Virus

A program that makes unbidden copies of itself. Sometimes these copies are added on to executable files, and other times they are part of Word or Excel documents, called macro viruses. The virus will usually have some effect on infected systems. Often, the intent of a virus is malicious. Sometimes the intent is not malicious, but due to the spreading of the virus, it becomes a malicious act.

Visitor

When a user arrives on a Web site, he or she is considered one visitor regardless of how many pages he or she looks at.

Visual Basic (VB)

This is a software product developed by Microsoft. Its purpose is to bring programming down to a drag-&-drop level to speed up development cycles. In many ways, that goal has been achieved. VB's main competitor is Borland's Delphi. Both programs offer similar functionality. The code for the program is BASIC and you can go in and edit if you want to.

Visual C++

This is a Microsoft product that is more complex than VB. It features a similar visual interface with drag-&-drop functionality, but the code is C++, which is more robust than BASIC. It is also much faster when compiled.

VLB

Abbreviation for VESA local bus.

VLSI

Abbreviation for *Very Large Scale Integration*. This refers to the amount of transistors incorporated in a chip. A VSLI processor has 100,000 or more transistors.

VRAM

Memory made specifically for video applications (such as a video card). Much faster and more expensive than DRAM.

Wait states

A fast processor must be able to synchronise slow-working peripherals. This is done by inserting an appropriate number of wait states, so that the slow peripheral can receive the transmitted data correctly.

WAV (Wave Audio Form)

This is a sound file format introduced in Windows 3.1 with the .wav file extension. Files with the .wav extension are digital representations of sound and typically take up a good deal of space to store (typically 50 Mb for a five minute song). If you use software to rip files from an audio CD, it is usually stored in .wav format. Standard Windows sounds are still in .wav format.

Web

Synonym for the World Wide Web, often referred to as the Web.

Web developer

Grown up Web masters are Web developers. Generally, if you are a Web developer, you have a range of Web skills from managing a Web server to coding HTML, CGI scripts, and even creating graphics as needed.

Web master

This is a blanket term that refers to the person responsible for running a Web site. It is associated more with server management and HTML coding than other Web development, such as CGI scripting.

Web portal

This is a term coined to describe the large search engine sites such as Yahoo! and Lycos which have branched off to become sites that offer a variety of services. The idea is that a Web user would surf the web by using only one Web site – the portal. For example, you go to a portal to do searches, get stock quotes, buy things, etc. It would be your everything site. Each portal site wants to offer one of each type of service so that a user never has to leave their site.

Web server

A machine or software that sends information as requested by a browser, using the WWW protocol called HTML, allowing people to view information or whatever you want to show them.

Web site

This term describes a particular company's, user's or organisation's Web pages served up by a Web server. It may be split across multiple servers or URLs, but it is one group of HTML pages with a particular association.

Wide Area Network (WAN)

Any network that spans more than one office, although some say it must span more than one building.

Wide SCSI

Wide SCSI is an expansion of the SCSI 2 standard. It allows for faster throughput by increasing the number of pins used to connect the drive to the controller from 50 to 68. Wide SCSI doubles the throughput of normal versions of SCSI, but is generally more expensive due to the additional pins.

Windows

This refers to a family of operating systems developed by Microsoft. The family includes Windows 3.x, 9x, NT and 2000. It can also refer to a rectangular shaped area on your screen that contains a program.

Windows 95

This is a 16- and 32-bit operating system that builds on DOS and Windows 3.x to support 32-bit operations, additional hardware and a more usable interface. This was a true breakthrough product for Microsoft, allowing game developers to run games inside their Windows OS instead of in DOS. It was designed for the consumer market.

Windows 98

This operating system was designed by Microsoft and adds additional hardware support and integrated browsing on to the Windows 95 platform. This OS is still partially 16-bit a full 15 years after Intel released their first 32-bit processor, the 386.

Windows NT (Windows New Technology)

This is a full 32-bit operating system developed by Microsoft to be a very stable operating system to be used on servers and business machines.

Wireless Application Protocol (WAP)

This is a proposed standard that allows for transfer of data securely between wireless devices, such as PDAs, cell phones, pagers or other combinations of those devices. WAP supports many different wireless networks.

Wizard

An enhancement to programs that makes them easier to operate by guiding you through what is required, step by step, to achieve your purpose.

Word

This is a group of bits of data regarded as a whole while programming or transferring data. Often a word is 8 bits in length, and is also referred to as a byte.

Workstation

This is typically a high powered computer, one step below a minicomputer, and a step above a microcomputer. The term often refers to powerful dual-processor computers used to generate 3D images, or manipulate 2D images or sound. Often, workstations require very powerful graphics setups.

World Wide Web

This is a means of communicating text, graphics, and other multimedia objects over the Internet. Web servers on the Internet are set to respond to requests by users sent on TCP/IP by sending HTML documents to the requester. The requester must use a browser to receive this data. Think of the Internet as a 100-lane highway, and the Web as one of those lanes. Of course, traffic in the Web lane is probably very high compared to traffic in most other lanes.

WORM

Abbreviation for *Write Once Read Many*. This is a type of drive/medium that allows you to write to it permanently. However, you cannot erase what you have written. CD-R is a form of WORM drive.

WRAM

VRAM constituents are also the newer Windows RAM memory designed for video cards. You have in addition some implemented functions to the faster version of graphic picture elements. The data throughput instalment could be increased by up to 50 per cent opposite the VRAMs.

WYSIWYG

Abbreviation for *What You See Is What You Get*. This term describes software that allows you to edit a document to show you on screen exactly what will print out. The Macintosh was one of the first computers to support WYSIWIG programs. This is why it became so popular in desktop publishing.

Xmodem

This is a protocol for transferring files during direct dial-up communications. Developed by Ward Christensen in 1977, Xmodem has basic error-checking to ensure that information is not lost or corrupted during transfer. It sends data in 128-byte blocks. Xmodem has undergone a couple of enhancements: Xmodem CRC uses a more reliable error-correction scheme, and Xmodem-1K transfers data faster by sending it in 1,024-byte blocks.

Ymodem

This is also a protocol for transferring files during direct dial-up communications. So named because it builds on the earlier Xmodem protocol, Ymodem sends data in 1,024-byte blocks and is consequently faster than Xmodem. However, it does not work well on noisy phone lines. Ymodem has undergone a few enhancements: Ymodem-Batch can send several files in one session, and Ymodem-G drops software error-correction, which speeds up the process by removing the overhead used by error-correction. This works because all modems since the V.32 era have error-correction built into their hardware.

ZIF socket

Abbreviation for *Zero Insertion Force Socket*. This is a socket designed to accept a PGA chip, such as most common CPUs produced today. The ZIF socket allows you to plug in a PGA chip with no pressure required. This is a big advantage because older sockets required you to push the chip in with equal force on all sides or risk bending the pins.

Zip disk drive

ZIP drives are comparable to a floppy disk drive. The media used has a capacity of 100 to 250 Mb.

Zmodem

This protocol has many error-correcting properties. It can detect if a bad block (of 1,024 bytes) has come through and ask to have it resent. If the transfer is interrupted for any reason, it can resume from where it left off. It is slightly slower than Ymodem-G, but is much more reliable.

Zone bit recording

ZBR is a recording method that takes the geometry of the various tracks on magnetic disks into account. It increases capacity by up to 40 per cent on the original disk size.

Solutions

Input devices and interfaces

1. The standard is MF II.
2. A code page contains country-specific information. It is loaded at start-up and remains in the background during work. PCs can be used without defining the hardware for specific countries.
3. a) and b) activate various functions in combination with other keys; c) stops the current operation; d) inserts text where the cursor is positioned; e) moves the cursor to the beginning of the line; f) moves the cursor to the end of the line; g) prints the current screen; h) they have various user-defined functions.
4. At the start, the BIOS has not loaded the English code page yet. Press "N" instead of "Y".
5. The movement of a ball is converted into a mouse movement as shown on the screen. A joystick activates contacts, which are converted to movements in all directions (up/down, left/right).
6. A mouse driver converts the electrical signals delivered by the mouse and sends them to the operating system to be interpreted.
7. The serial interface COM1.
8. Two serials (COM1 and COM2), a parallel (LPT1) and the game interface (GAM).
9. Serial communication will transmit only one data bit at a time, while parallel interfaces transfer eight data bits at once. Parallel interfaces are thus faster.
10. The joystick becomes the operator.

Memory and storage

1. A file contains information. Files can be combined in a folder which is then stored on a disk drive.
2. Using drag-&-drop, objects can quickly be moved to a different position.
3. Hard disks are faster and can store larger amounts of data.
4. The read/write head touches and a head crash occurs on the data carrier interface. All data saved on that hard disk is destroyed.
5. Formatting means to create a structure on the data carrier, usually a floppy disk, to enable it to save files. CD-ROMs do not require formatting because this is visual media.
6. Streamers are used for storing and backing up large amounts of data. Different data can be accessed on magnetic tapes.
7. Double clock frequency also means double operating speed within a processor, therefore it is twice as fast.
8. A byte contains eight bits.
9. "American Standard Code for Information of Interchange". Data can be exchanged between items of equipment using this code, which is recognised worldwide.
10. Clock speed, processor, memory, bus system, clock.

Printers and graphic systems

1. Printers can be attached both to serial and parallel interfaces. Parallel communication is faster, and longer distances can be bridged between PC and printer.
2. "dpi" (dots per inch) for printers and "points per row and per column" (pixels) in graphics.
3. Dot-matrix printers are robust, cheap and can print relatively well. They are noisy, however, and their print quality has been bettered by rival technologies. If you need to print carbon copies, then you will need to use a dot-matrix printer.
4. The picture repeating rate (refresh rate) displays the picture as a series of repeated pictures within a second. The unit of measurement is Hz (hertz). 60 Hz is the most common frequency for the VGA standard, and a graphic driver is needed to achieve a favourable picture repeating rate.
5. A graphic processor can set up graphic operations independently. The best-known example is the 3DFX. A graphics processor relieves the main processor and the bus system.
6. Printers and monitors handle colours differently. This means that their colour representation is different.
7. The user sits closer to the computer monitor and spends longer working on the PC than watching TV. A picture repeating rate of 60 Hz is required for ergonomically sound working conditions.
8. A printer spooler application programs the printer's printing workload and stores data, sending documents to print one after the other.
9. Video Graphics Array.
10. 14", 15", 17" and 20" are typical sizes. The resolution depends on the size, and therefore a bigger screen provides higher resolution, so a 17" monitor or bigger is required for graphics applications.

The Internet and going on-line

1. A computer, a telephone line, and a modem or ISDN adapter.
2. A modem transmits digital information on analog lines. A modem consists of a "modulator" and a "demodulator". A modem is always connected to a serial interface.
3. An ISDN adapter is the interface between a PC and the digital ISDN BT network. It connects at 64,000 bps.
4. A CFOS driver emulates drivers for an ISDN adapter.
5. An Internet Service Provider connects you to the Internet. Examples of ISPs are CompuServe, AOL and MSN.
6. Transmission protocol checks the transfer of data.
7. Transfer Control Protocol/Internet Protocol. It is the assignment protocol of the Internet. It is even being used in private networks around the world.
8. A browser is the basic software of the Internet. You use it to "browse" through the Internet.
9. Microsoft Internet Explorer (version 5.1) and Netscape Communicator (version 4.7).
10. You should be as careful as you would be in real life.

Software

1. WordPad and Internet Explorer.
2. It is mass-produced and can be purchased at any computer shop, therefore the cost of producing it is low.
3. "Bundled software" is enclosed with hardware products or PC systems.
4. This software is tailor-made for an individual user's needs. It can be adapted, even after designing, but it is very expensive.
5. Public Domain software is completely free, while shareware charges (registration charges) are due if you want to keep a product after the trial period.
6. Versions with reduced performance functions are called "light". The full product contains all functions and can be purchased as an upgrade.
7. Word for Windows and Lotus WordPro.
8. Database software can be used for keeping an address book, an appointment diary or for monitoring information such as stock levels in a warehouse.
9. Spreadsheets offer the required functions.
10. An office package contains several applications which are frequently used for daily office work. Examples of this are products by Microsoft (Office) and Sun Microsystems (StarOffice).

File extensions

Chapter 5 introduced file extensions and discussed what these extensions mean for the user. The following table lists the most common file extensions, in alphabetical order.

Extension	Represents	Program	Function
$$$	Temporary file	OS/2	Used to keep track of archived files
1ST	First	Different Word Processing	Read Info first!
ARC	Compressed archive	ARC (archive program for system enhancement)	Compressed data
ARJ	Robert Jung	ARJ (Robert Jung shareware program)	Compressed data
AVI	Audio video interface	Video for Windows	Audio Video (Windows document designed by Microsoft)
BAK	Back-up file	Backup Program	For compressing data
BAS	Basic file	z.B. Quick-Basic by Microsoft (MS-DOS)	For designing in text form
BAT	Batch file	MS-DOS	For creating MS-DOS routines

Extension	Represents	Program	Function
BMP	Bitmap file	Microsoft Paint	Creating bitmap graphics
CDR	CorelDraw file	CorelDraw	Vector drawings
CFG	Configuration file	Various	Program configuration
DAT	Data file	Various	Data file
DBF	dBase file	dBase Program	Data file
DLL	Dynamic link library	Windows or OS/2	Object library
DOC	Document	Word Processing, e.g. Microsoft Word	Word document
DRV	Driver	Operating system	Equipment driver
EPS	Encapsulated Postscript file	Any graphics program	Graphic data
EXE	Executable program	Operating system	Executable program
FAQ	Frequently asked	Text viewer	Text file
FAX	Fax	Fax program	Sent or received fax documents
FOX	Fox-Pro	Database Foxpro by Microsoft	Data file
GIF	Image file	Graphics program	Compressed image file
HLP	Help	Microsoft Windows and applications	Help document for on-line help

Extension	Represents	Program	Function
HTML	HyperText Markup Language file	Internet browser	HyperText-document
ICO	Icon	Microsoft Windows	Small graphic icon
IDX	Index	Various Databases	Index file
INI	Initialisation file	Various programs including Microsoft Windows	Initialisation configuration
JPG	Image file	Various graphics programs	Compressed file
LOG	Log file	Various programs	Protocol file
MID	Music file	Various music programs	MIDI music file
MOD	Module	Various music programs	Sound module
MOV	Movie	Various video programs	Video file
MPG	Image file	Various decoder program	Compressed video file
PAS	Pascal	Turbo Pascal or Borland	Source code
PCD	Photo-CD	Kodak Photo-CD Viewer	Image file
PCX	Pixel File	Various graphics programs	Image file
RTF	Rich Text Format	Various word processors	Formatted Word document
SCR	Screensaver	Microsoft Windows	Screensaver
SIK	Back-up file	Microsoft Word	Back-up copy of a file

Extension	Represents	Program	Function
SWP	Swap file	Microsoft Windows	Windows file
TMP	Temporary file	Various	Back-up copy of file
TXT	Text file	Various	Unformatted text document
XLS	Excel file	Microsoft Excel	Spreadsheet

Disk Formats

The following table shows you the disk formats currently in use:

Format	Capacity	Disk type		Density
3,5"	720 Kbyte	Double sided	Double density	135 TPI
3,5"	1.44 Mbyte	Double sided	High density	135 TPI
3,5"	2.88 Mbyte	Double sided	High density	96 TPI

How long can cables be?

In Chapter 4 we introduced parallel and serial interfaces and discussed the recommended length for cables in order for them to transport data without interference.

The following table specifies the maximum permitted lengths for the most frequently used cables:

Use	**Maximum length**
SCART	Maximum 3 m
RS232 (Modem, Mouse)	Specification: maximum 15 m up to 100 m
Parellel Cable (printer)	Maximum 5 m (depending on equipment: can be up to 20 m)
Monitor	Maximum 3 m (very sensitive to length)
Telephone	Extensions: approx. 500 m

Operating systems

In Chapter 1, we explained the function and structure of an operating system. The following list gives you a summary of the current available operating systems and will be useful to you when deciding which operating system you should use.

1. MS-DOS

The oldest operating system of the personal computer. It requires a high degree of training and detailed knowledge of its syntax and commands. Under DOS, instructions were always entered via the keyboard; the mouse was not supported.

The overall structure of the operating system is obsolete and is only used in specific circumstances. If you find yourself having to use an old computer, you may find this relic.

2. Windows 3. x

With the development of Microsofts Windows systems, graphical operating systems had arrived to the PC world. Versions 3.x were based on MS-DOS, and used the same settings.

Special network versions of Windows 3.1 or Windows 3.11 can still be occasionally found in use. Windows 3.x systems have been replaced by Windows 95 and 98.

3. Windows 95

Microsoft introduced this Windows operating system in September 1995. Windows 95 brought in numerous technical innovations. Hardware could be used, simply and comfortably, thanks to Plug & Play, and the eight-character rule for file names was also changed.

Windows 95 has excellent network and Internet compatibility, as well as a simplified and user-friendly approach. This is why it claims to be the ideal operating system both for the home user and for smaller networks.

It is also compatible with DOS and all applications which were developed under it, because they were already compatible with Windows 3.x.

4. Windows 98

Windows 98 is an enhanced version of Windows 95. The Internet function has been substantially extended. Numerous applications which were already integrated in Windows 95 functions have been further improved.

However, Windows 98 does not represent a technological quantum leap, compared to the jump from Windows 3. x to Windows 95 .

5. Windows 98, second edition

Some further enhancements have been added to the second edition of Windows 98. One of the most important new features is that it is fully geared up for Internet use, because all the applications are Internet-compatible.

Windows 98 second edition is heavily biased towards the Internet. Internet Explorer 5 is now an integral part of the operating system.

6. Windows NT 4.0

With Windows NT, Microsoft targeted the professional computer world. One reason for the high distribution in the industry is the system's stability, its access and safety mechanisms, and a new, more efficient file system (NTFS) than the one used in Windows 98. Windows NT costs three times as much as Windows 98.

The user interface is identical to that of Windows 98, so working with NT is easy to get used to if you are familiar with Windows 98.

7. Windows 2000

Windows 2000 is the successor to Windows NT 4 and Windows 98. It brings together the advantages of both operating systems. Windows 2000 is delivered in four versions, to cater for various user needs.

8. Mac OS/2

With the Operating System Version 2, the "other" computer giant (Apple) has been trying to compete with IBM's market leadership, and Microsoft's eminence in the operating system segment, but it has only met with some success.

The graphically-oriented, efficient operating system uses the "window" technique.

Software applications for the OS/2 are few and far between, which goes some way to explaining the relatively low use of OS/2, compared with Windows.

9. UNIX/Linux

UNIX is strictly speaking not an operating system, but it describes an operating system category, which follows a standardised technology. Linux is a special version of UNIX.

UNIX is an operating system for computer lovers and programmers; it is a standard for networks within universities and for many large and complicated networks.

This system requires knowledge-based command sequences, and is more specialised and less immediately user-friendly than the other systems listed here, but development is proceeding rapidly. Linux provides an alternative to Windows for the more experienced user.

Index

Symbols

A

B

C

D

M

N

O

P

Q

X

Z